SUPER HOROSCOPE
LIBRA
2010
SEPTEMBER 23 – OCTOBER 22

BERKLEY BOOKS, NEW YORK

THE BERKLEY PUBLISHING GROUP
Published by the Penguin Group
Penguin Group (USA) Inc.
375 Hudson Street, New York, New York 10014, USA
Penguin Group (Canada), 90 Eglinton Avenue East, Suite 700, Toronto, Ontario M4P 2Y3, Canada
(a division of Pearson Penguin Canada Inc.)
Penguin Books Ltd., 80 Strand, London WC2R 0RL, England
Penguin Group Ireland, 25 St. Stephen's Green, Dublin 2, Ireland (a division of Penguin Books Ltd.)
Penguin Group (Australia), 250 Camberwell Road, Camberwell, Victoria 3124, Australia
(a division of Pearson Australia Group Pty. Ltd.)
Penguin Books India Pvt. Ltd., 11 Community Centre, Panchsheel Park, New Delhi—110 017, India
Penguin Group (NZ), 67 Apollo Drive, Rosedale, North Shore 0632, New Zealand
(a division of Pearson New Zealand Ltd.)
Penguin Books (South Africa) (Pty.) Ltd., 24 Sturdee Avenue, Rosebank, Johannesburg 2196,
South Africa

Penguin Books Ltd., Registered Offices: 80 Strand, London WC2R 0RL, England

2010 SUPER HOROSCOPE LIBRA

The publishers regret that they cannot answer individual letters requesting personal horoscope information.

A Berkley Book / published by arrangement with the author

Copyright © 1974, 1978, 1979, 1980, 1981, 1982 by Grosset & Dunlap, Inc.

Copyright © 1983, 1984 by Charter Communications, Inc.

Copyright © 1985, 1986, 1987, 1988, 1989, 1990, 1991, 1992, 1993, 1994, 1995, 1996, 1997, 1998, 1999, 2000, 2001, 2002, 2003, 2004, 2005, 2006, 2007, 2008 by The Berkley Publishing Group.

Copyright © 2009 by Penguin Group (USA) Inc.
Cover design by Steven Ferlauto.

All rights reserved.
No part of this book may be reproduced, scanned, or distributed in any printed or electronic form without permission. Please do not participate in or encourage piracy of copyrighted materials in violation of the author's rights. Purchase only authorized editions.
BERKLEY® is a registered trademark of Penguin Group (USA) Inc.
The "B" design is a trademark of Penguin Group (USA) Inc.

PRINTING HISTORY
Berkley trade paperback edition / July 2009

ISBN: 978-0-425-22656-8

Library of Congress Cataloging-in-Publication Data

ISSN: 1535-8976

PRINTED IN THE UNITED STATES OF AMERICA

10 9 8 7 6 5 4 3 2 1

If you purchased this book without a cover, you should be aware that this book is stolen property. It was reported as "unsold and destroyed" to the publisher, and neither the author nor the publisher has received any payment for this "stripped book."

CONTENTS

THE CUSP-BORN LIBRA 4
   The Cusps of Libra 5
THE ASCENDANT: LIBRA RISING .6
   Rising Signs for Libra 8
THE PLACE OF ASTROLOGY IN TODAY'S WORLD 10
   Astrology and Relationships 10
   The Challenge of Love 11
   Astrology and Science 12
   Know Thyself—Why? 14
WHAT IS A HOROSCOPE? 16
   The Zodiac 16
   The Sun Sign and the Cusp 17
   The Rising Sign and the Zodiacal Houses 17
   The Planets in the Houses 20
   How To Use These Predictions 21
HISTORY OF ASTROLOGY 22
SPECIAL OVERVIEW 2011–2020 28
THE SIGNS OF THE ZODIAC 31
   Dominant Characteristics 31
   Sun Sign Personalities 56
   Key Words 58
   The Elements and Qualities of the Signs 59
THE PLANETS OF THE SOLAR SYSTEM 67
   The Planets and the Signs They Rule 67
   Characteristics of the Planets 68
THE MOON IN EACH SIGN 78
MOON TABLES 85
   Time Conversions 85
   Moon Sign Dates for 2010 86
   Moon Phases for 2010 90
   Fishing Guide for 2010 90
   Planting Guide for 2010 91
   Moon's Influence Over Plants 91
   Moon's Influence Over Health and Daily Affairs 92
LIBRA 93
   Character Analysis 94
   Love and Marriage 99
LIBRA LUCKY NUMBERS FOR 2010 128
LIBRA YEARLY FORECAST FOR 2010 129
LIBRA DAILY FORECAST FOR 2010 133
   November and December Daily Forecasts for 2009 231

THE CUSP-BORN LIBRA

Are you *really* a Libra? If your birthday falls around the fourth week in September, at the very beginning of Libra, will you still retain the traits of Virgo, the sign of the Zodiac before Libra? And what if you were born late in October—are you more Scorpio than Libra? Many people born at the edge, or cusp, of a sign have great difficulty in determining exactly what sign they are. If you are one of these people, here's how you can figure it out, once and for all.

Consult the cusp table on the facing page, then locate the year of your birth. The table will tell you the precise days on which the Sun entered and left your sign for the year of your birth. In that way you can determine if you are a true Libra—or whether you are a Virgo or Scorpio—according to the variations in cusp dates from year to year (see also page 17).

If you were born at the beginning or end of Libra, yours is a lifetime reflecting a process of subtle transformation. Your life on Earth will symbolize a significant change in consciousness, for you are either about to enter a whole new way of living or are leaving one behind.

If you were born at the beginning of Libra, you may want to read the horoscope book for Virgo as well as Libra, for Virgo holds the keys to much of the complexity of your spirit. Virgo reflects certain hidden weaknesses, uncertainties, and your secret wishes. You are eager to get involved with another person, yet you are pulled back often from total involvement by your sense of propriety or your wish to be pure and unspoiled. You hover between poetic romanticism and stiff mental analyzing.

At best, your powers of criticism serve you to develop your potentials and enhance the life of your partner. In that way, you are helpful and loving, considerate and faithful—a pure marriage of mind and body, head and heart.

If you were born at the end of Libra, you may want to read the horoscope book for Scorpio as well as Libra. Scorpio dominates your finances, money, assets, potentials, and your values in general. Although your sexual expectancies can be naive, unrealistic, and even adolescent, you are passionate, excitable, and highly seductive.

You may vacillate between a desire to please another and a fanatical determination to maintain control and survive on your own. You can love with a fatal obsession, where you will blind your eyes to keep peace in a relationship—then suddenly declare war. Although you could prolong the agony of a situation in order to avoid a confrontation, you are the personification of awakening passion and a spirit that longs for the joys of companionship and the simple harmonies of life.

THE CUSPS OF LIBRA

DATES SUN ENTERS LIBRA (LEAVES VIRGO)

September 23 every year from 1900 to 2010, except for the following:

September 22					September 24
1948	1968	1981	1992	2001	1903
52	72	84	93	2004	07
56	76	85	96	2005	
60	77	88	97	2008	
64	80	89	2000	2009	

DATES SUN LEAVES LIBRA (ENTERS SCORPIO)

October 23 every year from 1900 to 2010, except for the following:

October 22	October 24			
1992	1902	1911	1923	1943
1996	03	14	27	47
2000	06	15	31	51
2004	07	18	35	55
2008	10	19	39	59

THE ASCENDANT: LIBRA RISING

Could you be a "double" Libra? That is, could you have Libra as your Rising sign as well as your Sun sign? The tables on pages 8–9 will tell you Libras what your Rising sign happens to be. Just find the hour of your birth, then find the day of your birth, and you will see which sign of the Zodiac is your Ascendant, as the Rising sign is called. The Ascendant is called that because it is the sign rising on the eastern horizon at the time of your birth. For a more detailed discussion of the Rising sign and the twelve houses of the Zodiac, see pages 17–20.

The Ascendant, or Rising sign, is placed on the 1st house in a horoscope, of which there are twelve houses. The 1st house represents your response to the environment—your unique response. Call it identity, personality, ego, self-image, facade, come-on, body-mind-spirit—whatever term best conveys to you the meaning of the you that acts and reacts in the world. It is a you that is always changing, discovering a new you. Your identity started with birth and early environment, over which you had little conscious control, and continues to experience, to adjust, to express itself. The 1st house also represents how others see you. Has anyone ever guessed your sign to be your Rising sign? People may respond to that personality, that facade, that body type governed by your Rising sign.

Your Ascendant, or Rising sign, modifies your basic Sun sign personality, and it affects the way you act out the daily predictions for your Sun sign. If your Rising sign indeed is Libra, what follows is a description of its effects on your horoscope. If your Rising sign is not Libra but some other sign of the Zodiac, you may wish to read the horoscope book for that sign as well.

With Libra on the Ascendant, Venus—the planet that rules Libra—is rising in your 1st house. Venus here gives you the kindest disposition, genial and likable, and an elegant bearing, always graceful with just a touch of showiness. Your mind is well disposed to learning all that is subtle and fine, artistic subjects in general, and your body is attuned to refined, symmetrical rhythms. You could unselfishly put yourself in the service of noble causes, or you could get carried away with a life of sensual pleasure. A vain pursuit of brilliant company or an endless search for the perfect lover could waste your talents.

Your need for partnership underscores most of your activities, not only your love experiences. You have a highly developed social consciousness which acts as a spur to other people. Your insistence on fairness and honesty maintains the standards of any group of which you are a member. You bring a well balanced sense of social values to bear on group activity. The group dynamic is reciprocal, as you benefit by being needed, feeling that people appreciate and admire you. Though satisfying, your social and cultural participation is not sufficient. You must find a love partner with whom you can share everyday living as well as more exalted purposes.

You are well adapted for a life in tandem with another person. Like the Scales, the zodiacal symbol of Libra, you need that sensitive presence of another to achieve balance, to come to rest, both sides of the scales poised in perfect agreement. Alone, you may at times be indecisive, even idle. Seeing all sides of a question and being loathe to choose one side may cause an inability to act. When partnered, you gain a sponsorship that frees you. You can then weigh matters, make decisions, exercise judgments. As arbiter, judge, lawyer, you have no peer.

You put your individual stamp of beauty and harmony on your environment. Style-conscious, with an eye for line, color, and movement, you express your artistic sensibilities in all your surroundings. A blend of loveliness and liveliness is what you seek. Sometimes you can be fickle, a faddist. You can bewilder your close circle by endless experimentation with what pleases you and feels right. This vacillation is equally true in your love life; you may exhaust a round of admirers before you choose to settle down.

More sensitive than most people to nuances, perhaps underneath the surface activity you sense something awry; you will shy away from any situation or suggestion of tastelessness and vulgarity. Ever seeking harmony, you may need to select and discard until you find the right blend. Through this selection process you never really lose your intensity. You are deeply imbued with the belief that you can and will find equilibrium; this belief constantly nourishes, renews your spirit. But you can lose other things, such as opportunities to utilize your talents or a chance to negotiate in a personal relationship.

The key words for you with Libra Rising are balance and harmony. You may need to settle for less than your idealized conceptions so that you can deeply experience, rather than merely visualize, what life and love have actually to offer.

RISING SIGNS FOR LIBRA

Hour of Birth*	Day of Birth		
	September 22–26	September 27–30	October 1–6
Midnight	Cancer	Cancer	Cancer
1 AM	Leo	Leo	Leo
2 AM	Leo	Leo	Leo
3 AM	Leo	Leo	Virgo
4 AM	Virgo	Virgo	Virgo
5 AM	Virgo	Virgo	Virgo
6 AM	Libra	Libra	Libra
7 AM	Libra	Libra	Libra
8 AM	Libra	Scorpio	Scorpio
9 AM	Scorpio	Scorpio	Scorpio
10 AM	Scorpio	Scorpio	Scorpio; Sagittarius 10/6
11 AM	Sagittarius	Sagittarius	Sagittarius
Noon	Sagittarius	Sagittarius	Sagittarius
1 PM	Sagittarius	Capricorn	Capricorn
2 PM	Capricorn	Capricorn	Capricorn
3 PM	Capricorn	Aquarius	Aquarius
4 PM	Aquarius	Aquarius	Aquarius; Pisces 10/3
5 PM	Pisces	Pisces	Pisces; Aries 10/6
6 PM	Aries	Aries	Aries
7 PM	Aries	Aries	Taurus
8 PM	Taurus	Taurus	Taurus; Gemini 10/2
9 PM	Gemini	Gemini	Gemini
10 PM	Gemini	Gemini	Gemini; Cancer 10/2
11 PM	Cancer	Cancer	Cancer

*Hour of birth given here is for Standard Time in any time zone. If your hour of birth was recorded in Daylight Saving Time, subtract one hour from it and consult that hour in the table above. For example, if you were born at 6 AM D.S.T., see 5 AM above.

Hour of Birth*	Day of Birth		
	October 7–12	October 13–18	October 19–24
Midnight	Leo	Leo	Leo
1 AM	Leo	Leo	Leo
2 AM	Leo	Leo; Virgo 10/15	Virgo
3 AM	Virgo	Virgo	Virgo
4 AM	Virgo	Virgo	Virgo; Libra 10/22
5 AM	Libra	Libra	Libra
6 AM	Libra	Libra	Libra
7 AM	Libra	Libra; Scorpio 10/15	Scorpio
8 AM	Scorpio	Scorpio	Scorpio
9 AM	Scorpio	Scorpio	Scorpio; Sagittarius 10/22
10 AM	Sagittarius	Sagittarius	Sagittarius
11 AM	Sagittarius	Sagittarius	Sagittarius
Noon	Sagittarius; Capricorn 10/11	Capricorn	Capricorn
1 PM	Capricorn	Capricorn	Capricorn
2 PM	Capricorn; Aquarius 10/11	Aquarius	Aquarius
3 PM	Aquarius	Aquarius; Pisces 10/17	Pisces
4 PM	Pisces	Pisces	Pisces; Aries 10/21
5 PM	Aries	Aries	Aries
6 PM	Aries; Taurus 10/10	Taurus	Taurus
7 PM	Taurus	Taurus; Gemini 10/18	Gemini
8 PM	Gemini	Gemini	Gemini
9 PM	Gemini	Gemini; Cancer 10/17	Cancer
10 PM	Cancer	Cancer	Cancer
11 PM	Cancer	Cancer	Cancer; Leo 10/22

*See note on facing page.

THE PLACE OF ASTROLOGY IN TODAY'S WORLD

Does astrology have a place in the fast-moving, ultra-scientific world we live in today? Can it be justified in a sophisticated society whose outriders are already preparing to step off the moon into the deep space of the planets themselves? Or is it just a hangover of ancient superstition, a psychological dummy for neurotics and dreamers of every historical age?

These are the kind of questions that any inquiring person can be expected to ask when they approach a subject like astrology which goes beyond, but never excludes, the materialistic side of life.

The simple, single answer is that astrology works. It works for many millions of people in the western world alone. In the United States there are 10 million followers and in Europe, an estimated 25 million. America has more than 4000 practicing astrologers, Europe nearly three times as many. Even down-under Australia has its hundreds of thousands of adherents. In the eastern countries, astrology has enormous followings, again, because it has been proved to work. In India, for example, brides and grooms for centuries have been chosen on the basis of their astrological compatibility.

Astrology today is more vital than ever before, more practicable because all over the world the media devotes much space and time to it, more valid because science itself is confirming the precepts of astrological knowledge with every new exciting step. The ordinary person who daily applies astrology intelligently does not have to wonder whether it is true nor believe in it blindly. He can see it working for himself. And, if he can use it—and this book is designed to help the reader to do just that—he can make living a far richer experience, and become a more developed personality and a better person.

Astrology and Relationships

Astrology is the science of relationships. It is not just a study of planetary influences on man and his environment. It is the study of man himself.

We are at the center of our personal universe, of all our relationships. And our happiness or sadness depends on how we act, how we relate to the people and things that surround us. The emotions that we generate have a distinct effect—for better or worse—on the world around us. Our friends and our enemies will confirm this. Just look in the mirror the next time you are angry. In other words, each of us is a kind of sun or planet or star radiating our feelings onthe environment around us. Our influence on our personal universe, whether loving, helpful, or destructive, varies with our changing moods, expressed through our individual character.

Our personal "radiations" are potent in the way they affect our moods and our ability to control them. But we usually are able to throw off our emotion in some sort of action—we have a good cry, walk it off, or tell someone our troubles—before it can build up too far and make us physically ill. Astrology helps us to understand the universal forces working on us, and through this understanding, we can become more properly adjusted to our surroundings so that we find ourselves coping where others may flounder.

The Challenge of Love

The challenge of love lies in recognizing the difference between infatuation, emotion, sex, and, sometimes, the intentional deceit of the other person. Mankind, with its record of broken marriages, despair, and disillusionment, is obviously not very good at making these distinctions.

Can astrology help?

Yes. In the same way that advance knowledge can usually help in any human situation. And there is probably no situation as human, as poignant, as pathetic and universal, as the failure of man's love.

Love, of course, is not just between man and woman. It involves love of children, parents, home, and friends. But the big problems usually involve the choice of partner.

Astrology has established degrees of compatibility that exist between people born under the various signs of the Zodiac. Because people are individuals, there are numerous variations and modifications. So the astrologer, when approached on mate and marriage matters, makes allowances for them. But the fact remains that some groups of people are suited for each other and some are not, and astrology has expressed this in terms of characteristics we all can study and use as a personal guide.

No matter how much enjoyment and pleasure we find in the different aspects of each other's character, if it is not an overall compatibility, the chances of our finding fulfillment or enduring happiness in each other are pretty hopeless. And astrology can help us to find someone compatible.

Astrology and Science

Closely related to our emotions is the "other side" of our personal universe, our physical welfare. Our body, of course, is largely influenced by things around us over which we have very little control. The phone rings, we hear it. The train runs late. We snag our stocking or cut our face shaving. Our body is under a constant bombardment of events that influence our daily lives to varying degrees.

The question that arises from all this is, what makes each of us act so that we have to involve other people and keep the ball of activity and evolution rolling? This is the question that both science and astrology are involved with. The scientists have attacked it from different angles: anthropology, the study of human evolution as body, mind and response to environment; anatomy, the study of bodily structure; psychology, the science of the human mind; and so on. These studies have produced very impressive classifications and valuable information, but because the approach to the problem is fragmented, so is the result. They remain "branches" of science. Science generally studies effects. It keeps turning up wonderful answers but no lasting solutions. Astrology, on the other hand, approaches the question from the broader viewpoint. Astrology began its inquiry with the totality of human experience and saw it as an effect. It then looked to find the cause, or at least the prime movers, and during thousands of years of observation of man and his *universal* environment came up with the extraordinary principle of planetary influence—or astrology, which, from the Greek, means the science of the stars.

Modern science, as we shall see, has confirmed much of astrology's foundations—most of it unintentionally, some of it reluctantly, but still, indisputably.

It is not difficult to imagine that there must be a connection between outer space and Earth. Even today, scientists are not too sure how our Earth was created, but it is generally agreed that it is only a tiny part of the universe. And as a part of the universe, people on Earth see and feel the influence of heavenly bodies in almost every aspect of our existence. There is no doubt that the Sun has the greatest influence on life on this planet. Without it there would be no life, for without it there would be no warmth, no division into day and night, no cycles of time or season at all. This is clear and easy to see. The influence of the Moon, on the other hand, is more subtle, though no less definite.

There are many ways in which the influence of the Moon manifests itself here on Earth, both on human and animal life. It is a well-known fact, for instance, that the large movements of water on our planet—that is the ebb and flow of the tides—are caused by the Moon's gravitational pull. Since this is so, it follows that these water movements do not occur only in the oceans, but that all bodies of water are affected, even down to the tiniest puddle.

The human body, too, which consists of about 70 percent water, falls within the scope of this lunar influence. For example the menstrual cycle of most women corresponds to the 28-day lunar month; the period of pregnancy in humans is 273 days, or equal to nine lunar months. Similarly, many illnesses reach a crisis at the change of the Moon, and statistics in many countries have shown that the crime rate is highest at the time of the Full Moon. Even human sexual desire has been associated with the phases of the Moon. But it is in the movement of the tides that we get the clearest demonstration of planetary influence, which leads to the irresistible correspondence between the so-called metaphysical and the physical.

Tide tables are prepared years in advance by calculating the future positions of the Moon. Science has known for a long time that the Moon is the main cause of tidal action. But only in the last few years has it begun to realize the possible extent of this influence on mankind. To begin with, the ocean tides do not rise and fall as we might imagine from our personal observations of them. The Moon as it orbits around Earth sets up a circular wave of attraction which pulls the oceans of the world after it, broadly in an east to west direction. This influence is like a phantom wave crest, a loop of power stretching from pole to pole which passes over and around the Earth like an invisible shadow. It travels with equal effect across the land masses and, as scientists were recently amazed to observe, caused oysters placed in the dark in the middle of the United States where there is no sea to open their shells to receive the nonexistent tide. If the land-locked oysters react to this invisible signal, what effect does it have on us who not so long ago in evolutionary time came out of the sea and still have its salt in our blood and sweat?

Less well known is the fact that the Moon is also the primary force behind the circulation of blood in human beings and animals, and the movement of sap in trees and plants. Agriculturists have established that the Moon has a distinct influence on crops, which explains why for centuries people have planted according to Moon cycles. The habits of many animals, too, are directed by the movement of the Moon. Migratory birds, for instance, depart only at or near the time of the Full Moon. And certain sea creatures, eels in particular, move only in accordance with certain phases of the Moon.

Know Thyself—Why?

In today's fast-changing world, everyone still longs to know what the future holds. It is the one thing that everyone has in common: rich and poor, famous and infamous, all are deeply concerned about tomorrow.

But the key to the future, as every historian knows, lies in the past. This is as true of individual people as it is of nations. You cannot understand your future without first understanding your past, which is simply another way of saying that you must first of all know yourself.

The motto "know thyself" seems obvious enough nowadays, but it was originally put forward as the foundation of wisdom by the ancient Greek philosophers. It was then adopted by the "mystery religions" of the ancient Middle East, Greece, Rome, and is still used in all genuine schools of mind training or mystical discipline, both in those of the East, based on yoga, and those of the West. So it is universally accepted now, and has been through the ages.

But how do you go about discovering what sort of person you are? The first step is usually classification into some sort of system of types. Astrology did this long before the birth of Christ. Psychology has also done it. So has modern medicine, in its way.

One system classifies people according to the source of the impulses they respond to most readily: the muscles, leading to direct bodily action; the digestive organs, resulting in emotion; or the brain and nerves, giving rise to thinking. Another such system says that character is determined by the endocrine glands, and gives us such labels as "pituitary," "thyroid," and "hyperthyroid" types. These different systems are neither contradictory nor mutually exclusive. In fact, they are very often different ways of saying the same thing.

Very popular, useful classifications were devised by Carl Jung, the eminent disciple of Freud. Jung observed among the different faculties of the mind, four which have a predominant influence on character. These four faculties exist in all of us without exception, but not in perfect balance. So when we say, for instance, that someone is a "thinking type," it means that in any situation he or she tries to be rational. Emotion, which may be the opposite of thinking, will be his or her weakest function. This thinking type can be sensible and reasonable, or calculating and unsympathetic. The emotional type, on the other hand, can often be recognized by exaggerated language—everything is either marvelous or terrible—and in extreme cases they even invent dramas and quarrels out of nothing just to make life more interesting.

The other two faculties are intuition and physical sensation. The sensation type does not only care for food and drink, nice clothes and furniture; he or she is also interested in all forms of physical experience. Many scientists are sensation types as are athletes and nature-lovers. Like sensation, intuition is a form of perception and we all possess it. But it works through that part of the mind which is not under conscious control—consequently it sees meanings and connections which are not obvious to thought or emotion. Inventors and original thinkers are always intuitive, but so, too, are superstitious people who see meanings where none exist.

Thus, sensation tells us what is going on in the world, feeling (that is, emotion) tells us how important it is to ourselves, thinking enables us to interpret it and work out what we should do about it, and intuition tells us what it means to ourselves and others. All four faculties are essential, and all are present in every one of us. But some people are guided chiefly by one, others by another. In addition, Jung also observed a division of the human personality into the extrovert and the introvert, which cuts across these four types.

A disadvantage of all these systems of classification is that one cannot tell very easily where to place oneself. Some people are reluctant to admit that they act to please their emotions. So they deceive themselves for years by trying to belong to whichever type they think is the "best." Of course, there is no best; each has its faults and each has its good points.

The advantage of the signs of the Zodiac is that they simplify classification. Not only that, but your date of birth is personal—it is unarguably yours. What better way to know yourself than by going back as far as possible to the very moment of your birth? And this is precisely what your horoscope is all about, as we shall see in the next section.

WHAT IS A HOROSCOPE?

If you had been able to take a picture of the skies at the moment of your birth, that photograph would be your horoscope. Lacking such a snapshot, it is still possible to recreate the picture—and this is at the basis of the astrologer's art. In other words, your horoscope is a representation of the skies with the planets in the exact positions they occupied at the time you were born.

The year of birth tells an astrologer the positions of the distant, slow-moving planets Jupiter, Saturn, Uranus, Neptune, and Pluto. The month of birth indicates the Sun sign, or birth sign as it is commonly called, as well as indicating the positions of the rapidly moving planets Venus, Mercury, and Mars. The day and time of birth will locate the position of our Moon. And the moment—the exact hour and minute—of birth determines the houses through what is called the Ascendant, or Rising sign.

With this information the astrologer consults various tables to calculate the specific positions of the Sun, Moon, and other planets relative to your birthplace at the moment you were born. Then he or she locates them by means of the Zodiac.

The Zodiac

The Zodiac is a band of stars (constellations) in the skies, centered on the Sun's apparent path around the Earth, and is divided into twelve equal segments, or signs. What we are actually dividing up is the Earth's path around the Sun. But from our point of view here on Earth, it seems as if the Sun is making a great circle around our planet in the sky, so we say it is the Sun's apparent path. This twelvefold division, the Zodiac, is a reference system for the astrologer. At any given moment the planets—and in astrology both the Sun and Moon are considered to be planets—can all be located at a specific point along this path.

Now where in all this are you, the subject of the horoscope? Your character is largely determined by the sign the Sun is in. So that is where the astrologer looks first in your horoscope, at your Sun sign.

The Sun Sign and the Cusp

There are twelve signs in the Zodiac, and the Sun spends approximately one month in each sign. But because of the motion of the Earth around the Sun—the Sun's apparent motion—the dates when the Sun enters and leaves each sign may change from year to year. Some people born near the cusp, or edge, of a sign have difficulty determining which is their Sun sign. But in this book a Table of Cusps is provided for the years 1900 to 2010 (page 5) so you can find out what your true Sun sign is.

Here are the twelve signs of the Zodiac, their ancient zodiacal symbol, and the dates when the Sun enters and leaves each sign for the year 2010. Remember, these dates may change from year to year.

ARIES	Ram	March 20–April 20
TAURUS	Bull	April 20–May 21
GEMINI	Twins	May 21–June 21
CANCER	Crab	June 21–July 22
LEO	Lion	July 22–August 23
VIRGO	Virgin	August 23–September 23
LIBRA	Scales	September 23–October 23
SCORPIO	Scorpion	October 23–November 22
SAGITTARIUS	Archer	November 22–December 21
CAPRICORN	Sea Goat	December 21–January 20
AQUARIUS	Water Bearer	January 20–February 18
PISCES	Fish	February 18–March 20

It is possible to draw significant conclusions and make meaningful predictions based simply on the Sun sign of a person. There are many people who have been amazed at the accuracy of the description of their own character based only on the Sun sign. But an astrologer needs more information than just your Sun sign to interpret the photograph that is your horoscope.

The Rising Sign and the Zodiacal Houses

An astrologer needs the exact time and place of your birth in order to construct and interpret your horoscope. The illustration on the next page shows the flat chart, or natural wheel, an astrologer uses. Note the inner circle of the wheel labeled 1 through 12. These 12 divisions are known as the houses of the Zodiac.

18 / WHAT IS A HOROSCOPE?

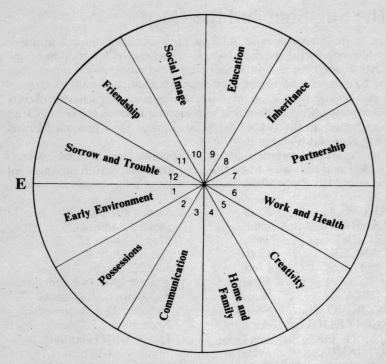

The 1st house always starts from the position marked E, which corresponds to the eastern horizon. The rest of the houses 2 through 12 follow around in a "counterclockwise" direction. The point where each house starts is known as a cusp, or edge.

The cusp, or edge, of the 1st house (point E) is where an astrologer would place your Rising sign, the Ascendant. And, as already noted, the exact time of your birth determines your Rising sign. Let's see how this works.

As the Earth rotates on its axis once every 24 hours, each one of the twelve signs of the Zodiac appears to be "rising" on the horizon, with a new one appearing about every 2 hours. Actually it is the turning of the Earth that exposes each sign to view, but in our astrological work we are discussing apparent motion. This Rising sign marks the Ascendant, and it colors the whole orientation of a horoscope. It indicates the sign governing the 1st house of the chart, and will thus determine which signs will govern all the other houses.

To visualize this idea, imagine two color wheels with twelve divisions superimposed upon each other. For just as the Zodiac is divided into twelve constellations that we identify as the signs, another twelvefold division is used to denote the houses. Now imagine one wheel (the signs) moving slowly while the other wheel (the houses) remains still. This analogy may help you see how the signs keep shifting the "color" of the houses as the Rising sign continues to change every two hours. To simplify things, a Table of Rising Signs has been provided (pages 8–9) for your specific Sun sign.

Once your Rising sign has been placed on the cusp of the 1st house, the signs that govern the rest of the 11 houses can be placed on the chart. In any individual's horoscope the signs do not necessarily correspond with the houses. For example, it could be that a sign covers part of two adjacent houses. It is the interpretation of such variations in an individual's horoscope that marks the professional astrologer.

But to gain a workable understanding of astrology, it is not necessary to go into great detail. In fact, we just need a description of the houses and their meanings, as is shown in the illustration above and in the table below.

THE 12 HOUSES OF THE ZODIAC

1st	Individuality, body appearance, general outlook on life	Personality house
2nd	Finance, possessions, ethical principles, gain or loss	Money house
3rd	Relatives, communication, short journeys, writing, education	Relatives house
4th	Family and home, parental ties, land and property, security	Home house
5th	Pleasure, children, creativity, entertainment, risk	Pleasure house
6th	Health, harvest, hygiene, work and service, employees	Health house
7th	Marriage and divorce, the law, partnerships and alliances	Marriage house
8th	Inheritance, secret deals, sex, death, regeneration	Inheritance house
9th	Travel, sports, study, philosophy and religion	Travel house
10th	Career, social standing, success and honor	Business house
11th	Friendship, social life, hopes and wishes	Friends house
12th	Troubles, illness, secret enemies, hidden agendas	Trouble house

The Planets in the Houses

An astrologer, knowing the exact time and place of your birth, will use tables of planetary motion in order to locate the planets in your horoscope chart. He or she will determine which planet or planets are in which sign and in which house. It is not uncommon, in an individual's horoscope, for there to be two or more planets in the same sign and in the same house.

The characteristics of the planets modify the influence of the Sun according to their natures and strengths.

Sun: Source of life. Basic temperament according to the Sun sign. The conscious will. Human potential.
Moon: Emotions. Moods. Customs. Habits. Changeable. Adaptive. Nurturing.
Mercury: Communication. Intellect. Reasoning power. Curiosity. Short travels.
Venus: Love. Delight. Charm. Harmony. Balance. Art. Beautiful possessions.
Mars: Energy. Initiative. War. Anger. Adventure. Courage. Daring. Impulse.
Jupiter: Luck. Optimism. Generous. Expansive. Opportunities. Protection.
Saturn: Pessimism. Privation. Obstacles. Delay. Hard work. Research. Lasting rewards after long struggle.
Uranus: Fashion. Electricity. Revolution. Independence. Freedom. Sudden changes. Modern science.
Neptune: Sensationalism. Theater. Dreams. Inspiration. Illusion. Deception.
Pluto: Creation and destruction. Total transformation. Lust for power. Strong obsessions.

Superimpose the characteristics of the planets on the functions of the house in which they appear. Express the result through the character of the Sun sign, and you will get the basic idea.

Of course, many other considerations have been taken into account in producing the carefully worked out predictions in this book: the aspects of the planets to each other; their strength according to position and sign; whether they are in a house of exaltation or decline; whether they are natural enemies or not; whether a planet occupies its own sign; the position of a planet in relation to its own house or sign; whether the sign is male or female; whether the sign is a fire, earth, water, or air sign. These are only a few of the colors on the astrologer's pallet which he or she must mix with the inspiration of the artist and the accuracy of the mathematician.

How To Use These Predictions

A person reading the predictions in this book should understand that they are produced from the daily position of the planets for a group of people and are not, of course, individually specialized. To get the full benefit of them our readers should relate the predictions to their own character and circumstances, coordinate them, and draw their own conclusions from them.

If you are a serious observer of your own life, you should find a definite pattern emerging that will be a helpful and reliable guide.

The point is that we always retain our free will. The stars indicate certain directional tendencies but we are not compelled to follow. We can do or not do, and wisdom must make the choice.

We all have our good and bad days. Sometimes they extend into cycles of weeks. It is therefore advisable to study daily predictions in a span ranging from the day before to several days ahead.

Daily predictions should be taken very generally. The word "difficult" does not necessarily indicate a whole day of obstruction or inconvenience. It is a warning to you to be cautious. Your caution will often see you around the difficulty before you are involved. This is the correct use of astrology.

In another section (pages 78–84), detailed information is given about the influence of the Moon as it passes through each of the twelve signs of the Zodiac. There are instructions on how to use the Moon Tables (pages 85–92), which provide Moon Sign Dates throughout the year as well as the Moon's role in health and daily affairs. This information should be used in conjunction with the daily forecasts to give a fuller picture of the astrological trends.

HISTORY OF ASTROLOGY

The origins of astrology have been lost far back in history, but we do know that reference is made to it as far back as the first written records of the human race. It is not hard to see why. Even in primitive times, people must have looked for an explanation for the various happenings in their lives. They must have wanted to know why people were different from one another. And in their search they turned to the regular movements of the Sun, Moon, and stars to see if they could provide an answer.

It is interesting to note that as soon as man learned to use his tools in any type of design, or his mind in any kind of calculation, he turned his attention to the heavens. Ancient cave dwellings reveal dim crescents and circles representative of the Sun and Moon, rulers of day and night. Mesopotamia and the civilization of Chaldea, in itself the foundation of those of Babylonia and Assyria, show a complete picture of astronomical observation and well-developed astrological interpretation.

Humanity has a natural instinct for order. The study of anthropology reveals that primitive people—even as far back as prehistoric times—were striving to achieve a certain order in their lives. They tried to organize the apparent chaos of the universe. They had the desire to attach meaning to things. This demand for order has persisted throughout the history of man. So that observing the regularity of the heavenly bodies made it logical that primitive peoples should turn heavenward in their search for an understanding of the world in which they found themselves so random and alone.

And they did find a significance in the movements of the stars. Shepherds tending their flocks, for instance, observed that when the cluster of stars now known as the constellation Aries was in sight, it was the time of fertility and they associated it with the Ram. And they noticed that the growth of plants and plant life corresponded with different phases of the Moon, so that certain times were favorable for the planting of crops, and other times were not. In this way, there grew up a tradition of seasons and causes connected with the passage of the Sun through the twelve signs of the Zodiac.

Astrology was valued so highly that the king was kept informed of the daily and monthly changes in the heavenly bodies, and the results of astrological studies regarding events of the future. Head astrologers were clearly men of great rank and position, and the office was said to be a hereditary one.

Omens were taken, not only from eclipses and conjunctions of the Moon or Sun with one of the planets, but also from storms and earthquakes. In the eastern civilizations, particularly, the reverence inspired by astrology appears to have remained unbroken since the very earliest days. In ancient China, astrology, astronomy, and religion went hand in hand. The astrologer, who was also an astronomer, was part of the official government service and had his own corner in the Imperial Palace. The duties of the Imperial astrologer, whose office was one of the most important in the land, were clearly defined, as this extract from early records shows:

> This exalted gentleman must concern himself with the stars in the heavens, keeping a record of the changes and movements of the Planets, the Sun and the Moon, in order to examine the movements of the terrestrial world with the object of prognosticating good and bad fortune. He divides the territories of the nine regions of the empire in accordance with their dependence on particular celestial bodies. All the fiefs and principalities are connected with the stars and from this their prosperity or misfortune should be ascertained. He makes prognostications according to the twelve years of the Jupiter cycle of good and evil of the terrestrial world. From the colors of the five kinds of clouds, he determines the coming of floods or droughts, abundance or famine. From the twelve winds, he draws conclusions about the state of harmony of heaven and earth, and takes note of good and bad signs that result from their accord or disaccord. In general, he concerns himself with five kinds of phenomena so as to warn the Emperor to come to the aid of the government and to allow for variations in the ceremonies according to their circumstances.

The Chinese were also keen observers of the fixed stars, giving them such unusual names as Ghost Vehicle, Sun of Imperial Concubine, Imperial Prince, Pivot of Heaven, Twinkling Brilliance, Weaving Girl. But, great astrologers though they may have been, the Chinese lacked one aspect of mathematics that the Greeks applied to astrology—deductive geometry. Deductive geometry was the basis of much classical astrology in and after the time of the Greeks, and this explains the different methods of prognostication used in the East and West.

Down through the ages the astrologer's art has depended, not so much on the uncovering of new facts, though this is important, as on the interpretation of the facts already known. This is the essence of the astrologer's skill.

But why should the signs of the Zodiac have any effect at all on the formation of human character? It is easy to see why people thought they did, and even now we constantly use astrological expressions in our everyday speech. The thoughts of "lucky star," "ill-fated," "star-crossed," "mooning around," are interwoven into the very structure of our language.

Wherever the concept of the Zodiac is understood and used, it could well appear to have an influence on the human character. Does this mean, then, that the human race, in whose civilization the idea of the twelve signs of the Zodiac has long been embedded, is divided into only twelve types? Can we honestly believe that it is really as simple as that? If so, there must be pretty wide ranges of variation within each type. And if, to explain the variation, we call in heredity and environment, experiences in early childhood, the thyroid and other glands, and also the four functions of the mind together with extroversion and introversion, then one begins to wonder if the original classification was worth making at all. No sensible person believes that his favorite system explains everything. But even so, he will not find the system much use at all if it does not even save him the trouble of bothering with the others.

In the same way, if we were to put every person under only one sign of the Zodiac, the system becomes too rigid and unlike life. Besides, it was never intended to be used like that. It may be convenient to have only twelve types, but we know that in practice there is every possible gradation between aggressiveness and timidity, or between conscientiousness and laziness. How, then, do we account for this?

A person born under any given Sun sign can be mainly influenced by one or two of the other signs that appear in their individual horoscope. For instance, famous persons born under the sign of Gemini include Henry VIII, whom nothing and no one could have induced to abdicate, and Edward VIII, who did just that. Obviously, then, the sign Gemini does not fully explain the complete character of either of them.

Again, under the opposite sign, Sagittarius, were both Stalin, who was totally consumed with the notion of power, and Charles V, who freely gave up an empire because he preferred to go into a monastery. And we find under Scorpio many uncompromising characters such as Luther, de Gaulle, Indira Gandhi, and Montgomery, but also Petain, a successful commander whose name later became synonymous with collaboration.

A single sign is therefore obviously inadequate to explain the differences between people; it can only explain resemblances, such as the combativeness of the Scorpio group, or the far-reaching devotion of Charles V and Stalin to their respective ideals—the Christian heaven and the Communist utopia.

But very few people have only one sign in their horoscope chart.

In addition to the month of birth, the day and, even more, the hour to the nearest minute if possible, ought to be considered. Without this, it is impossible to have an actual horoscope, for the word horoscope literally means "a consideration of the hour."

The month of birth tells you only which sign of the Zodiac was occupied by the Sun. The day and hour tell you what sign was occupied by the Moon. And the minute tells you which sign was rising on the eastern horizon. This is called the Ascendant, and, as some astrologers believe, it is supposed to be the most important thing in the whole horoscope.

The Sun is said to signify one's heart, that is to say, one's deepest desires and inmost nature. This is quite different from the Moon, which signifies one's superficial way of behaving. When the ancient Romans referred to the Emperor Augustus as a Capricorn, they meant that he had the Moon in Capricorn. Or, to take another example, a modern astrologer would call Disraeli a Scorpion because he had Scorpio Rising, but most people would call him Sagittarius because he had the Sun there. The Romans would have called him Leo because his Moon was in Leo.

So if one does not seem to fit one's birth month, it is always worthwhile reading the other signs, for one may have been born at a time when any of them were rising or occupied by the Moon. It also seems to be the case that the influence of the Sun develops as life goes on, so that the month of birth is easier to guess in people over the age of forty. The young are supposed to be influenced mainly by their Ascendant, the Rising sign, which characterizes the body and physical personality as a whole.

It is nonsense to assume that all people born at a certain time will exhibit the same characteristics, or that they will even behave in the same manner. It is quite obvious that, from the very moment of its birth, a child is subject to the effects of its environment, and that this in turn will influence its character and heritage to a decisive extent. Also to be taken into account are education and economic conditions, which play a very important part in the formation of one's character as well.

People have, in general, certain character traits and qualities which, according to their environment, develop in either a positive or a negative manner. Therefore, selfishness (inherent selfishness, that is) might emerge as unselfishness; kindness and consideration as cruelty and lack of consideration toward others. In the same way, a naturally constructive person may, through frustration, become destructive, and so on. The latent characteristics with which people are born can, therefore, through environment and good or bad training, become something that would appear to be its opposite, and so give the lie to the astrologer's description of their character. But this is not the case. The true character is still there, but it is buried deep beneath these external superficialities.

Careful study of the character traits of various signs of the Zodiac are of immeasurable help, and can render beneficial service to the intelligent person. Undoubtedly, the reader will already have discovered that, while he is able to get on very well with some people, he just "cannot stand" others. The causes sometimes seem inexplicable. At times there is intense dislike, at other times immediate sympathy. And there is, too, the phenomenon of love at first sight, which is also apparently inexplicable. People appear to be either sympathetic or unsympathetic toward each other for no apparent reason.

Now if we look at this in the light of the Zodiac, we find that people born under different signs are either compatible or incompatible with each other. In other words, there are good and bad interrelating factors among the various signs. This does not, of course, mean that humanity can be divided into groups of hostile camps. It would be quite wrong to be hostile or indifferent toward people who happen to be born under an incompatible sign. There is no reason why everybody should not, or cannot, learn to control and adjust their feelings and actions, especially after they are aware of the positive qualities of other people by studying their character analyses, among other things.

Every person born under a certain sign has both positive and negative qualities, which are developed more or less according to our free will. Nobody is entirely good or entirely bad, and it is up to each of us to learn to control ourselves on the one hand and at the same time to endeavor to learn about ourselves and others.

It cannot be emphasized often enough that it is free will that determines whether we will make really good use of our talents and abilities. Using our free will, we can either overcome our failings or allow them to rule us. Our free will enables us to exert sufficient willpower to control our failings so that they do not harm ourselves or others.

Astrology can reveal our inclinations and tendencies. Astrology can tell us about ourselves so that we are able to use our free will to overcome our shortcomings. In this way astrology helps us do our best to become needed and valuable members of society as well as helpmates to our family and our friends. Astrology also can save us a great deal of unhappiness and remorse.

Yet it may seem absurd that an ancient philosophy could be a prop to modern men and women. But below the materialistic surface of modern life, there are hidden streams of feeling and thought. Symbology is reappearing as a study worthy of the scholar; the psychosomatic factor in illness has passed from the writings of the crank to those of the specialist; spiritual healing in all its forms is no longer a pious hope but an accepted phenomenon. And it is into this context that we consider astrology, in the sense that it is an analysis of human types.

Astrology and medicine had a long journey together, and only parted company a couple of centuries ago. There still remain in medical language such astrological terms as "saturnine," "choleric," and "mercurial," used in the diagnosis of physical tendencies. The herbalist, for long the handyman of the medical profession, has been dominated by astrology since the days of the Greeks. Certain herbs traditionally respond to certain planetary influences, and diseases must therefore be treated to ensure harmony between the medicine and the disease.

But the stars are expected to foretell and not only to diagnose.

Astrological forecasting has been remarkably accurate, but often it is wide of the mark. The brave person who cares to predict world events takes dangerous chances. Individual forecasting is less clear cut; it can be a help or a disillusionment. Then we come to the nagging question: if it is possible to foreknow, is it right to foretell? This is a point of ethics on which it is hard to pronounce judgment. The doctor faces the same dilemma if he finds that symptoms of a mortal disease are present in his patient and that he can only prognosticate a steady decline. How much to tell an individual in a crisis is a problem that has perplexed many distinguished scholars. Honest and conscientious astrologers in this modern world, where so many people are seeking guidance, face the same problem.

Five hundred years ago it was customary to call in a learned man who was an astrologer who was probably also a doctor and a philosopher. By his knowledge of astrology, his study of planetary influences, he felt himself qualified to guide those in distress. The world has moved forward at a fantastic rate since then, and yet people are still uncertain of themselves. At first sight it seems fantastic in the light of modern thinking that they turn to the most ancient of all studies, and get someone to calculate a horoscope for them. But is it really so fantastic if you take a second look? For astrology is concerned with tomorrow, with survival. And in a world such as ours, tomorrow and survival are the keywords for the twenty-first century.

SPECIAL OVERVIEW 2011–2020

The second decade of the twenty-first century opens on major planetary shifts that set the stage for challenge, opportunity, and change. The personal planets—notably Jupiter and Saturn—and the generational planets—Uranus, Neptune, and Pluto—have all moved forward into new signs of the zodiac. These fresh planetary influences act to shape unfolding events and illuminate pathways to the future.

Jupiter, the big planet that attracts luck, spends about one year in each zodiacal sign. It takes approximately twelve years for Jupiter to travel through all twelve signs of the zodiac in order to complete a cycle. In 2011 a new Jupiter cycle is initiated with Jupiter transiting Aries, the first sign of the zodiac. As each year progresses over the course of the decade, Jupiter moves forward into the next sign, following the natural progression of the zodiac. Jupiter visits Taurus in 2012, Gemini in 2013,, Cancer in 2014, Leo in 2015, Virgo in 2016, Libra in 2017, Scorpio in 2018, Sagittarius in 2019, Capricorn in 2020. Then in late December 2020 Jupiter enters Aquarius just two weeks before the decade closes. Jupiter's vibrations are helpful and fruitful, a source of good luck and a protection against bad luck. Opportunity swells under Jupiter's powerful rays. Learning takes leaps of faith.

Saturn, the beautiful planet of reason and responsibility, spends about two and a half years in each zodiacal sign. A complete Saturn cycle through all twelve signs of the zodiac takes about twenty-nine to thirty years. Saturn is known as the lawgiver: setting boundaries and codes of conduct, urging self-discipline and structure within a creative framework. The rule of law, the role of government, the responsibility of the individual are all sourced from Saturn. Saturn gives as it takes. Once a lesson is learned, Saturn's reward is just and full.

Saturn transits Libra throughout 2011 until early autumn of 2012. Here Saturn seeks to harmonize, to balance, to bring order out of chaos. Saturn in Libra ennobles the artist, the judge, the high-minded, the honest. Saturn next visits Scorpio from autumn 2012 until late December 2014. With Saturn in Scorpio, tactic and strategy combine to get workable solutions and desired results. Saturn's problem-solving tools here can harness dynamic energy for the common good. Saturn in Sagittarius, an idealistic and humanistic transit that stretches from December 2014 into the last day of autumn 2017, promotes activism over mere dogma and debate. Saturn in Sagittarius can be a driving force for good. Saturn tours Capricorn, the sign that Saturn rules, from the first day of winter 2017 into early spring 2020. Saturn in Capricorn is a consolidating transit, bringing things forth and into fruition. Here a plan can be made right, made whole, then launched for success. Saturn starts to visit Aquarius, a sign that Saturn corules and a very good sign for Saturn to visit, in the very last year of the decade. Saturn in Aquarius fosters team spirit, the unity of effort amid diversity. The transit of Saturn in Aquarius until early 2023 represents a period of enlightened activism and unprecedented growth.

Uranus, Neptune, and Pluto spend more than several years in each sign. They produce the differences in attitude, belief, behavior, and taste that distinguish one generation from another—and so are called the generational planets.

Uranus, planet of innovation and surprise, is known as the awakener. Uranus spends seven to eight years in each sign. Uranus started a new cycle when it entered Aries, the first sign of the zodiac, in May 2010. Uranus tours Aries until May 2018. Uranus in Aries accents originality, freedom, independence, unpredictability. There can be a start-stop quality to undertakings given this transit. Despite contradiction and confrontation, significant invention and productivity mark this transit. Uranus next visits Taurus through the end of the decade into 2026. Strategic thinking and timely action characterize the transit of Uranus in Taurus. Here intuition is backed up by common sense, leading to fresh discoveries upon which new industries can be built.

Neptune spends about fourteen years in each sign. Neptune, the visionary planet, enters Pisces, the sign Neptune rules and the final sign of the zodiac, in early April 2011. Neptune journeys through Pisces until 2026 to complete the Neptune cycle of visiting all twelve zodiacal signs. Neptune's tour of Pisces ushers in a long period of great potentiality: universal understanding, universal good, universal love, universal generosity, universal forgiveness—the universal spirit affects all. Neptune in Pisces can oversee the fruition of such noble aims as human rights for all and liberation from all forms of tyranny. Neptune in Pisces is a pervasive influence that changes concepts, consciences, attitudes, actions. The impact of Neptune in Pisces is to illuminate and to inspire.

Pluto, dwarf planet of beginnings and endings, entered the earthy sign of Capricorn in 2008 and journeys there for sixteen years into late 2024. Pluto in Capricorn over the course of this extensive visit has the capacity to change the landscape as well as the humanscape. The transforming energy of Pluto combines with the persevering power of Capricorn to give depth and character to potential change. Pluto in Capricorn brings focus and cohesion to disparate, diverse creativities. As new forms arise and take root, Pluto in Capricorn organizes the rebuilding process. Freedom versus limitation, freedom versus authority is in the framework during this transit. Reasonableness struggles with recklessness to solve divisive issues. Pluto in Capricorn teaches important lessons about adversity, and the lessons will be learned.

THE SIGNS OF THE ZODIAC

Dominant Characteristics

Aries: March 21–April 20

The Positive Side of Aries

The Aries has many positive points to his character. People born under this first sign of the Zodiac are often quite strong and enthusiastic. On the whole, they are forward-looking people who are not easily discouraged by temporary setbacks. They know what they want out of life and they go out after it. Their personalities are strong. Others are usually quite impressed by the Ram's way of doing things. Quite often they are sources of inspiration for others traveling the same route. Aries men and women have a special zest for life that can be contagious; for others, they are a fine example of how life should be lived.

The Aries person usually has a quick and active mind. He is imaginative and inventive. He enjoys keeping busy and active. He generally gets along well with all kinds of people. He is interested in mankind, as a whole. He likes to be challenged. Some would say he thrives on opposition, for it is when he is set against that he often does his best. Getting over or around obstacles is a challenge he generally enjoys. All in all, Aries is quite positive and young-thinking. He likes to keep abreast of new things that are happening in the world. Aries are often fond of speed. They like things to be done quickly, and this sometimes aggravates their slower colleagues and associates.

The Aries man or woman always seems to remain young. Their whole approach to life is youthful and optimistic. They never say die, no matter what the odds. They may have an occasional setback, but it is not long before they are back on their feet again.

The Negative Side of Aries

Everybody has his less positive qualities—and Aries is no exception. Sometimes the Aries man or woman is not very tactful in communicating with others; in his hurry to get things done he is apt to be a little callous or inconsiderate. Sensitive people are likely to find him somewhat sharp-tongued in some situations. Often in his eagerness to get the show on the road, he misses the mark altogether and cannot achieve his aims.

At times Aries can be too impulsive. He can occasionally be stubborn and refuse to listen to reason. If things do not move quickly enough to suit the Aries man or woman, he or she is apt to become rather nervous or irritable. The uncultivated Aries is not unfamiliar with moments of doubt and fear. He is capable of being destructive if he does not get his way. He can overcome some of his emotional problems by steadily trying to express himself as he really is, but this requires effort.

Taurus: April 21–May 20

The Positive Side of Taurus

The Taurus person is known for his ability to concentrate and for his tenacity. These are perhaps his strongest qualities. The Taurus man or woman generally has very little trouble in getting along with others; it's his nature to be helpful toward people in need. He can always be depended on by his friends, especially those in trouble.

Taurus generally achieves what he wants through his ability to persevere. He never leaves anything unfinished but works on something until it has been completed. People can usually take him at his word; he is honest and forthright in most of his dealings. The Taurus person has a good chance to make a success of his life because of his many positive qualities. The Taurus who aims high seldom falls short of his mark. He learns well by experience. He is thorough and does not believe in shortcuts of any kind. The Bull's thoroughness pays off in the end, for through his deliberateness he learns how to rely on himself and what he has learned. The Taurus person tries to get along with others, as a rule. He is not

overly critical and likes people to be themselves. He is a tolerant person and enjoys peace and harmony—especially in his home life.

Taurus is usually cautious in all that he does. He is not a person who believes in taking unnecessary risks. Before adopting any one line of action, he will weigh all of the pros and cons. The Taurus person is steadfast. Once his mind is made up it seldom changes. The person born under this sign usually is a good family person—reliable and loving.

The Negative Side of Taurus

Sometimes the Taurus man or woman is a bit too stubborn. He won't listen to other points of view if his mind is set on something. To others, this can be quite annoying. Taurus also does not like to be told what to do. He becomes rather angry if others think him not too bright. He does not like to be told he is wrong, even when he is. He dislikes being contradicted.

Some people who are born under this sign are very suspicious of others—even of those persons close to them. They find it difficult to trust people fully. They are often afraid of being deceived or taken advantage of. The Bull often finds it difficult to forget or forgive. His love of material things sometimes makes him rather avaricious and petty.

Gemini: May 21–June 20

The Positive Side of Gemini

The person born under this sign of the Heavenly Twins is usually quite bright and quick-witted. Some of them are capable of doing many different things. The Gemini person very often has many different interests. He keeps an open mind and is always anxious to learn new things.

Gemini is often an analytical person. He is a person who enjoys making use of his intellect. He is governed more by his mind than by his emotions. He is a person who is not confined to one view; he can often understand both sides to a problem or question. He knows how to reason, how to make rapid decisions if need be.

He is an adaptable person and can make himself at home almost anywhere. There are all kinds of situations he can adapt to. He is a person who seldom doubts himself; he is sure of his talents and his ability to think and reason. Gemini is generally most satisfied when he is in a situation where he can make use of his intellect. Never short of imagination, he often has strong talents for invention. He is rather a modern person when it comes to life; Gemini almost always moves along with the times—perhaps that is why he remains so youthful throughout most of his life.

Literature and art appeal to the person born under this sign. Creativity in almost any form will interest and intrigue the Gemini man or woman.

The Gemini is often quite charming. A good talker, he often is the center of attraction at any gathering. People find it easy to like a person born under this sign because he can appear easygoing and usually has a good sense of humor.

The Negative Side of Gemini

Sometimes the Gemini person tries to do too many things at one time—and as a result, winds up finishing nothing. Some Twins are easily distracted and find it rather difficult to concentrate on one thing for too long a time. Sometimes they give in to trifling fancies and find it rather boring to become too serious about any one thing. Some of them are never dependable, no matter what they promise.

Although the Gemini man or woman often appears to be well-versed on many subjects, this is sometimes just a veneer. His knowledge may be only superficial, but because he speaks so well he gives people the impression of erudition. Some Geminis are sharp-tongued and inconsiderate; they think only of themselves and their own pleasure.

Cancer: June 21–July 20

The Positive Side of Cancer

The Moon Child's most positive point is his understanding nature. On the whole, he is a loving and sympathetic person. He would never go out of his way to hurt anyone. The Cancer man or woman is often very kind and tender; they give what they can to others. They hate to see others suffering and will do what they can to help someone in less fortunate circumstances than themselves. They are often very concerned about the world. Their interest in people generally goes beyond that of just their own families and close friends; they have a deep sense of community and respect humanitarian values. The Moon Child means what he says, as a rule; he is honest about his feelings.

The Cancer man or woman is a person who knows the art of patience. When something seems difficult, he is willing to wait until the situation becomes manageable again. He is a person who knows how to bide his time. Cancer knows how to concentrate on one thing at a time. When he has made his mind up he generally sticks with what he does, seeing it through to the end.

Cancer is a person who loves his home. He enjoys being surrounded by familiar things and the people he loves. Of all the signs, Cancer is the most maternal. Even the men born under this sign often have a motherly or protective quality about them. They like to take care of people in their family—to see that they are well loved and well provided for. They are usually loyal and faithful. Family ties mean a lot to the Cancer man or woman. Parents and in-laws are respected and loved. Young Cancer responds very well to adults who show faith in him. The Moon Child has a strong sense of tradition. He is very sensitive to the moods of others.

The Negative Side of Cancer

Sometimes Cancer finds it rather hard to face life. It becomes too much for him. He can be a little timid and retiring, when things don't go too well. When unfortunate things happen, he is apt to just shrug and say, "Whatever will be will be." He can be fatalistic to a fault. The uncultivated Cancer is a bit lazy. He doesn't have very much ambition. Anything that seems a bit difficult he'll gladly leave to others. He may be lacking in initiative. Too sensitive, when he feels he's been injured, he'll crawl back into his shell and nurse his imaginary wounds. The immature Moon Child often is given to crying when the smallest thing goes wrong.

Some Cancers find it difficult to enjoy themselves in environments outside their homes. They make heavy demands on others, and need to be constantly reassured that they are loved. Lacking such reassurance, they may resort to sulking in silence.

Leo: July 21–August 21

The Positive Side of Leo

Often Leos make good leaders. They seem to be good organizers and administrators. Usually they are quite popular with others. Whatever group it is that they belong to, the Leo man or woman is almost sure to be or become the leader. Loyalty, one of the Lion's noblest traits, enables him or her to maintain this leadership position.

Leo is generous most of the time. It is his best characteristic. He or she likes to give gifts and presents. In making others happy, the Leo person becomes happy himself. He likes to splurge when spending money on others. In some instances it may seem that the Lion's generosity knows no boundaries. A hospitable person, the Leo man or woman is very fond of welcoming people to his house and entertaining them. He is never short of company.

Leo has plenty of energy and drive. He enjoys working toward some specific goal. When he applies himself correctly, he gets what he wants most often. The Leo person is almost never unsure of himself. He has plenty of confidence and aplomb. He is a person who is direct in almost everything he does. He has a quick mind and can make a decision in a very short time.

He usually sets a good example for others because of his ambitious manner and positive ways. He knows how to stick to something once he's started. Although Leo may be good at making a joke, he is not superficial or glib. He is a loving person, kind and thoughtful.

There is generally nothing small or petty about the Leo man or woman. He does what he can for those who are deserving. He is a person others can rely upon at all times. He means what he says. An honest person, generally speaking, he is a friend who is valued and sought out.

The Negative Side of Leo

Leo, however, does have his faults. At times, he can be just a bit too arrogant. He thinks that no one deserves a leadership position except him. Only he is capable of doing things well. His opinion of himself is often much too high. Because of his conceit, he is sometimes rather unpopular with a good many people. Some Leos are too materialistic; they can only think in terms of money and profit.

Some Leos enjoy lording it over others—at home or at their place of business. What is more, they feel they have the right to. Egocentric to an impossible degree, this sort of Leo cares little about how others think or feel. He can be rude and cutting.

Virgo: August 22–September 22

The Positive Side of Virgo

The person born under the sign of Virgo is generally a busy person. He knows how to arrange and organize things. He is a good planner. Above all, he is practical and is not afraid of hard work.

Often called the sign of the Harvester, Virgo knows how to attain what he desires. He sticks with something until it is finished. He never shirks his duties, and can always be depended upon. The Virgo person can be thoroughly trusted at all times.

The man or woman born under this sign tries to do everything to perfection. He doesn't believe in doing anything halfway. He always aims for the top. He is the sort of a person who is always learning and constantly striving to better himself—not because he wants more money or glory, but because it gives him a feeling of accomplishment.

The Virgo man or woman is a very observant person. He is sensitive to how others feel, and can see things below the surface of a situation. He usually puts this talent to constructive use.

It is not difficult for the Virgo to be open and earnest. He believes in putting his cards on the table. He is never secretive or underhanded. He's as good as his word. The Virgo person is generally plainspoken and down to earth. He has no trouble in expressing himself.

The Virgo person likes to keep up to date on new developments in his particular field. Well-informed, generally, he sometimes has a keen interest in the arts or literature. What he knows, he knows well. His ability to use his critical faculties is well-developed and sometimes startles others because of its accuracy.

Virgos adhere to a moderate way of life; they avoid excesses. Virgo is a responsible person and enjoys being of service.

The Negative Side of Virgo

Sometimes a Virgo person is too critical. He thinks that only he can do something the way it should be done. Whatever anyone else does is inferior. He can be rather annoying in the way he quibbles over insignificant details. In telling others how things should be done, he can be rather tactless and mean.

Some Virgos seem rather emotionless and cool. They feel emotional involvement is beneath them. They are sometimes too tidy, too neat. With money they can be rather miserly. Some Virgos try to force their opinions and ideas on others.

Libra: September 23–October 22

The Positive Side of Libra

Libras love harmony. It is one of their most outstanding character traits. They are interested in achieving balance; they admire beauty and grace in things as well as in people. Generally speaking, they are kind and considerate people. Libras are usually very sympathetic. They go out of their way not to hurt another person's feelings. They are outgoing and do what they can to help those in need.

People born under the sign of Libra almost always make good friends. They are loyal and amiable. They enjoy the company of others. Many of them are rather moderate in their views; they believe in keeping an open mind, however, and weighing both sides of an issue fairly before making a decision.

Alert and intelligent, Libra, often known as the Lawgiver, is always fair-minded and tries to put himself in the position of the other person. They are against injustice; quite often they take up for the underdog. In most of their social dealings, they try to be tactful and kind. They dislike discord and bickering, and most Libras strive for peace and harmony in all their relationships.

The Libra man or woman has a keen sense of beauty. They appreciate handsome furnishings and clothes. Many of them are artistically inclined. Their taste is usually impeccable. They know how to use color. Their homes are almost always attractively arranged and inviting. They enjoy entertaining people and see to it that their guests always feel at home and welcome.

Libra gets along with almost everyone. He is well-liked and socially much in demand.

The Negative Side of Libra

Some people born under this sign tend to be rather insincere. So eager are they to achieve harmony in all relationships that they will even go so far as to lie. Many of them are escapists. They find facing the truth an ordeal and prefer living in a world of make-believe.

In a serious argument, some Libras give in rather easily even when they know they are right. Arguing, even about something they believe in, is too unsettling for some of them.

Libras sometimes care too much for material things. They enjoy possessions and luxuries. Some are vain and tend to be jealous.

Scorpio: October 23–November 22

The Positive Side of Scorpio

The Scorpio man or woman generally knows what he or she wants out of life. He is a determined person. He sees something through to the end. Scorpio is quite sincere, and seldom says anything he doesn't mean. When he sets a goal for himself he tries to go about achieving it in a very direct way.

The Scorpion is brave and courageous. They are not afraid of hard work. Obstacles do not frighten them. They forge ahead until they achieve what they set out for. The Scorpio man or woman has a strong will.

Although Scorpio may seem rather fixed and determined, inside he is often quite tender and loving. He can care very much for others. He believes in sincerity in all relationships. His feelings about someone tend to last; they are profound and not superficial.

The Scorpio person is someone who adheres to his principles no matter what happens. He will not be deterred from a path he believes to be right.

Because of his many positive strengths, the Scorpion can often achieve happiness for himself and for those that he loves.

He is a constructive person by nature. He often has a deep understanding of people and of life, in general. He is perceptive and unafraid. Obstacles often seem to spur him on. He is a positive person who enjoys winning. He has many strengths and resources; challenge of any sort often brings out the best in him.

The Negative Side of Scorpio

The Scorpio person is sometimes hypersensitive. Often he imagines injury when there is none. He feels that others do not bother to recognize him for his true worth. Sometimes he is given to excessive boasting in order to compensate for what he feels is neglect.

Scorpio can be proud, arrogant, and competitive. They can be sly when they put their minds to it and they enjoy outwitting persons or institutions noted for their cleverness.

Their tactics for getting what they want are sometimes devious and ruthless. They don't care too much about what others may think. If they feel others have done them an injustice, they will do their best to seek revenge. The Scorpion often has a sudden, violent temper; and this person's interest in sex is sometimes quite unbalanced or excessive.

Sagittarius: November 23–December 20

The Positive Side of Sagittarius

People born under this sign are honest and forthright. Their approach to life is earnest and open. Sagittarius is often quite adult in his way of seeing things. They are broad-minded and tolerant people. When dealing with others the person born under the sign of the Archer is almost always open and forthright. He doesn't believe in deceit or pretension. His standards are high. People who associate with Sagittarius generally admire and respect his tolerant viewpoint.

The Archer trusts others easily and expects them to trust him. He is never suspicious or envious and almost always thinks well of others. People always enjoy his company because he is so friendly and easygoing. The Sagittarius man or woman is often good-humored. He can always be depended upon by his friends, family, and co-workers.

The person born under this sign of the Zodiac likes a good joke every now and then. Sagittarius is eager for fun and laughs, which makes him very popular with others.

A lively person, he enjoys sports and outdoor life. The Archer is fond of animals. Intelligent and interesting, he can begin an animated

conversation with ease. He likes exchanging ideas and discussing various views.

He is not selfish or proud. If someone proposes an idea or plan that is better than his, he will immediately adopt it. Imaginative yet practical, he knows how to put ideas into practice.

The Archer enjoys sport and games, and it doesn't matter if he wins or loses. He is a forgiving person, and never sulks over something that has not worked out in his favor.

He is seldom critical, and is almost always generous.

The Negative Side of Sagittarius

Some Sagittarius are restless. They take foolish risks and seldom learn from the mistakes they make. They don't have heads for money and are often mismanaging their finances. Some of them devote much of their time to gambling.

Some are too outspoken and tactless, always putting their feet in their mouths. They hurt others carelessly by being honest at the wrong time. Sometimes they make promises which they don't keep. They don't stick close enough to their plans and go from one failure to another. They are undisciplined and waste a lot of energy.

Capricorn: December 21–January 19

The Positive Side of Capricorn

The person born under the sign of Capricorn, known variously as the Mountain Goat or Sea Goat, is usually very stable and patient. He sticks to whatever tasks he has and sees them through. He can always be relied upon and he is not averse to work.

An honest person, Capricorn is generally serious about whatever he does. He does not take his duties lightly. He is a practical person and believes in keeping his feet on the ground.

Quite often the person born under this sign is ambitious and knows how to get what he wants out of life. The Goat forges ahead and never gives up his goal. When he is determined about something, he almost always wins. He is a good worker—a hard worker. Although things may not come easy to him, he will not complain, but continue working until his chores are finished.

He is usually good at business matters and knows the value of money. He is not a spendthrift and knows how to put something away for a rainy day; he dislikes waste and unnecessary loss.

Capricorn knows how to make use of his self-control. He can apply himself to almost anything once he puts his mind to it. His ability to concentrate sometimes astounds others. He is diligent and does well when involved in detail work.

The Capricorn man or woman is charitable, generally speaking, and will do what is possible to help others less fortunate. As a friend, he is loyal and trustworthy. He never shirks his duties or responsibilities. He is self-reliant and never expects too much of the other fellow. He does what he can on his own. If someone does him a good turn, then he will do his best to return the favor.

The Negative Side of Capricorn

Like everyone, Capricorn, too, has faults. At times, the Goat can be overcritical of others. He expects others to live up to his own high standards. He thinks highly of himself and tends to look down on others.

His interest in material things may be exaggerated. The Capricorn man or woman thinks too much about getting on in the world and having something to show for it. He may even be a little greedy.

He sometimes thinks he knows what's best for everyone. He is too bossy. He is always trying to organize and correct others. He may be a little narrow in his thinking.

Aquarius: January 20–February 18

The Positive Side of Aquarius

The Aquarius man or woman is usually very honest and forthright. These are his two greatest qualities. His standards for himself are generally very high. He can always be relied upon by others. His word is his bond.

Aquarius is perhaps the most tolerant of all the Zodiac personalities. He respects other people's beliefs and feels that everyone is entitled to his own approach to life.

He would never do anything to injure another's feelings. He is never unkind or cruel. Always considerate of others, the Water

Bearer is always willing to help a person in need. He feels a very strong tie between himself and all the other members of mankind.

The person born under this sign, called the Water Bearer, is almost always an individualist. He does not believe in teaming up with the masses, but prefers going his own way. His ideas about life and mankind are often quite advanced. There is a saying to the effect that the average Aquarius is fifty years ahead of his time.

Aquarius is community-minded. The problems of the world concern him greatly. He is interested in helping others no matter what part of the globe they live in. He is truly a humanitarian sort. He likes to be of service to others.

Giving, considerate, and without prejudice, Aquarius have no trouble getting along with others.

The Negative Side of Aquarius

Aquarius may be too much of a dreamer. He makes plans but seldom carries them out. He is rather unrealistic. His imagination has a tendency to run away with him. Because many of his plans are impractical, he is always in some sort of a dither.

Others may not approve of him at all times because of his unconventional behavior. He may be a bit eccentric. Sometimes he is so busy with his own thoughts that he loses touch with the realities of existence.

Some Aquarius feel they are more clever and intelligent than others. They seldom admit to their own faults, even when they are quite apparent. Some become rather fanatic in their views. Their criticism of others is sometimes destructive and negative.

Pisces: February 19–March 20

The Positive Side of Pisces

Known as the sign of the Fishes, Pisces has a sympathetic nature. Kindly, he is often dedicated in the way he goes about helping others. The sick and the troubled often turn to him for advice and assistance. Possessing keen intuition, Pisces can easily understand people's deepest problems.

He is very broad-minded and does not criticize others for their faults. He knows how to accept people for what they are. On the whole, he is a trustworthy and earnest person. He is loyal to his friends and will do what he can to help them in time of need. Generous and good-natured, he is a lover of peace; he is often willing to help others solve their differences. People who have taken a wrong turn in life often interest him and he will do what he can to persuade them to rehabilitate themselves.

He has a strong intuitive sense and most of the time he knows how to make it work for him. Pisces is unusually perceptive and often knows what is bothering someone before that person, himself, is aware of it. The Pisces man or woman is an idealistic person, basically, and is interested in making the world a better place in which to live. Pisces believes that everyone should help each other. He is willing to do more than his share in order to achieve cooperation with others.

The person born under this sign often is talented in music or art. He is a receptive person; he is able to take the ups and downs of life with philosophic calm.

The Negative Side of Pisces

Some Pisces are often depressed; their outlook on life is rather glum. They may feel that they have been given a bad deal in life and that others are always taking unfair advantage of them. Pisces sometimes feel that the world is a cold and cruel place. The Fishes can be easily discouraged. The Pisces man or woman may even withdraw from the harshness of reality into a secret shell of his own where he dreams and idles away a good deal of his time.

Pisces can be lazy. He lets things happen without giving the least bit of resistance. He drifts along, whether on the high road or on the low. He can be lacking in willpower.

Some Pisces people seek escape through drugs or alcohol. When temptation comes along they find it hard to resist. In matters of sex, they can be rather permissive.

Sun Sign Personalities

ARIES: Hans Christian Andersen, Pearl Bailey, Marlon Brando, Wernher Von Braun, Charlie Chaplin, Joan Crawford, Da Vinci, Bette Davis, Doris Day, W.C. Fields, Alec Guinness, Adolf Hitler, William Holden, Thomas Jefferson, Nikita Khrushchev, Elton John, Arturo Toscanini, J.P. Morgan, Paul Robeson, Gloria Steinem, Sarah Vaughn, Vincent van Gogh, Tennessee Williams

TAURUS: Fred Astaire, Charlotte Brontë, Carol Burnett, Irving Berlin, Bing Crosby, Salvador Dali, Tchaikovsky, Queen Elizabeth II, Duke Ellington, Ella Fitzgerald, Henry Fonda, Sigmund Freud, Orson Welles, Joe Louis, Lenin, Karl Marx, Golda Meir, Eva Peron, Bertrand Russell, Shakespeare, Kate Smith, Benjamin Spock, Barbra Streisand, Shirley Temple, Harry Truman

GEMINI: Ruth Benedict, Josephine Baker, Rachel Carson, Carlos Chavez, Walt Whitman, Bob Dylan, Ralph Waldo Emerson, Judy Garland, Paul Gauguin, Allen Ginsberg, Benny Goodman, Bob Hope, Burl Ives, John F. Kennedy, Peggy Lee, Marilyn Monroe, Joe Namath, Cole Porter, Laurence Olivier, Harriet Beecher Stowe, Queen Victoria, John Wayne, Frank Lloyd Wright

CANCER: "Dear Abby," Lizzie Borden, David Brinkley, Yul Brynner, Pearl Buck, Marc Chagall, Princess Diana, Babe Didrikson, Mary Baker Eddy, Henry VIII, John Glenn, Ernest Hemingway, Lena Horne, Oscar Hammerstein, Helen Keller, Ann Landers, George Orwell, Nancy Reagan, Rembrandt, Richard Rodgers, Ginger Rogers, Rubens, Jean-Paul Sartre, O.J. Simpson

LEO: Neil Armstrong, James Baldwin, Lucille Ball, Emily Brontë, Wilt Chamberlain, Julia Child, William J. Clinton, Cecil B. De Mille, Ogden Nash, Amelia Earhart, Edna Ferber, Arthur Goldberg, Alfred Hitchcock, Mick Jagger, George Meany, Annie Oakley, George Bernard Shaw, Napoleon, Jacqueline Onassis, Henry Ford, Francis Scott Key, Andy Warhol, Mae West, Orville Wright

VIRGO: Ingrid Bergman, Warren Burger, Maurice Chevalier, Agatha Christie, Sean Connery, Lafayette, Peter Falk, Greta Garbo, Althea Gibson, Arthur Godfrey, Goethe, Buddy Hackett, Michael Jackson, Lyndon Johnson, D.H. Lawrence, Sophia Loren, Grandma Moses, Arnold Palmer, Queen Elizabeth I, Walter Reuther, Peter Sellers, Lily Tomlin, George Wallace

LIBRA: Brigitte Bardot, Art Buchwald, Truman Capote, Dwight D. Eisenhower, William Faulkner, F. Scott Fitzgerald, Gandhi, George Gershwin, Micky Mantle, Helen Hayes, Vladimir Horowitz, Doris Lessing, Martina Navratalova, Eugene O'Neill, Luciano Pavarotti, Emily Post, Eleanor Roosevelt, Bruce Springsteen, Margaret Thatcher, Gore Vidal, Barbara Walters, Oscar Wilde

SCORPIO: Vivien Leigh, Richard Burton, Art Carney, Johnny Carson, Billy Graham, Grace Kelly, Walter Cronkite, Marie Curie, Charles de Gaulle, Linda Evans, Indira Gandhi, Theodore Roosevelt, Rock Hudson, Katherine Hepburn, Robert F. Kennedy, Billie Jean King, Martin Luther, Georgia O'Keeffe, Pablo Picasso, Jonas Salk, Alan Shepard, Robert Louis Stevenson

SAGITTARIUS: Jane Austen, Louisa May Alcott, Woody Allen, Beethoven, Willy Brandt, Mary Martin, William F. Buckley, Maria Callas, Winston Churchill, Noel Coward, Emily Dickinson, Walt Disney, Benjamin Disraeli, James Doolittle, Kirk Douglas, Chet Huntley, Jane Fonda, Chris Evert Lloyd, Margaret Mead, Charles Schulz, John Milton, Frank Sinatra, Steven Spielberg

CAPRICORN: Muhammad Ali, Isaac Asimov, Pablo Casals, Dizzy Dean, Marlene Dietrich, James Farmer, Ava Gardner, Barry Goldwater, Cary Grant, J. Edgar Hoover, Howard Hughes, Joan of Arc, Gypsy Rose Lee, Martin Luther King, Jr., Rudyard Kipling, Mao Tse-tung, Richard Nixon, Gamal Nasser, Louis Pasteur, Albert Schweitzer, Stalin, Benjamin Franklin, Elvis Presley

AQUARIUS: Marian Anderson, Susan B. Anthony, Jack Benny, John Barrymore, Mikhail Baryshnikov, Charles Darwin, Charles Dickens, Thomas Edison, Clark Gable, Jascha Heifetz, Abraham Lincoln, Yehudi Menuhin, Mozart, Jack Nicklaus, Ronald Reagan, Jackie Robinson, Norman Rockwell, Franklin D. Roosevelt, Gertrude Stein, Charles Lindbergh, Margaret Truman

PISCES: Edward Albee, Harry Belafonte, Alexander Graham Bell, Chopin, Adelle Davis, Albert Einstein, Golda Meir, Jackie Gleason, Winslow Homer, Edward M. Kennedy, Victor Hugo, Mike Mansfield, Michelangelo, Edna St. Vincent Millay, Liza Minelli, John Steinbeck, Linus Pauling, Ravel, Renoir, Diana Ross, William Shirer, Elizabeth Taylor, George Washington

The Signs and Their Key Words

		POSITIVE	NEGATIVE
ARIES	self	courage, initiative, pioneer instinct	brash rudeness, selfish impetuosity
TAURUS	money	endurance, loyalty, wealth	obstinacy, gluttony
GEMINI	mind	versatility	capriciousness, unreliability
CANCER	family	sympathy, homing instinct	clannishness, childishness
LEO	children	love, authority, integrity	egotism, force
VIRGO	work	purity, industry, analysis	faultfinding, cynicism
LIBRA	marriage	harmony, justice	vacillation, superficiality
SCORPIO	sex	survival, regeneration	vengeance, discord
SAGITTARIUS	travel	optimism, higher learning	lawlessness
CAPRICORN	career	depth	narrowness, gloom
AQUARIUS	friends	human fellowship, genius	perverse unpredictability
PISCES	confinement	spiritual love, universality	diffusion, escapism

The Elements and Qualities of The Signs

Every sign has both an *element* and a *quality* associated with it. The element indicates the basic makeup of the sign, and the quality describes the kind of activity associated with each.

Element	Sign	Quality	Sign
FIRE	ARIES LEO SAGITTARIUS	CARDINAL	ARIES LIBRA CANCER CAPRICORN
EARTH	TAURUS VIRGO CAPRICORN	FIXED	TAURUS LEO SCORPIO AQUARIUS
AIR	GEMINI LIBRA AQUARIUS		
WATER	CANCER SCORPIO PISCES	MUTABLE	GEMINI VIRGO SAGITTARIUS PISCES

Signs can be grouped together according to their element and quality. Signs of the same element share many basic traits in common. They tend to form stable configurations and ultimately harmonious relationships. Signs of the same quality are often less harmonious, but they share many dynamic potentials for growth as well as profound fulfillment.

Further discussion of each of these sign groupings is provided on the following pages.

The Fire Signs

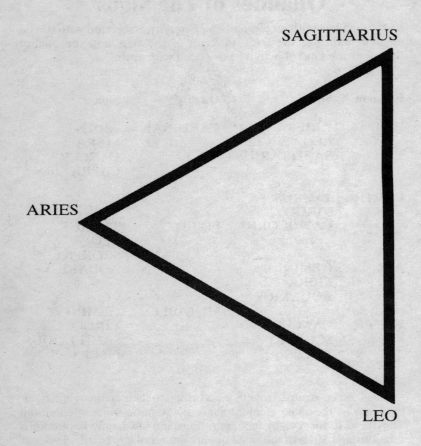

This is the fire group. On the whole these are emotional, volatile types, quick to anger, quick to forgive. They are adventurous, powerful people and act as a source of inspiration for everyone. They spark into action with immediate exuberant impulses. They are intelligent, self-involved, creative, and idealistic. They all share a certain vibrancy and glow that outwardly reflects an inner flame and passion for living.

The Earth Signs

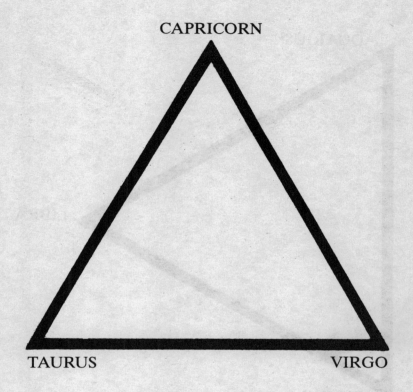

This is the earth group. They are in constant touch with the material world and tend to be conservative. Although they are all capable of spartan self-discipline, they are earthy, sensual people who are stimulated by the tangible, elegant, and luxurious. The thread of their lives is always practical, but they do fantasize and are often attracted to dark, mysterious, emotional people. They are like great cliffs overhanging the sea, forever married to the ocean but always resisting erosion from the dark, emotional forces that thunder at their feet.

The Air Signs

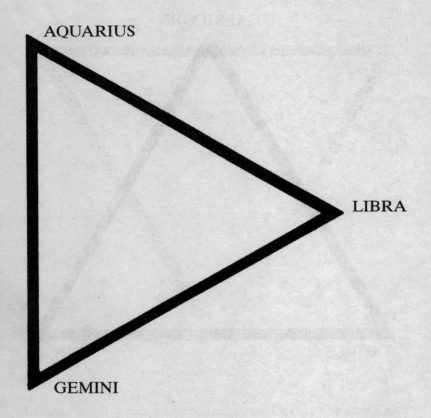

This is the air group. They are light, mental creatures desirous of contact, communication, and relationship. They are involved with people and the forming of ties on many levels. Original thinkers, they are the bearers of human news. Their language is their sense of word, color, style, and beauty. They provide an atmosphere suitable and pleasant for living. They add change and versatility to the scene, and it is through them that we can explore new territory of human intelligence and experience.

The Water Signs

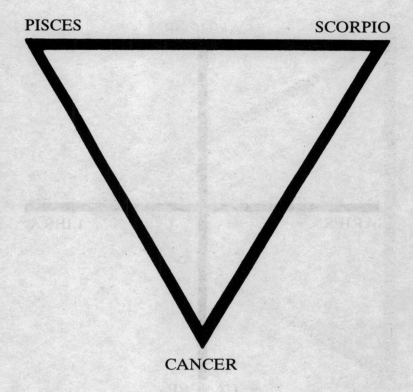

This is the water group. Through the water people, we are all joined together on emotional, nonverbal levels. They are silent, mysterious types whose magic hypnotizes even the most determined realist. They have uncanny perceptions about people and are as rich as the oceans when it comes to feeling, emotion, or imagination. They are sensitive, mystical creatures with memories that go back beyond time. Through water, life is sustained. These people have the potential for the depths of darkness or the heights of mysticism and art.

The Cardinal Signs

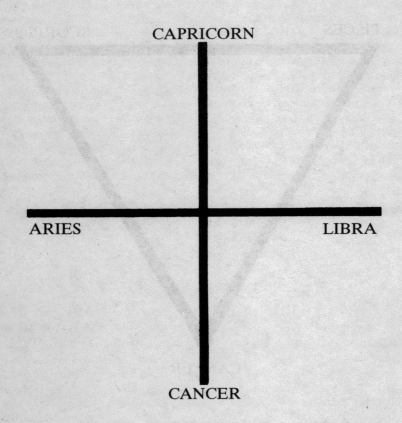

Put together, this is a clear-cut picture of dynamism, activity, tremendous stress, and remarkable achievement. These people know the meaning of great change since their lives are often characterized by significant crises and major successes. This combination is like a simultaneous storm of summer, fall, winter, and spring. The danger is chaotic diffusion of energy; the potential is irrepressible growth and victory.

The Fixed Signs

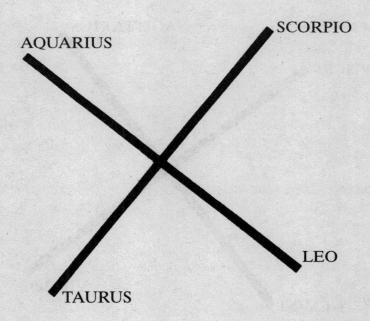

Fixed signs are always establishing themselves in a given place or area of experience. Like explorers who arrive and plant a flag, these people claim a position from which they do not enjoy being deposed. They are staunch, stalwart, upright, trusty, honorable people, although their obstinacy is well-known. Their contribution is fixity, and they are the angels who support our visible world.

The Mutable Signs

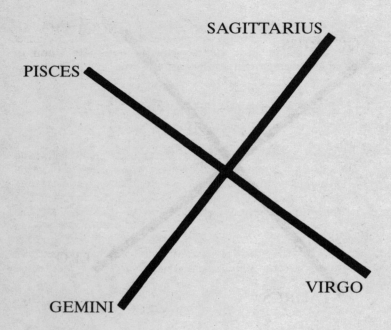

Mutable people are versatile, sensitive, intelligent, nervous, and deeply curious about life. They are the translators of all energy. They often carry out or complete tasks initiated by others. Combinations of these signs have highly developed minds; they are imaginative and jumpy and think and talk a lot. At worst their lives are a Tower of Babel. At best they are adaptable and ready creatures who can assimilate one kind of experience and enjoy it while anticipating coming changes.

THE PLANETS OF THE SOLAR SYSTEM

This section describes the planets of the solar system. In astrology, both the Sun and the Moon are considered to be planets. Because of the Moon's influence in our day-to-day lives, the Moon is described in a separate section following this one.

The Planets and the Signs They Rule

The signs of the Zodiac are linked to the planets in the following way. Each sign is governed or ruled by one or more planets. No matter where the planets are located in the sky at any given moment, they still rule their respective signs, and when they travel through the signs they rule, they have special dignity and their effects are stronger.

Following is a list of the planets and the signs they rule. After looking at the list, read the definitions of the planets and see if you can determine how the planet ruling *your* Sun sign has affected your life.

SIGNS	RULING PLANETS
Aries	Mars, Pluto
Taurus	Venus
Gemini	Mercury
Cancer	Moon
Leo	Sun
Virgo	Mercury
Libra	Venus
Scorpio	Mars, Pluto
Sagittarius	Jupiter
Capricorn	Saturn
Aquarius	Saturn, Uranus
Pisces	Jupiter, Neptune

Characteristics of the Planets

The following pages give the meaning and characteristics of the planets of the solar system. They all travel around the Sun at different speeds and different distances. Taken with the Sun, they all distribute individual intelligence and ability throughout the entire chart.

The planets modify the influence of the Sun in a chart according to their own particular natures, strengths, and positions. Their positions must be calculated for each year and day, and their function and expression in a horoscope will change as they move from one area of the Zodiac to another.

We start with a description of the sun.

THE SUN

SUN

This is the center of existence. Around this flaming sphere all the planets revolve in endless orbits. Our star is constantly sending out its beams of light and energy without which no life on Earth would be possible. In astrology it symbolizes everything we are trying to become, the center around which all of our activity in life will always revolve. It is the symbol of our basic nature and describes the natural and constant thread that runs through everything that we do from birth to death on this planet.

To early astrologers, the Sun seemed to be another planet because it crossed the heavens every day, just like the rest of the bodies in the sky.

It is the only star near enough to be seen well—it is, in fact, a dwarf star. Approximately 860,000 miles in diameter, it is about ten times as wide as the giant planet Jupiter. The next nearest star is nearly 300,000 times as far away, and if the Sun were located as far away as most of the bright stars, it would be too faint to be seen without a telescope.

Everything in the horoscope ultimately revolves around this singular body. Although other forces may be prominent in the charts of some individuals, still the Sun is the total nucleus of being and symbolizes the complete potential of every human being alive. It is vitality and the life force. Your whole essence comes from the position of the Sun.

You are always trying to express the Sun according to its position by house and sign. Possibility for all development is found in the Sun, and it marks the fundamental character of your personal radiations all around you.

It is the symbol of strength, vigor, wisdom, dignity, ardor, and generosity, and the ability for a person to function as a mature individual. It is also a creative force in society. It is consciousness of the gift of life.

The underdeveloped solar nature is arrogant, pushy, undependable, and proud, and is constantly using force.

MERCURY

Mercury is the planet closest to the Sun. It races around our star, gathering information and translating it to the rest of the system. Mercury represents your capacity to understand the desires of your own will and to translate those desires into action.

In other words it is the planet of mind and the power of communication. Through Mercury we develop an ability to think, write, speak, and observe—to become aware of the world around us. It colors our attitudes and vision of the world, as well as our capacity to communicate our inner responses to the outside world. Some people who have serious disabilities in their power of verbal communication have often wrongly been described as people lacking intelligence.

Although this planet (and its position in the horoscope) indicates your power to communicate your thoughts and perceptions to the world, intelligence is something deeper. Intelligence is distributed throughout all the planets. It is the relationship of the planets to each other that truly describes what we call intelligence. Mercury rules speaking, language, mathematics, draft and design, students, messengers, young people, offices, teachers, and any pursuits where the mind of man has wings.

VENUS

Venus is beauty. It symbolizes the harmony and radiance of a rare and elusive quality: beauty itself. It is refinement and delicacy, softness and charm. In astrology it indicates grace, balance, and the aesthetic sense. Where Venus is we see beauty, a gentle drawing in of energy and the need for satisfaction and completion. It is a special touch that finishes off rough edges. It is sensitivity, and affection, and it is always the place for that other elusive phenomenon: love. Venus describes our sense of what is beautiful and loving. Poorly developed, it is vulgar, tasteless, and self-indulgent. But its ideal is the flame of spiritual love—Aphrodite, goddess of love, and the sweetness and power of personal beauty.

MARS

Mars is raw, crude energy. The planet next to Earth but outward from the Sun is a fiery red sphere that charges through the horoscope with force and fury. It represents the way you reach out for new adventure and new experience. It is energy and drive, initiative, courage, and daring. It is the power to start something and see it through. It can be thoughtless, cruel and wild, angry and hostile, causing cuts, burns, scalds, and wounds. It can stab its way through a chart, or it can be the symbol of healthy spirited adventure, well-channeled constructive power to begin and keep up the drive. If you have trouble starting things, if you lack the get-up-and-go to start the ball rolling, if you lack aggressiveness and self-confidence, chances are there's another planet influencing your Mars. Mars rules soldiers, butchers, surgeons, salesmen—any field that requires daring, bold skill, operational technique, or self-promotion.

JUPITER

This is the largest planet of the solar system. Scientists have recently learned that Jupiter reflects more light than it receives from the Sun. In a sense it is like a star itself. In astrology it rules good luck and good cheer, health, wealth, optimism, happiness, success, and joy. It is the symbol of opportunity and always opens the way for new possibilities in your life. It rules exuberance, enthusiasm, wisdom, knowledge, generosity, and all forms of expansion in general. It rules actors, statesmen, clerics, professional people, religion, publishing, and the distribution of many people over large areas.

Sometimes Jupiter makes you think you deserve everything, and you become sloppy, wasteful, careless and rude, prodigal and lawless, in the illusion that nothing can ever go wrong. Then there is the danger of overconfidence, exaggeration, undependability, and overindulgence.

Jupiter is the minimization of limitation and the emphasis on spirituality and potential. It is the thirst for knowledge and higher learning.

SATURN

Saturn circles our system in dark splendor with its mysterious rings, forcing us to be awakened to whatever we have neglected in the past. It will present real puzzles and problems to be solved, causing delays, obstacles, and hindrances. By doing so, Saturn stirs our own sensitivity to those areas where we are laziest.

Here we must patiently develop *method*, and only through painstaking effort can our ends be achieved. It brings order to a horoscope and imposes reason just where we are feeling least reasonable. By creating limitations and boundary, Saturn shows the consequences of being human and demands that we accept the changing cycles inevitable in human life. Saturn rules time, old age, and sobriety. It can bring depression, gloom, jealousy, and greed, or serious acceptance of responsibilities out of which success will develop. With Saturn there is nothing to do but face facts. It rules laborers, stones, granite, rocks, and crystals of all kinds.

THE OUTER PLANETS:
URANUS, NEPTUNE, PLUTO

Uranus, Neptune, Pluto are the outer planets. They liberate human beings from cultural conditioning, and in that sense are the lawbreakers. In early times it was thought that Saturn was the last planet of the system—the outer limit beyond which we could never go. The discovery of the next three planets ushered in new phases of human history, revolution, and technology.

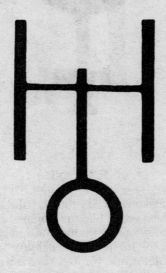

URANUS

Uranus rules unexpected change, upheaval, revolution. It is the symbol of total independence and asserts the freedom of an individual from all restriction and restraint. It is a breakthrough planet and indicates talent, originality, and genius in a horoscope. It usually causes last-minute reversals and changes of plan, unwanted separations, accidents, catastrophes, and eccentric behavior. It can add irrational rebelliousness and perverse bohemianism to a personality or a streak of unaffected brilliance in science and art. It rules technology, aviation, and all forms of electrical and electronic advancement. It governs great leaps forward and topsy-turvy situations, and *always* turns things around at the last minute. Its effects are difficult to predict, since it rules sudden last-minute decisions and events that come like lightning out of the blue.

NEPTUNE

Neptune dissolves existing reality the way the sea erodes the cliffs beside it. Its effects are subtle like the ringing of a buoy's bell in the fog. It suggests a reality higher than definition can usually describe. It awakens a sense of higher responsibility often causing guilt, worry, anxieties, or delusions. Neptune is associated with all forms of escape and can make things seem a certain way so convincingly that you are absolutely sure of something that eventually turns out to be quite different.

It is the planet of illusion and therefore governs the invisible realms that lie beyond our ordinary minds, beyond our simple factual ability to prove what is "real." Treachery, deceit, disillusionment, and disappointment are linked to Neptune. It describes a vague reality that promises eternity and the divine, yet in a manner so complex that we cannot really fathom it at all. At its worst Neptune is a cheap intoxicant; at its best it is the poetry, music, and inspiration of the higher planes of spiritual love. It has dominion over movies, photographs, and much of the arts.

PLUTO

Pluto lies at the outpost of our system and therefore rules finality in a horoscope—the final closing of chapters in your life, the passing of major milestones and points of development from which there is no return. It is a final wipeout, a closeout, an evacuation. It is a distant, subtle but powerful catalyst in all transformations that occur. It creates, destroys, then recreates. Sometimes Pluto starts its influence with a minor event or insignificant incident that might even go unnoticed. Slowly but surely, little by little, everything changes, until at last there has been a total transformation in the area of your life where Pluto has been operating. It rules mass thinking and the trends that society first rejects, then adopts, and finally outgrows.

Pluto rules the dead and the underworld—all the powerful forces of creation and destruction that go on all the time beneath, around, and above us. It can bring a lust for power with strong obsessions.

It is the planet that rules the metamorphosis of the caterpillar into a butterfly, for it symbolizes the capacity to change totally and forever a person's lifestyle, way of thought, and behavior.

THE MOON IN EACH SIGN

The Moon is the nearest planet to the Earth. It exerts more observable influence on us from day to day than any other planet. The effect is very personal, very intimate, and if we are not aware of how it works it can make us quite unstable in our ideas. And the annoying thing is that at these times we often see our own instability but can do nothing about it. A knowledge of what can be expected may help considerably. We can then be prepared to stand strong against the Moon's negative influences and use its positive ones to help us to get ahead. Who has not heard of going with the tide?

The Moon reflects, has no light of its own. It reflects the Sun—the life giver—in the form of vital movement. The Moon controls the tides, the blood rhythm, the movement of sap in trees and plants. Its nature is inconstancy and change so it signifies our moods, our superficial behavior—walking, talking, and especially thinking. Being a true reflector of other forces, the Moon is cold, watery like the surface of a still lake, brilliant and scintillating at times, but easily ruffled and disturbed by the winds of change.

The Moon takes about 27⅓ days to make a complete transit of the Zodiac. It spends just over 2¼ days in each sign. During that time it reflects the qualities, energies, and characteristics of the sign and, to a degree, the planet which rules the sign. When the Moon in its transit occupies a sign incompatible with our own birth sign, we can expect to feel a vague uneasiness, perhaps a touch of irritableness. We should not be discouraged nor let the feeling get us down, or, worse still, allow ourselves to take the discomfort out on others. Try to remember that the Moon has to change signs within 55 hours and, provided you are not physically ill, your mood will probably change with it. It is amazing how frequently depression lifts with the shift in the Moon's position. And, of course, when the Moon is transiting a sign compatible or sympathetic to yours, you will probably feel some sort of stimulation or just be plain happy to be alive.

In the horoscope, the Moon is such a powerful indicator that competent astrologers often use the sign it occupied at birth as the birth sign of the person. This is done particularly when the Sun is on the cusp, or edge, of two signs. Most experienced astrologers, however, coordinate both Sun and Moon signs by reading and confirming from one to the other and secure a far more accurate and personalized analysis.

For these reasons, the Moon tables which follow this section (see pages 86–92) are of great importance to the individual. They show the days and the exact times the Moon will enter each sign of the Zodiac for the year. Remember, you have to adjust the indicated times to local time. The corrections, already calculated for most of the main cities, are at the beginning of the tables. What follows now is a guide to the influences that will be reflected to the Earth by the Moon while it transits each of the twelve signs. The influence is at its peak about 26 hours after the Moon enters a sign. As you read the daily forecast, check the Moon sign for any given day and glance back at this guide.

MOON IN ARIES
This is a time for action, for reaching out beyond the usual self-imposed limitations and faint-hearted cautions. If you have plans in your head or on your desk, put them into practice. New ventures, applications, new jobs, new starts of any kind—all have a good chance of success. This is the period when original and dynamic impulses are being reflected onto Earth. Such energies are extremely vital and favor the pursuit of pleasure and adventure in practically every form. Sick people should feel an improvement. Those who are well will probably find themselves exuding confidence and optimism. People fond of physical exercise should find their bodies growing with tone and well-being. Boldness, strength, determination should characterize most of your activities with a readiness to face up to old challenges. Yesterday's problems may seem petty and exaggerated—so deal with them. Strike out alone. Self-reliance will attract others to you. This is a good time for making friends. Business and marriage partners are more likely to be impressed with the man and woman of action. Opposition will be overcome or thrown aside with much less effort than usual. CAUTION: Be dominant but not domineering.

MOON IN TAURUS
The spontaneous, action-packed person of yesterday gives way to the cautious, diligent, hardworking "thinker." In this period ideas will probably be concentrated on ways of improving finances. A great deal of time may be spent figuring out and going over schemes

and plans. It is the right time to be careful with detail. People will find themselves working longer than usual at their desks. Or devoting more time to serious thought about the future. A strong desire to put order into business and financial arrangements may cause extra work. Loved ones may complain of being neglected and may fail to appreciate that your efforts are for their ultimate benefit. Your desire for system may extend to criticism of arrangements in the home and lead to minor upsets. Health may be affected through overwork. Try to secure a reasonable amount of rest and relaxation, although the tendency will be to "keep going" despite good advice. Work done conscientiously in this period should result in a solid contribution to your future security. CAUTION: Try not to be as serious with people as the work you are engaged in.

MOON IN GEMINI

The humdrum of routine and too much work should suddenly end. You are likely to find yourself in an expansive, quicksilver world of change and self-expression. Urges to write, to paint, to experience the freedom of some sort of artistic outpouring, may be very strong. Take full advantage of them. You may find yourself finishing something you began and put aside long ago. Or embarking on something new which could easily be prompted by a chance meeting, a new acquaintance, or even an advertisement. There may be a yearning for a change of scenery, the feeling to visit another country (not too far away), or at least to get away for a few days. This may result in short, quick journeys. Or, if you are planning a single visit, there may be some unexpected changes or detours on the way. Familiar activities will seem to give little satisfaction unless they contain a fresh element of excitement or expectation. The inclination will be toward untried pursuits, particularly those that allow you to express your inner nature. The accent is on new faces, new places. CAUTION: Do not be too quick to commit yourself emotionally.

MOON IN CANCER

Feelings of uncertainty and vague insecurity are likely to cause problems while the Moon is in Cancer. Thoughts may turn frequently to the warmth of the home and the comfort of loved ones. Nostalgic impulses could cause you to bring out old photographs and letters and reflect on the days when your life seemed to be much more rewarding and less demanding. The love and understanding of parents and family may be important, and, if it is not forthcoming, you may have to fight against bouts of self-pity. The cordiality of friends and the thought of good times with them that are sure to be repeated will help to restore you to a happier frame of mind. The desire to be alone may follow minor setbacks or rebuffs at this time, but solitude is unlikely to help. Better to get on the telephone or visit someone. This period often causes peculiar dreams and upsurges of imaginative thinking which can be helpful to authors of occult and mystical works. Preoccupation with the personal world of simple human needs can overshadow any material strivings. CAUTION: Do not spend too much time thinking—seek the company of loved ones or close friends.

MOON IN LEO

New horizons of exciting and rather extravagant activity open up. This is the time for exhilarating entertainment, glamorous and lavish parties, and expensive shopping sprees. Any merrymaking that relies upon your generosity as a host has every chance of being a spectacular success. You should find yourself right in the center of the fun, either as the life of the party or simply as a person whom happy people like to be with. Romance thrives in this heady atmosphere and friendships are likely to explode unexpectedly into serious attachments. Children and younger people should be attracted to you and you may find yourself organizing a picnic or a visit to a fun-fair, the movies, or the beach. The sunny company and vitality of youthful companions should help you to find some unsuspected energy. In career, you could find an opening for promotion or advancement. This should be the time to make a direct approach. The period favors those engaged in original research. CAUTION: Bask in popularity, not in flattery.

MOON IN VIRGO

Off comes the party cap and out steps the busy, practical worker. He wants to get his personal affairs straight, to rearrange them, if necessary, for more efficiency, so he will have more time for more work. He clears up his correspondence, pays outstanding bills, makes numerous phone calls. He is likely to make inquiries, or sign up for some new insurance and put money into gilt-edged investment. Thoughts probably revolve around the need for future security—to tie up loose ends and clear the decks. There may be a tendency to be "finicky," to interfere in the routine of others, particularly friends and family members. The motive may be a genuine desire to help with suggestions for updating or streamlining their affairs, but these will probably not be welcomed. Sympathy may be felt for less fortunate sections of the community and a flurry of some sort of voluntary service is likely. This may be accompanied by strong feelings of responsibility on several fronts and health may suffer from extra efforts made. CAUTION: Everyone may not want your help or advice.

MOON IN LIBRA
These are days of harmony and agreement and you should find yourself at peace with most others. Relationships tend to be smooth and sweet-flowing. Friends may become closer and bonds deepen in mutual understanding. Hopes will be shared. Progress by cooperation could be the secret of success in every sphere. In business, established partnerships may flourish and new ones get off to a good start. Acquaintances could discover similar interests that lead to congenial discussions and rewarding exchanges of some sort. Love, as a unifying force, reaches its optimum. Marriage partners should find accord. Those who wed at this time face the prospect of a happy union. Cooperation and tolerance are felt to be stronger than dissension and impatience. The argumentative are not quite so loud in their bellowings, nor as inflexible in their attitudes. In the home, there should be a greater recognition of the other point of view and a readiness to put the wishes of the group before selfish insistence. This is a favorable time to join an art group. CAUTION: Do not be too independent—let others help you if they want to.

MOON IN SCORPIO
Driving impulses to make money and to economize are likely to cause upsets all around. No area of expenditure is likely to be spared the ax, including the household budget. This is a time when the desire to cut down on extravagance can become near fanatical. Care must be exercised to try to keep the aim in reasonable perspective. Others may not feel the same urgent need to save and may retaliate. There is a danger that possessions of sentimental value will be sold to realize cash for investment. Buying and selling of stock for quick profit is also likely. The attention turns to organizing, reorganizing, tidying up at home and at work. Neglected jobs could suddenly be done with great bursts of energy. The desire for solitude may intervene. Self-searching thoughts could disturb. The sense of invisible and mysterious energies in play could cause some excitability. The reassurance of loves ones may help. CAUTION: Be kind to the people you love.

MOON IN SAGITTARIUS
These are days when you are likely to be stirred and elevated by discussions and reflections of a religious and philosophical nature. Ideas of faraway places may cause unusual response and excitement. A decision may be made to visit someone overseas, perhaps a person whose influence was important to your earlier character development. There could be a strong resolution to get away from

present intellectual patterns, to learn new subjects, and to meet more interesting people. The superficial may be rejected in all its forms. An impatience with old ideas and unimaginative contacts could lead to a change of companions and interests. There may be an upsurge of religious feeling and metaphysical inquiry. Even a new insight into the significance of astrology and other occult studies is likely under the curious stimulus of the Moon in Sagittarius. Physically, you may express this need for fundamental change by spending more time outdoors: sports, gardening, long walks appeal. CAUTION: Try to channel any restlessness into worthwhile study.

MOON IN CAPRICORN
Life in these hours may seem to pivot around the importance of gaining prestige and honor in the career, as well as maintaining a spotless reputation. Ambitious urges may be excessive and could be accompanied by quite acquisitive drives for money. Effort should be directed along strictly ethical lines where there is no possibility of reproach or scandal. All endeavors are likely to be characterized by great earnestness, and an air of authority and purpose which should impress those who are looking for leadership or reliability. The desire to conform to accepted standards may extend to sharp criticism of family members. Frivolity and unconventional actions are unlikely to amuse while the Moon is in Capricorn. Moderation and seriousness are the orders of the day. Achievement and recognition in this period could come through community work or organizing for the benefit of some amateur group. CAUTION: Dignity and esteem are not always self-awarded.

MOON IN AQUARIUS
Moon in Aquarius is in the second last sign of the Zodiac where ideas can become disturbingly fine and subtle. The result is often a mental "no-man's land" where imagination cannot be trusted with the same certitude as other times. The dangers for the individual are the extremes of optimism and pessimism. Unless the imagination is held in check, situations are likely to be misread, and rosy conclusions drawn where they do not exist. Consequences for the unwary can be costly in career and business. Best to think twice and not speak or act until you think again. Pessimism can be a cruel self-inflicted penalty for delusion at this time. Between the two extremes are strange areas of self-deception which, for example, can make the selfish person think he is actually being generous. Eerie dreams which resemble the reality and even seem to continue into the waking state are also possible. CAUTION: Look for the fact and not just for the image in your mind.

MOON IN PISCES

Everything seems to come to the surface now. Memory may be crystal clear, throwing up long-forgotten information which could be valuable in the career or business. Flashes of clairvoyance and intuition are possible along with sudden realizations of one's own nature, which may be used for self-improvement. A talent, never before suspected, may be discovered. Qualities not evident before in friends and marriage partners are likely to be noticed. As this is a period in which the truth seems to emerge, the discovery of false characteristics is likely to lead to disenchantment or a shift in attachments. However, when qualities are accepted, it should lead to happiness and deeper feeling. Surprise solutions could bob up for old problems. There may be a public announcement of the solving of a crime or mystery. People with secrets may find someone has "guessed" correctly. The secrets of the soul or the inner self also tend to reveal themselves. Religious and philosophical groups may make some interesting discoveries. CAUTION: Not a time for activities that depend on secrecy.

NOTE: When you read your daily forecasts, use the Moon Sign Dates that are provided in the following section of Moon Tables. Then you may want to glance back here for the Moon's influence in a given sign.

MOON TABLES

CORRECTION FOR NEW YORK TIME, FIVE HOURS WEST OF GREENWICH

Atlanta, Boston, Detroit, Miami, Washington, Montreal,
  Ottawa, Quebec, Bogota, Havana, Lima, Santiago ... Same time
Chicago, New Orleans, Houston, Winnipeg, Churchill,
  Mexico City .... Deduct 1 hour
Albuquerque, Denver, Phoenix, El Paso, Edmonton,
  Helena .... Deduct 2 hours
Los Angeles, San Francisco, Reno, Portland,
  Seattle, Vancouver .... Deduct 3 hours
Honolulu, Anchorage, Fairbanks, Kodiak .... Deduct 5 hours
Nome, Samoa, Tonga, Midway .... Deduct 6 hours
Halifax, Bermuda, San Juan, Caracas, La Paz,
  Barbados .... Add 1 hour
St. John's, Brasilia, Rio de Janeiro, Sao Paulo,
  Buenos Aires, Montevideo .... Add 2 hours
Azores, Cape Verde Islands .... Add 3 hours
Canary Islands, Madeira, Reykjavik .... Add 4 hours
London, Paris, Amsterdam, Madrid, Lisbon,
  Gibraltar, Belfast, Raba .... Add 5 hours
Frankfurt, Rome, Oslo, Stockholm, Prague,
  Belgrade .... Add 6 hours
Bucharest, Beirut, Tel Aviv, Athens, Istanbul, Cairo,
  Alexandria, Cape Town, Johannesburg .... Add 7 hours
Moscow, Leningrad, Baghdad, Dhahran,
  Addis Ababa, Nairobi, Teheran, Zanzibar ...... Add 8 hours
Bombay, Calcutta, Sri Lanka .... Add 10½
Hong Kong, Shanghai, Manila, Peking, Perth ..... Add 13 hours
Tokyo, Okinawa, Darwin, Pusan .... Add 14 hours
Sydney, Melbourne, Port Moresby, Guam .... Add 15 hours
Auckland, Wellington, Suva, Wake .... Add 17 hours

2010 MOON SIGN DATES— NEW YORK TIME

JANUARY
Day Moon Enters
1. Leo 9:42 pm
2. Leo
3. Virgo 9:54 pm
4. Virgo
5. Libra 11:59 pm
6. Libra
7. Libra
8. Scorp. 5:01 am
9. Scorp.
10. Sagitt. 1:11 pm
11. Sagitt.
12. Capric. 11:55 pm
13. Capric.
14. Capric.
15. Aquar. 12:18 pm
16. Aquar.
17. Aquar.
18. Pisces 1:18 am
19. Pisces
20. Aries 1:37 pm
21. Aries
22. Taurus 11:41 pm
23. Taurus
24. Taurus
25. Gemini 6:12 am
26. Gemini
27. Cancer 9:02 am
28. Cancer
29. Leo 9:11 am
30. Leo
31. Virgo 8:24 am

FEBRUARY
Day Moon Enters
1. Virgo
2. Libra 8:43 am
3. Libra
4. Scorp. 11:57 am
5. Scorp.
6. Sagitt. 7:05 pm
7. Sagitt.
8. Sagitt.
9. Capric. 5:45 am
10. Capric.
11. Aquar. 6:25 pm
12. Aquar.
13. Aquar.
14. Pisces 7:24 am
15. Pisces
16. Aries 7:31 pm
17. Aries
18. Aries
19. Taurus 5:56 am
20. Taurus
21. Gemini 1:48 pm
22. Gemini
23. Cancer 6:30 pm
24. Cancer
25. Leo 8:09 pm
26. Leo
27. Virgo 7:53 pm
28. Virgo

MARCH
Day Moon Enters
1. Libra 7:32 pm
2. Libra
3. Scorp. 9:12 pm
4. Scorp.
5. Scorp.
6. Sagitt. 1:37 am
7. Sagitt.
8. Capric. 12:14 pm
9. Capric.
10. Capric.
11. Aquar. 12:43 am
12. Aquar.
13. Pisces 1:45 pm
14. Pisces
15. Pisces
16. Aries 1:33 am
17. Aries
18. Taurus 11:30 am
19. Taurus
20. Gemini 7:29 pm
21. Gemini
22. Gemini
23. Cancer 1:17 am
24. Cancer
25. Leo 4:40 am
26. Leo
27. Virgo 5:58 am
28. Virgo
29. Libra 6:22 am
30. Libra
31. Scorp. 7:42 am

Daylight saving time to be considered where applicable.

2010 MOON SIGN DATES— NEW YORK TIME

APRIL
Day Moon Enters
1. Scorp.
2. Sagitt. 11:54 am
3. Sagitt.
4. Capric. 8:08 pm
5. Capric.
6. Capric.
7. Aquar. 7:52 am
8. Aquar.
9. Pisces 8:49 pm
10. Pisces
11. Pisces
12. Aries 8:32 am
13. Aries
14. Taurus 5:56 pm
15. Taurus
16. Taurus
17. Gemini 1:09 am
18. Gemini
19. Cancer 6:40 am
20. Cancer
21. Leo 10:43 am
22. Leo
23. Virgo 1:25 pm
24. Virgo
25. Libra 3:18 pm
26. Libra
27. Scorp. 5:30 pm
28. Scorp.
29. Sagitt. 9:37 pm
30. Sagitt.

MAY
Day Moon Enters
1. Sagitt.
2. Capric. 5:01 am
3. Capric.
4. Aquar. 3:53 pm
5. Aquar.
6. Aquar.
7. Pisces 4:35 am
8. Pisces
9. Aries 4:30 pm
10. Aries
11. Aries
12. Taurus 1:49 am
13. Taurus
14. Gemini 8:19 am
15. Gemini
16. Cancer 12:47 pm
17. Cancer
18. Leo 4:07 pm
19. Leo
20. Virgo 6:59 pm
21. Virgo
22. Libra 9:51 pm
23. Libra
24. Libra
25. Scorp. 1:18 am
26. Scorp.
27. Sagitt. 6:17 am
28. Sagitt.
29. Capric. 1:45 pm
30. Capric.
31. Capric.

JUNE
Day Moon Enters
1. Aquar. 12:09 am
2. Aquar.
3. Pisces 12:35 pm
4. Pisces
5. Pisces
6. Aries 12:51 am
7. Aries
8. Taurus 10:42 am
9. Taurus
10. Gemini 5:12 pm
11. Gemini
12. Cancer 8:51 pm
13. Cancer
14. Leo 10:55 pm
15. Leo
16. Leo
17. Virgo 12:42 am
18. Virgo
19. Libra 3:14 am
20. Libra
21. Scorp. 7:15 am
22. Scorp.
23. Sagitt. 1:11 pm
24. Sagitt.
25. Capric. 9:22 pm
26. Capric.
27. Capric.
28. Aquar. 7:53 am
29. Aquar.
30. Pisces 8:11 pm

Daylight saving time to be considered where applicable.

2010 MOON SIGN DATES— NEW YORK TIME

JULY
Day Moon Enters
1. Pisces
2. Pisces
3. Aries 8:45 am
4. Aries
5. Taurus 7:30 pm
6. Taurus
7. Taurus
8. Gemini 2:52 am
9. Gemini
10. Cancer 6:39 am
11. Cancer
12. Leo 7:55 am
13. Leo
14. Virgo 8:16 am
15. Virgo
16. Libra 9:25 am
17. Libra
18. Scorp. 12:43 pm
19. Scorp.
20. Sagitt. 6:50 pm
21. Sagitt.
22. Sagitt.
23. Capric. 3:40 am
24. Capric.
25. Aquar. 2:39 pm
26. Aquar.
27. Aquar.
28. Pisces 3:01 am
29. Pisces
30. Aries 3:43 pm
31. Aries

AUGUST
Day Moon Enters
1. Aries
2. Taurus 3:14 am
3. Taurus
4. Gemini 11:55 am
5. Gemini
6. Cancer 4:51 pm
7. Cancer
8. Leo 6:24 pm
9. Leo
10. Virgo 6:02 pm
11. Virgo
12. Libra 5:44 pm
13. Libra
14. Scorp. 7:27 pm
15. Scorp.
16. Scorp.
17. Sagitt. 12:35 am
18. Sagitt.
19. Capric. 9:18 am
20. Capric.
21. Aquar. 8:38 pm
22. Aquar.
23. Aquar.
24. Pisces 9:12 am
25. Pisces
26. Aries 9:50 pm
27. Aries
28. Aries
29. Taurus 9:36 am
30. Taurus
31. Gemini 7:20 pm

SEPTEMBER
Day Moon Enters
1. Gemini
2. Gemini
3. Cancer 1:52 am
4. Cancer
5. Leo 4:46 am
6. Leo
7. Virgo 4:54 am
8. Virgo
9. Libra 4:02 am
10. Libra
11. Scorp. 4:22 am
12. Scorp.
13. Sagitt. 7:53 am
14. Sagitt.
15. Capric. 3:31 pm
16. Capric.
17. Capric.
18. Aquar. 2:36 am
19. Aquar.
20. Pisces 3:16 pm
21. Pisces
22. Pisces
23. Aries 3:48 am
24. Aries
25. Taurus 3:18 pm
26. Taurus
27. Taurus
28. Gemini 1:12 am
29. Gemini
30. Cancer 8:47 am

Daylight saving time to be considered where applicable.

2010 MOON SIGN DATES—
NEW YORK TIME

OCTOBER Day Moon Enters		NOVEMBER Day Moon Enters		DECEMBER Day Moon Enters	
1. Cancer		1. Virgo		1. Libra	
2. Leo	1:22 pm	2. Virgo		2. Scorp.	9:45 am
3. Leo		3. Libra	12:20 am	3. Scorp.	
4. Virgo	3:01 pm	4. Libra		4. Sagitt.	1:00 pm
5. Virgo		5. Scorp.	1:17 am	5. Sagitt.	
6. Libra	2:53 pm	6. Scorp.		6. Capric.	6:17 pm
7. Libra		7. Sagitt.	3:29 am	7. Capric.	
8. Scorp.	2:53 pm	8. Sagitt.		8. Capric.	
9. Scorp.		9. Capric.	8:38 am	9. Aquar.	2:32 am
10. Sagitt.	5:10 pm	10. Capric.		10. Aquar.	
11. Sagitt.		11. Aquar.	5:33 pm	11. Pisces	1:42 pm
12. Capric.	11:18 pm	12. Aquar.		12. Pisces	
13. Capric.		13. Aquar.		13. Pisces	
14. Capric.		14. Pisces	5:25 am	14. Aries	2:16 am
15. Aquar.	9:25 am	15. Pisces		15. Aries	
16. Aquar.		16. Aries	6:00 pm	16. Taurus	1:50 pm
17. Pisces	9:53 pm	17. Aries		17. Taurus	
18. Pisces		18. Aries		18. Gemini	10:38 pm
19. Pisces		19. Taurus	5:05 am	19. Gemini	
20. Aries	10:24 am	20. Taurus		20. Gemini	
21. Aries		21. Gemini	1:47 pm	21. Cancer	4:23 am
22. Taurus	9:31 pm	22. Gemini		22. Cancer	
23. Taurus		23. Cancer	8:15 pm	23. Leo	7:52 am
24. Taurus		24. Cancer		24. Leo	
25. Gemini	6:49 am	25. Cancer		25. Virgo	10:15 am
26. Gemini		26. Leo	1:02 am	26. Virgo	
27. Cancer	2:15 pm	27. Leo		27. Libra	12:39 pm
28. Cancer		28. Virgo	4:35 am	28. Libra	
29. Leo	7:40 pm	29. Virgo		29. Scorp.	3:51 pm
30. Leo		30. Libra	7:16 am	30. Scorp.	
31. Virgo	10:52 pm			31. Sagitt.	8:22 pm

Daylight saving time to be considered where applicable.

2010 PHASES OF THE MOON— NEW YORK TIME

New Moon	First Quarter	Full Moon	Last Quarter
Dec. 15 ('09)	Dec. 24 ('09)	Dec. 31 ('09)	Jan. 7
Jan. 15	Jan. 23	Jan. 30	Feb. 5
Feb. 13	Feb. 21	Feb. 28	March 7
March 15	March 23	March 29	April 6
April 14	April 21	April 28	May 5
May 13	May 20	May 27	June 4
June 12	June 18	June 26	July 4
July 11	July 18	July 25	August 3
August 9	August 16	August 24	Sept. 1
Sept. 8	Sept. 15	Sept. 23	Sept. 30
Oct. 7	Oct. 14	Oct. 22	Oct. 30
Nov. 6	Nov. 13	Nov. 21	Nov. 28
Dec. 5	Dec. 13	Dec. 21	Dec. 27

Each phase of the Moon lasts approximately seven to eight days, during which the Moon's shape gradually changes as it comes out of one phase and goes into the next.

There will be a solar eclipse during the New Moon phase on January 15 and July 11.

There will be a lunar eclipse during the Full Moon phase on June 26 and December 21.

2010 FISHING GUIDE

	Good	Best
January	3-4-16-28-29-30-31	2-6-23-27
February	1-2-13-21-26-27-28	5-25
March	1-7-15-27-28-29	2-3-24-30-31
April	13-22-24-29	1-2-3-8-26-27-28
May	1-7-14-20-27-28-29	25-26-30
June	12-24-25-28-29	4-19-26-27
July	4-22-26-27	11-17-23-24-28
August	10-16-21-22-23-27-28	3-24-25
September	1-8-14-19-20-23-24-25	21-22-26
October	21-22-23-25-26-30	1-7-14-19-24
November	13-17-18-22-23-28	6-19-20-24
December	5-19-20-21-23-24	13-17-22-28

2010 PLANTING GUIDE

	Aboveground Crops	Root Crops
January	18-19-23-24-28	1-6-7-8-9-13-14
February	15-16-20-24	2-3-4-5-9-10
March	19-20-23-24	2-3-4-5-9-10-14-30-31
April	15-16-19-20-26-27	1-5-6-10-11-28
May	17-23-24-25-26	2-3-7-8-13-30-31
June	13-14-19-20-21-22	4-9-10-26-27
July	17-18-19-20-23-24	1-2-6-28-29
August	13-14-15-16-20-21	3-7-8-25-26-30-31
September	9-10-11-12-16-17-21	3-4-26-27
October	7-8-9-13-14-18-19	1-7-24-28
November	10-11-15-16-19-20	3-4-5-24-25-30
December	7-8-12-13-17-18	1-2-3-22-28-29-30-31

	Pruning	Weeds and Pests
January	1-8-9	2-3-4-5-11-12-30-31
February	5-6	1-7-8-12-28
March	4-5-15	6-7-11-12
April	1-10-11-28-29	3-4-8-9-13-30
May	7-8	1-5-6-10-28
June	4	1-2-6-7-11-29-30
July	1-2-28-29	3-4-8-26-27-31
August	7-8-25-26	1-5-9-27-28
September	3-4	1-2-5-6-7-23-24-28-29
October	1-28	3-4-5-26-30-31
November	24-25	1-2-22-23-26-27-28-29
December	3-4-22-30-31	5-24-25-26

MOON'S INFLUENCE OVER PLANTS

Centuries ago it was established that seeds planted when the Moon is in signs and phases called Fruitful will produce more growth than seeds planted when the Moon is in a Barren sign.

Fruitful Signs: Taurus, Cancer, Libra, Scorpio, Capricorn, Pisces
Barren Signs: Aries, Gemini, Leo, Virgo, Sagittarius, Aquarius
Dry Signs: Aries, Gemini, Sagittarius, Aquarius

Activity	Moon In
Mow lawn, trim plants	**Fruitful sign:** 1st & 2nd quarter
Plant flowers	**Fruitful sign:** 2nd quarter; best in Cancer and Libra
Prune	**Fruitful sign:** 3rd & 4th quarter
Destroy pests; spray	**Barren sign:** 4th quarter
Harvest potatoes, root crops	**Dry sign:** 3rd & 4th quarter; Taurus, Leo, and Aquarius

MOON'S INFLUENCE OVER YOUR HEALTH

ARIES	Head, brain, face, upper jaw
TAURUS	Throat, neck, lower jaw
GEMINI	Hands, arms, lungs, shoulders, nervous system
CANCER	Esophagus, stomach, breasts, womb, liver
LEO	Heart, spine
VIRGO	Intestines, liver
LIBRA	Kidneys, lower back
SCORPIO	Sex and eliminative organs
SAGITTARIUS	Hips, thighs, liver
CAPRICORN	Skin, bones, teeth, knees
AQUARIUS	Circulatory system, lower legs
PISCES	Feet, tone of being

Try to avoid work being done on that part of the body when the Moon is in the sign governing that part.

MOON'S INFLUENCE OVER DAILY AFFAIRS

The Moon makes a complete transit of the Zodiac every 27 days 7 hours and 43 minutes. In making this transit the Moon forms different aspects with the planets and consequently has favorable or unfavorable bearings on affairs and events for persons according to the sign of the Zodiac under which they were born.

When the Moon is in conjunction with the Sun it is called a New Moon; when the Moon and Sun are in opposition it is called a Full Moon. From New Moon to Full Moon, first and second quarter—which takes about two weeks—the Moon is increasing or waxing. From Full Moon to New Moon, third and fourth quarter, the Moon is decreasing or waning.

Activity	Moon In
Business: buying and selling new, requiring public support	Sagittarius, Aries, Gemini, Virgo 1st and 2nd quarter
meant to be kept quiet	3rd and 4th quarter
Investigation	3rd and 4th quarter
Signing documents	1st & 2nd quarter, Cancer, Scorpio, Pisces
Advertising	2nd quarter, Sagittarius
Journeys and trips	1st & 2nd quarter, Gemini, Virgo
Renting offices, etc.	Taurus, Leo, Scorpio, Aquarius
Painting of house/apartment	3rd & 4th quarter, Taurus, Scorpio, Aquarius
Decorating	Gemini, Libra, Aquarius
Buying clothes and accessories	Taurus, Virgo
Beauty salon or barber shop visit	1st & 2nd quarter, Taurus, Leo, Libra, Scorpio, Aquarius
Weddings	1st & 2nd quarter

Libra

LIBRA

Character Analysis

People born under the sign of Libra are generally quite kind and sympathetic. They dislike seeing others suffer and do what they can to help those in dire straits. Another outstanding characteristic of a Libra is love of harmony and beauty. They generally have a deep appreciation for all forms of art. Libra only feels comfortable in places that radiate harmony and beauty. They are often willing to sacrifice to make their environment suit their tastes.

Libras like people. They are often afraid of being alone. They love company. Others like them for their charm and gentle ways. They are happiest when with others. A Libra alone is likely to fall into a depressed state easily. Being with others helps them to keep their spirits up even during difficult moments. A Libra rarely goes through life alone. They need permanent and reliable relationships. Often they marry early in life.

Libra has a kind and gentle nature. They would never go out of their way to hurt someone. Libra is considerate of others feelings. They will always keep up their end of a bargain. He or she is cooperative and courteous—sometimes to a fault.

The Libra man or woman is someone who is constantly weighing both sides of a problem. This characteristic is represented by the Scales, which is the zodiacal symbol for Libra. Libras are difficult people to satisfy. They want to make sure they are right in all the decisions they make. They may take a long time before coming to a decision. They may even change their minds several times in the process of weighing the pros and cons.

Balance is central to the Libra man or woman, just as balance typifies the function of the Scales. Outwardly Libra remains calm and intelligent in order to present the face of harmony, while inwardly he or she is mulling over the consequences of a proposed action. Libra's interest in harmony extends to social and business relationships. These individuals seldom hold a grudge. They put unpleasant things out of mind. Libra easily forgives and forgets.

Both men and women born under this sign are a bit soft in their dispositions. Sometimes others take advantage of this. The Libra person searches for a world where all things are beautiful and well-balanced—a place where harmony reigns. Because such a search would be useless in the real world, Libra takes refuge in daydreaming and flights of fancy. The harshness they might meet in life makes them unhappy. They may have an intricate fantasy world where they retreat when the going gets too rough.

Libra is gentle and easygoing. They seldom go where they know they are not wanted. Their interest in beauty and art leads them along the less troublesome and conflicting roads of life.

Libra can often achieve what he wants through friendly persuasion. Because of his calm, others often find him a port in a storm. He will tell people what he knows they want to hear in order to bolster their confidence and to avoid unpleasantness. He is tactful and knows how to use his gentleness to his own advantage. People may try to take advantage of him, but when he has his wits about him, this is rather difficult. Even when others think they see through him, they find him a difficult nut to crack. He is so strong in his ways of persuasion that he is almost never undermined.

The Libra man or woman is even-tempered generally, but can flare up when cornered. Still and all, they cool off quite rapidly and are willing to let bygones be bygones. Libra understands others quite deeply because of his sympathetic nature; it is quite easy for him to put himself in another's place. He is considerate of other people's opinions no matter how wrong they may seem.

Libra is fair-minded. He dislikes it when someone is mistreated or cheated out of a chance that is rightfully his. Injustice infuriates him. In all matters, he tries to make the right decision. He may take his time about coming to a conclusion.

In most social affairs, Libra is quite popular and charming. People like Libras because of their pleasant, easygoing ways. Most Libras have a lot of friends. All kinds of people attract Libra. They seldom make preferences on a superficial basis.

Harmony plays an important part in the life of every Libra. He or she will try to preserve it at all costs. Harsh realities disturb the Libra man or woman so at times they are given to lying in order to preserve peace and harmony.

Health

Libras are generally well-groomed and graceful. Their features, for the most part, are small. They are interested in maintaining good health and would never do anything that might encourage illness—even in a slight way. Quite often the man or woman born under this sign is not terribly vigorous and may require lots of rest in order to feel fit. Although they may never say no to a social obligation, Libra often tires quickly as a result of socializing. If they do not have proper rest, they are easily irritated.

Still, Libra is built well and strongly. In spite of this, they are not what you could really call strong. Their resistance is not always what it should be; they can catch colds easily. Still, they have remarkable powers of recovery and do not stay out of commission for very long. In spite of the fact that Libra is delicate, they are surprisingly resilient.

The weakest points of a Libra's body are the kidneys, spine, and loins. When they do fall ill, one of these three points is often affected.

Libra women are often remarkably beautiful. They seldom have problems attracting the opposite sex. Their voices are generally soft and their eyes lively.

Even though the Libra man may not look terribly strong, he is often capable of handling work that would exhaust someone who is bigger or seemingly more vigorous.

Libras become somewhat out of sorts when ill. Being sick tends to make them finicky and ill-humored. They like sympathy when in this condition. When their whims are not satisfied, they may complain about being neglected or unloved.

Occupation

The Libra man or woman is usually pleasant to work with. They like to cooperate with others. They will not oppose authority unless they feel it is unjust. Libra is flexible. It is not difficult for them to shift from one phase of an operation to another.

Environment may have an uncommonly strong influence on Libra. It may spur him or her on to greater heights or slow them down. Sometimes Libra needs to be inspired by the activities of those working in the immediate vicinity. They will sometimes look at the other fellow to see how he is working before they begin on their own.

Libra likes to work in pleasant surroundings. They abhor filth and disorder. They do what they can to bring about the working conditions best suited to their nature. Libra people are not attracted to work that is likely to be strenuous or untidy.

Libra people make good business partners. They are quite good at making the proper decisions at the right time. The person born under this sign knows how to weigh the pros and cons of an argument or problem. People often turn to Libra to make the right decision. Others find it easy to believe in Libra's powers of reasoning. They seldom make a wrong move. Libra can always be relied upon to do what is proper.

On the whole Libra is rather moderate or conservative in most things. This stems from their desire to avoid extremes—especially if they are apt to bring about controversy. Secrets are safe with Libra, especially if they might do someone some harm.

The person born under this sign is often quite intelligent. They have the ability to reason well and to analyze. Philosophical argument does not frighten them, and they can hold their own in almost any intellectual debate. They have a talent for objectivity, putting themselves in another's shoes quite easily. As a mediator Libra is excellent. People born under the sign of the Scales also make good diplomats.

Often called the Lawgiver, the Libra man or woman plays a powerful role as a mediator. In law, Libra can be of service to many, maintaining the peacekeeping and arbitration functions of society. These men and woman make competent judges and lawyers.

Libra can view things calmly and rationally. He or she is not easily swayed by emotions if truth or justice is at stake. Libra wants what is good for everybody concerned. They tend to look at things the way they are. They are not prone to make a mountain out of a molehill. In moments of confusion, Libra's mind is as clear as a bell.

Because of their natural objectivity, many Libras turn out to be admirable scientists and mathematicians. Also, Libra knows how to criticize without hurting. So these men and women could do well as reviewers of books, plays, films, and art in general.

Most Libras are good in creative matters. Anything to do with art or aesthetics appeals to them most of the time. Some of them make good painters, writers, or musicians. The person under this sign sometimes ignores surges of inspiration when they overcome him for fear of being too self-indulgent. The strong Libra knows how to seize these moments to further creative aims and interests. Some of the greatest painters in the world were born under the sign of Libra.

Because Libra is so good at persuasion, they make invaluable salespeople. They possess so much charm that their customers often buy more than they originally intended. Because of their rare beauty, Libra men and women often do well in the field of modeling or acting.

Libra is capable of spending more money than they actually have. During their lifetime, great sums are apt to come into their hands. They do not care too much about money, though. They are generous to a fault, and find it hard to refuse people who claim they are in need.

Libra usually has expensive tastes. They find it hard to save money. Because they like people and a busy social life, the person born under this sign often spends considerable sums in entertainment. Luxuries are as important to Libra at times as necessities are to someone else.

In spite of their light ways with money, Libra is no fool. They know well how to discourage someone who is only interested in them for their finances.

Home and Family

Home is important to the average Libra. It must be a place where they can relax and feel comfortable. It must radiate charm, beauty, and harmony. A popular person, the Libra man or woman loves to entertain. Nothing excites them more than company of good friends and acquaintances. Libra usually makes a good host. They know how to put guests at ease. People like to visit Libra because of their charming and easygoing ways.

The furnishings in a Libra's home are usually of excellent taste. They like ornamental furnishings, things that are often a bit ostentatious. No Libra home is without its paintings or pieces of sculpture. The Libra woman or man is often excellent at interior decorating. They may have a habit of changing the interior of their house quite often.

The Libra person is refined in nature and is not fond of getting their hands soiled. They would rather leave the rough tasks for others to do. If they have enough money, they'll see to it that someone comes to the house several times a week to clean up. There are always flowers and plants in the Libra home. In general, they are fond of light gardening.

There is usually a definite relationship between the Libra woman and her home. It usually complements or supplements her charm and personality.

The person born under Libra is generally a good parent. He or she does what they can to bring up youngsters properly. Libra never tries to influence the children unnecessarily. Libra lets them develop along natural lines, never forcing them into a mold he or she has designed. One thing a Libra respects in a child is originality and individuality.

The Libra parent is far from strict, yet the children seldom turn out spoiled. The Libra mother or father will correct or punish whenever it is absolutely necessary. Most of the time, the children listen to them because of their calm sure way. Kids have faith in their Libra parent and usually respect their judgment. Children like being with Libra adults because in them they have a sympathetic friend—someone who can understand their point of view.

Libras as children are often happy and friendly. Parents find them ideal because they are so agreeable and cooperative. They never challenge their parents' authority and do what is expected of them most of the time. Libra children are often creative. Whenever they show signs of artistic ability, they should be encouraged. Some of them are great daydreamers at school and have to be encouraged and inspired in order to do their best.

Social Relationships

The Libra man or woman usually makes a good friend because of their even disposition and easygoing ways. Others turn to Libra in time of need. He or she always is able to advise someone in a helpful manner. Generally, Libra is honest and sincere in their dealings with associates and friends. However, he or she may feel a bit envious if friends have nicer things.

Libras do not enjoy being alone and perhaps this is the reason they are so friendly. They enjoy being popular and well-liked. They seldom disappoint people who believe in them. All in all, they are quite cooperative and easy to get along with. They can be counted on to do the right thing at all times.

The person born under this sign usually becomes angry rather quickly. However, he quickly gets over it and is willing to kiss and make up within a short time after his explosion. Whatever he does he will try to avoid hurting someone else's feelings. He is not cruel or petty. That is not his nature.

The Libra person is a good conversationalist. Often at parties they are the center of attention. People generally have the impression that Libra is well-informed and rather aristocratic. Whenever Libra is upset or disturbed—off balance, so to speak—they try not to let it show.

Love and Marriage

In matters of love and romance, Libra is without equal. They are well-informed on everything that has to do with romance. Love is essential to Libras because they are born under the love planet Venus. As sons and daughters of Venus, Libras are affectionate and gentle, truly considerate of their mate or lover.

At times, the Libra man or woman may be uncertain of their feelings. They may go through a series of love affairs before they really know what they are looking for in a mate. Libra is fickle. He or she can be quite passionate in a love affair, then some days later break it off or lose interest for no apparent reason. It is just one of Libra's ways—difficult as it may be to understand.

Libra is easily attracted to members of the opposite sex and enjoys their company immensely. People find the Libra charm difficult to resist. Some people born under this seventh sign of the Zodiac are somewhat sentimental and are easily moved. This quality often appeals to their lovers or admirers. When Libras desire to transfer their affection, they usually do so with much tact and consideration.

Libras are often passionate lovers in spite of their calm and gentle ways. Their calm fronts often hide a hot temperament. When in love, they'll forsake their usual lamb-like ways for those of a ram.

The Libra woman expects to be handled with kid gloves by the man who professes to love her. She enjoys small courtesies and enjoys having things done for her.

Libra people are generally quite well suited for marriage or permanent love relationships. Although they may go from one romance to the other quite easily, what they are always in search of is permanent union. They are quite domestic by nature and enjoy setting up house and attending to family affairs. Some of them marry quite young. Although they may not be faithful at all times, they are honest in their intention of being steadfast.

The Libra person enjoys home life. A place for entertaining and sharing the company of loved ones, the home is something special. Libra is usually a very considerate partner. A mate may find it a difficult task keeping up. Libra's ease in social relationships is a quality that is rare to come by.

In spite of an occasional post-marital fling that they may find difficult to pass up from time to time, Libras shun all thoughts of divorce or separation. They do what they can to keep the marriage together and will try to keep serious faults under wraps. Libra is not likely to be open about indiscretions for fear of upsetting a mate and the relationship.

Romance and the Libra Woman

Libra women are quite passionate and affectionate. Most of them possess a mysterious charm which makes them much in demand with the opposite sex. The Libra woman is never short of admirers. She may have a difficult time trying to make up her mind about which one to settle down with, but she does what she can to enjoy herself during her state of indecision. She may go from one affair to the other without any regrets or misgivings. Others may accuse her of being a great flirt, but in all love relationships she is quite sincere. She is changeable and impulsive, though, which makes it hard for her to be consistent in her affections at times.

The Libra woman adjusts to married life very well. When she has found the right man, she is willing to do all she can to keep their life a peaceful and harmonious one. In spite of her inclination to flirt, the Libra woman usually remains faithful after she has married. At times, she may find herself strongly attracted to another man. But she knows how to control herself and would do nothing that might jeopardize her marriage.

The Libra woman is usually poised and charming in a standoffish way. Underneath, however, she may be very passionate and loving. Her husband may find her more romantic than he expected. She is the kind of woman most men adore. There is something helpless yet seductive about her. She is not the sort of woman who would like to wear the pants in the family. She is only too glad to let someone else manage everything. She likes being taken care of.

Although she may seem terribly dependent and clinging, when the situation calls for her to take things over, she can do this quite ably. She's the kind of a woman who generally gets things her own way. Her charm and beauty are indeed irresistible.

The Libra woman makes an ideal wife. She knows how to arrange things in a home so that they radiate peace, harmony, and beauty. When guests arrive, she knows how to make them feel comfortable immediately. She makes an excellent hostess. Her husband is apt to find her an invaluable companion. He can discuss things with her at his ease. The Libra woman is quite intelligent and has no difficulty in discussing matters that many women fail to understand or master.

She is a lover of a busy social life. However, she would be willing to give up all the glitter and laughter of party going if it interfered with her duties as a wife or mother.

Her tastes are rather expensive. She may run up bills without giving it much thought. If her husband can afford her extravagance, chances are he won't complain. He is apt to feel that his charming wife is worth the extra expense.

The Libra woman makes an understanding mother. It is important to her that her children get a chance to develop their real personalities. She is quite persuasive in a gentle way.

Romance and the Libra Man

Libra men have no trouble at all in attracting members of the opposite sex. Women find them charming and handsome. They are usually quite considerate of their women friends and know how to make them feel important and loved. The Libra man is quite a lover. He is not at a loss when it comes to romancing, for he finds love one of the most important things there is about life.

One fault, however, is the Libra man's ability to change from one love to another with appalling ease. He is always sincere in his love interests, but sometimes he finds it difficult to remain in love with the same person for a long period of time.

Women like him because he seems to know what is right; he never does the wrong thing, no matter what the occasion. His interest in the arts and such matters impress women. His sensitivity is another quality they often admire. The Libra man does not stint when it comes to demonstrating his affection for the woman he believes he loves. However, he is quite crestfallen if the woman should indicate that she is not ready to reciprocate.

Once he settles down, the Libra man makes a good husband and father. He is well suited to family life. Home is important to him. He likes to entertain close friends and relatives frequently. He is generally a very considerate and lively host. It is important that the Libra man find the right woman for his married life. If he has selected someone who finds it difficult to show the same interest in him that he shows in her, he will begin to look elsewhere for companionship. However, he is interested in having stability in his home and will do what he can to keep things in order.

He may be difficult to please at times, particularly if his wife does not share his refined tastes. If his wife has a practical mind, so much the better. Generally, Libra has a poor head for financial matters and is apt to let money slip through his fingers like water.

As a father he is quite considerate and encouraging. He is anxious to see his children express themselves as they desire. Yet he will not tolerate spoiled behavior. Children respect his gentle ways, and they do what they can to please him.

Woman—Man

LIBRA WOMAN
ARIES MAN
In some ways, the Aries man resembles his zodiacal symbol the Ram, roaming the meadow in search of good grazing land. He has an insatiable thirst for knowledge. He's ambitious and is apt to have his finger in many pies. He can do with a woman like you—someone attractive, quick-witted, and smart.

He is not interested in a clinging vine for a mate. He wants someone who is there when he needs her, someone who listens and understands what he says, someone who can give advice if he should ever need it—which is not likely to be often. The Aries man wants a woman who will look good on his arm without hanging on it too heavily.

He is looking for a woman who has both feet on the ground and yet is mysterious and enticing—a kind of domestic Helen of Troy whose face or fine dinner can launch a thousand business deals if need be. That woman he's in search of sounds a little like you, doesn't she? If the shoe fits, put it on. You won't regret it.

The Aries man makes a good husband. He is faithful and attentive. He is an affectionate kind of man. He'll make you feel needed and loved. Love is a serious matter for the Aries man. He does not believe in flirting or playing the field—especially after he's found the woman of his dreams. He'll expect you to be as constant in your affection as he is in his. He'll expect you to be one hundred percent his; he won't put up with any nonsense while romancing you.

The Aries man may be fairly progressive and modern about many things. However, when it comes to pants wearing, he's downright conventional: it's strictly male attire. The best role you can take in the relationship is a supporting one. He's the boss and that's that. Once you have learned to accept the role playing, you'll find the going easy.

The Aries man, with his endless energy and drive, likes to relax in the comfort of his home at the end of the day. The good homemaker can be sure of holding his love. He's keen on watching the news from a comfortable armchair. If you see to it that everything in the house is where he expects to find it, you'll have no difficulty keeping the relationship on an even keel.

Life and love with an Aries man may be just the medicine you need. He'll be a good provider. He'll spoil you if he's financially able to do so.

Aries is your zodiacal mate, as well as your zodiacal opposite, so the Aries-Libra couple will make wonderful parents together. Kids take to Aries like ducks to water. His quick mind and energetic behavior appeal to the young. His ability to jump from one thing to another will delight the kids and keep them active. The Aries father is young at heart and will spoil children every chance he gets. You will set standards for their growing up and see to it that they observe social etiquette and good manners.

LIBRA WOMAN
TAURUS MAN

If you've got your heart set on a man born under the sign of Taurus, you'll have to learn the art of being patient. Taurus take their time about everything—even love.

The steady and deliberate Taurus man is a little slow on the draw. It may take him quite a while before he gets around to popping that question. For the woman who doesn't mind twiddling her thumbs, the waiting and anticipating will almost always pay off in the end. Taurus men want to make sure that every step they take is a good one—particularly if they feel that the path they're on is one that leads to the altar.

If you are in the mood for a whirlwind romance, you had better cast your net in shallower waters. Moreover, most Taurus prefer to do the angling themselves. They are not keen on women taking the lead. If she does, he might drop her like a dead fish. If you let yourself get caught on his terms, you'll find that he's fallen for you—hook, line, and sinker.

The Taurus man is fond of a comfortable home life. It is very important to him. If you keep those home fires burning you will have no trouble keeping that flame in your Bull's heart aglow. You have a talent for homemaking; use it. Your taste in furnishings is excellent. You know how to make a house come to life with colors and decorations.

Taurus, the strong, steady, and protective Bull, may not be your idea of a man on the move. Still, he's reliable. Perhaps he could be the anchor for your dreams and plans. He could help you to acquire a more balanced outlook and approach to your life. If you're given to impulsiveness, he could help you to curb it. He's the man who is always there when you need him.

When you tie the knot with a man born under Taurus, you can put away fears about creditors pounding on the front door. Taurus are practical about everything including bill paying. When he carries you over that threshold, you can be certain that the entire house is paid for, not only the doorsill.

As a wife, you won't have to worry about putting aside your many interests for the sake of back-breaking house chores. Your Taurus hubby will see to it that you have all the latest time-saving appliances and comforts.

Taurus, born under the planet Venus just as you are, has much affection for the children, and he has no trouble demonstrating his love and warmth. Yet the Taurus father does not believe in spoiling the kids. He believes that children have a place, and that place is mainly to be seen but not heard. He is an excellent disciplinarian. With your cooperation, he will see to it that the youngsters grow up to be polite, obedient, and respectful.

LIBRA WOMAN
GEMINI MAN

The Gemini man is quite a catch. Many a woman has set her cap for him and failed to bag him. Generally, Gemini men are intelligent, witty, and outgoing. Many of them tend to be versatile and multitalented. The Gemini man could easily wind up being your better half.

One thing that causes a Twin's mind and affection to wander is a bore. But it is unlikely that a socially chic woman like Libra would ever allow herself to be accused of being that. The Gemini man who has caught your heart will admire you for your ideas and intellect— perhaps even more than for your homemaking talents and good looks.

The woman who hitches up with a Twin needn't feel that once she's made her marriage vows she'll have to store her interests and ambition in the attic somewhere. The Gemini man will admire you for your zeal and liveliness. He's the kind of guy who won't scowl if you let him shift for himself in the kitchen once in a while. In fact, he'll enjoy the challenge of wrestling with pots and pans himself for a change. Chances are, too, that he might turn out to be a better cook than you—that is, if he isn't already.

The man born under the sign of the Twins is a very active person. There aren't many women who have enough pep to keep up with him, but this should be no problem for the airy Libra female.

The Gemini man is a dreamer, planner, and idealist. A woman with a strong personality could easily fill the role of rudder for her Gemini's ship-without-a-sail. If you are a cultivated, purposeful woman, he won't mind it too much. The intelligent Twin is often aware of his shortcomings and doesn't resent it if someone with better bearings than himself gives him a shove in the right direction— when it's needed. The average Gemini does not have serious ego hang-ups and will even accept a well-deserved chewing out from his mate quite good-naturedly.

When you team up with a Gemini man, you'll probably always have a houseful of people to entertain—interesting people, too, which suits your Libra sociability. Geminis find it hard to tolerate antisocial characters who have little to say.

People born under Gemini generally have two sides to their natures, as different as night and day. It's very easy for them to be happy-go-lucky one minute, then down in the dumps the next. They hate to be bored and will generally do anything to make their lives interesting, vivid, and action-packed.

Gemini men are always attractive to the opposite sex. He'll flirt occasionally, but it will never amount to anything serious.

The Gemini father and the Libra mother combine the airy qualities basic to both your zodiacal signs, and as a result the children will grow up in a very open, tolerant environment. The Gemini father is a pushover for the kids. He loves them so much, he generally lets them do what they want. His sense of humor is infectious, so the youngsters will naturally come to see the fun and funny sides of life. You will have to introduce a few rules and regulations.

LIBRA WOMAN
CANCER MAN

Chances are you won't hit it off too well with the man born under Cancer if your plans are love. But then, Cupid has been known to do some pretty unlikely things. The Cancer man is very sensitive— thin-skinned and occasionally moody. You've got to keep on your toes—and not step on his—if you're determined to make a go of the relationship.

The Cancer man may be lacking in some of the qualities you seek in a man. But when it comes to being faithful and being a good provider, he's hard to beat.

The perceptive woman will not mistake the Crab's quietness for sullenness or his thriftiness for penny-pinching. In some respects, he is like that wise old owl out on a limb; he may look like he's dozing but actually he hasn't missed a thing.

Cancer people often possess a well of knowledge about human behavior. They can come across with some pretty helpful advice to those in trouble or in need. He can certainly guide you in making investments both in time and money. He may not say much, but he's always got his wits about him.

The Crab may not be the match or catch for the sociable Libra woman. At times, you are likely to find him downright dull. True to his sign, he can be fairly cranky and crabby when handled the wrong way. He is perhaps more sensitive than he should be.

If you're smarter than your Cancer friend, be smart enough not to let him know. Never give him the idea that you think he's a little short on brainpower. It would send him scurrying back into his shell—and all that ground lost in the relationship will perhaps never be recovered.

The Crab is most himself at home. Once settled down for the night or the weekend, wild horses couldn't drag him farther than the gatepost—that is, unless those wild horses were dispatched by his mother. The Crab is sometimes a Momma's boy. If his mate does not put her foot down, he will see to it that his mother always comes first. No self-respecting wife would ever allow herself to play second fiddle to her mother-in-law. With a little bit of tact, however, she'll find that slipping into that number-one position is as easy as pie (that legendary one his mother used to bake).

If you pamper your Cancer man, you'll find that Mother turns up less and less, at the front door as well as in conversations.

Cancers make proud, patient, and protective fathers. But they can be a little too protective. Their sheltering instincts can interfere with a youngster's natural inclination to test the waters outside the home. Still, the Cancer father doesn't want to see his kids learning about life the hard way from the streets. Your qualities of grace and refinement, fairness and tolerance will help the youngsters cope with a variety of life situations.

LIBRA WOMAN
LEO MAN

For the woman who enjoys being swept off her feet in a romantic whirlwind fashion, Leo is the sign of love. When the Lion puts his mind to romancing, he doesn't stint. It's all wining and dining and dancing till the wee hours of the morning.

Leo is all heart and knows how to make his woman feel like a woman. The girl in constant search of a man she can look up to need go no farther: Leo is ten-feet tall—in spirit if not in stature. He's a man not only in full control of his faculties but in full control of just about any situation he finds himself in. He's a winner.

The Leo man may not look like Tarzan, but he knows how to roar and beat his chest if he has to. The woman who has had her fill of weak-kneed men finds in a Leo someone she can at last lean upon. He can support you not only physically but spiritually as well. He's good at giving advice that pays off.

Leos are direct people. They don't believe in wasting time or effort. They almost never make unwise investments.

Many Leos rise to the top of their profession. Through example, they often prove to be a source of great inspiration to others.

Although he's a ladies' man, the Leo man is very particular about his ladies. His standards are high when it comes to love interests. The idealistic and cultivated Libra should have no trouble keeping her balance on the pedestal the Lion sets her on. Leo believes that romance should be played on a fair give-and-take basis. He won't stand for any monkey business in a love relationship. It's all or nothing.

You'll find him a frank, off-the-shoulder person. He generally says what is on his mind.

If you decide upon a Leo man for a mate, you must be prepared to stand behind him full force. He expects it—and usually deserves it. He's the head of the house and can handle that position without a hitch. He knows how to go about breadwinning. If he has his way, and most Leos do have their own way, he'll see to it that you'll have all the luxuries you crave and the comforts you need.

It's unlikely that the romance in your marriage will ever die out. Lions need love like flowers need sunshine. They're ever-amorous and generally expect full attention and affection from their mates. Leos are fond of going out on the town. They love to give parties, as well as go to them.

Leo fathers have a tendency to spoil the children—up to a point. That point is reached when the children become the center of attention, and Leo feels neglected. Then the Leo father becomes strict and insists that his rules be followed. You will have your hands full pampering both your Leo mate and the children. As long as he comes first in your affections, the family will be happy and loving.

**LIBRA WOMAN
VIRGO MAN**
The Virgo man is all business—at least he may seem so to you. He is usually very cool, calm, and collected. He's perhaps too much of

a fussbudget to wake up deep romantic interests in the Venus-born Libra woman.

Torrid romancing to Virgo is just so much sentimental mush. He can do without it and can make that quite evident in short order. He's keen on chastity and, if necessary, he can lead a sedentary, sexless life without caring too much about the fun others think he's missing.

In short, you might find the Virgo man a first-class dud. He doesn't have much of an imagination; flights of fancy don't interest him. He is always correct and likes to be handled correctly. Almost everything about him is orderly, with a place for everything and everything in its place.

He does have an honest-to-goodness heart, believe it or not. The woman who finds herself strangely attracted to his cool, feet-flat-on-the-ground ways will discover that his is a constant heart, not one that goes in for flings or sordid affairs. Virgos take an awfully long time to warm up to someone. A practical man, even in matters of the heart, he wants to know just what kind of person you are before he takes a chance on you.

The impulsive date had better not make the mistake of kissing her Virgo friend on the street—even if it's only a peck on the cheek. He's not at all demonstrative and hates public displays of affection. Love, according to him, should be kept within the confines of one's home—with the curtains drawn.

Once he believes that you are on the level with him as far as your love is concerned, you'll see how fast he can lose his cool. Virgos are considerate, gentle lovers. He'll spend a long time, though, getting to know you. He'll like you before he loves you.

A romance with a Virgo man can be a sometime—or, rather, a one-time—thing. If the bottom ever falls out, don't bother reaching for the adhesive tape. Nine times out of ten he won't care about patching up. He's a once-burnt-twice-shy guy. When he crosses your telephone number out of his address book, he's crossing you out of his life—for good.

Neat as a pin, he's thumbs-down on what he considers sloppy housekeeping. An ashtray with just one stubbed out cigarette in it can annoy him even if it's only two seconds old. Glassware should always sparkle and shine if you want to keep him happy.

If you marry him, keep your sunny-side up.

The Virgo father appreciates courtesy, good manners, and proper etiquette as much, if not more, than you do. He will instill a sense of order in the household, and he expects the children to respect his wishes. He is very concerned about the kids' health and hygiene, so he may try to restrict their freedom. You'll have to step in and let the youngsters break a few rules now and then.

LIBRA WOMAN
LIBRA MAN
If there's a Libra man in your life, you may have found the male complement to your side of the Libra equation for balance and harmony. Men born under this sign have a way with women. You'll always feel at ease in a Libra's company. You can be yourself when you're with him.

The Libra man can be moody at times. His moodiness is often puzzling. One moment he comes on hard and strong with declarations of his love, the next moment you find that he's left you like yesterday's mashed potatoes. He'll come back, though; don't worry. Libras are like that. Deep down inside he really knows what he wants even though he may not appear to.

You'll appreciate his admiration of beauty and harmony. If you're dressed to the teeth and never looked lovelier, you'll get a ready compliment—and one that's really deserved. Libras don't indulge in idle flattery. If they don't like something, they are tactful enough to remain silent.

Libras will go to great lengths to preserve peace and harmony—even tell a fat lie if necessary. They don't like showdowns or disagreeable confrontations. The frank woman is all for getting whatever is bothering her off her chest and out into the open, even if it comes out all wrong. To the Libra man, making a clean breast of everything seems like sheer folly sometimes.

One of you Libras may lose your patience while waiting for the other to make up your mind. It takes ages sometimes for Libra to make a decision. You both weigh all sides carefully before committing to anything. You both dillydally—at least about small things—and often find it difficult to come to a decision.

All in all, the Libra man is kind, considerate, and fair. He is interested in the real truth. He'll try to balance everything out until he has all the correct answers. It's not difficult for him to see both sides of a story.

Libras are not show-offs. Generally, they are well-balanced, modest people. Honest, wholesome, and affectionate, they are serious about every love encounter they have. If he should find that the woman he's dating is not really suited to him, he will end the relationship in such a tactful manner that no hard feelings will come about.

The Libra father is patient and fair. He can be firm without exercising undue strictness or discipline. Although he can be a harsh judge at times, with the kids he will radiate sweetness and light in the hope that they will grow up imitating his gentle manner. Together, the Libra couple will set a sterling example of graciousness and charm for the youngsters to follow.

LIBRA WOMAN
SCORPIO MAN

Many find the Scorpio's sting a fate worse than death. When his anger breaks loose, you had better clear out of the vicinity.

The average Scorpio may strike you as a brute. He'll stick pins into the balloons of your plans and dreams if they don't line up with what he thinks is right. If you do anything to irritate him—just anything—you'll wish you hadn't. He'll give you a sounding out that would make you pack your bags and go back to mother—if you were that kind of woman.

The Scorpio man hates being tied down to home life. He would rather be out on the battlefield of life, belting away at whatever he feels is a just and worthy cause, instead of staying home nestled in a comfortable armchair with the evening paper. If you are a woman who has a homemaking streak, don't keep those home fires burning too brightly, too long; you may run out of firewood.

As passionate as he is in business affairs and politics, the Scorpio man still has plenty of pepper and ginger stored away for lovemaking.

Most women are easily attracted to him—perhaps you are no exception. Those who allow a man born under this sign to sweep them off their feet soon find that they are dealing with a cauldron of seething excitement. The Scorpio is passionate with a capital P, you can be sure of that. But he's capable of dishing out as much pain as pleasure.

Scorpios are blunt. An insult is likely to whiz out of his mouth quicker than a compliment.

If you're the kind of woman who can keep a stiff upper lip, take it on the chin, turn a deaf ear, and all that, because you feel you are still under his love spell in spite of everything—lots of luck.

If you have decided to take the bitter with the sweet, prepare yourself for a lot of ups and downs. Chances are you won't have as much time for your own affairs and interests as you'd like. The Scorpio's love of power may cause you to be at his constant beck and call.

Scorpios like fathering large families. He is proud of his children, but often he fails to live up to his responsibilities as a parent. In spite of the extremes in his personality, the Scorpio man is able to transform the conflicting characteristics within himself when he becomes a father. When he takes his fatherly duties seriously, he is a powerful teacher. He believes in preparing his children for the hard knocks life sometimes delivers. He is adept with difficult youngsters because he knows how to tap the best in each child.

LIBRA WOMAN
SAGITTARIUS MAN

If you've set your cap for a man born under the sign of Sagittarius, you may have to apply an awful lot of strategy before you can persuade him to get down on bended knee. Although some Sagittarius may be marriage-shy, they're not ones to skitter away from romance. You'll find a love relationship with an Archer—whether a fling or the real thing—a very enjoyable experience.

As a rule, Sagittarius are bright, happy, healthy people. They have a strong sense of fair play. Often they are a source of inspiration to others. They are full of drive and ideas.

You'll be taken by the Archer's infectious grin and his light-hearted friendly nature. If you do wind up being the woman in his life, you'll find that he's apt to treat you more like a buddy than the love of his life. It's just his way. Sagittarius is often more chummy than romantic.

You'll admire his broad-mindedness in most matters—including those of the heart. If, while dating you, he claims that he still wants to play the field, he'll expect you to enjoy the same liberty. Once he's promised to love, honor, and obey, however, he does just that. Marriage for him, once he's taken that big step, is very serious business.

The Sagittarius man is quick-witted. He has a genuine interest in equality. He hates prejudice and injustice. Generally, Archers are good at sports. They love the great outdoors and respect wildlife and wilderness in all its forms.

He's not much of a homebody. Quite often he's occupied with faraway places either in his daydreams or in reality. He enjoys being on the move. He's got ants in his pants and refuses to sit still for long stretches at a time. Humdrum routine—especially at home—bores him.

He likes to surprise people. At the drop of a hat, he may ask you to hop on a plane and dine in some foreign port—most likely down the road and not too far from home by car. He also likes to tease.

He'll take great pride in showing you off to his friends. He'll always be considerate of your feelings. He will never embarrass or disappoint you intentionally.

His friendly, sunshiny nature is capable of attracting many people. Like you, he's very tolerant when it comes to friends. You will most likely spend a great deal of time helping him entertain people and being the gracious Libra hostess for his big parties.

The Sagittarius father can be all thumbs when it comes to tiny tots. He will dote on any son or daughter dutifully, but he may be bewildered by the newborn. The Archer usually becomes comfortable with youngsters once they have passed through the baby stage. As soon as the children are old enough to walk and talk, the Sagittarius dad encourages each and every visible sign of talent and skill in his kids.

LIBRA WOMAN
CAPRICORN MAN

A with-it Libra woman like you is likely to find the average Capricorn man a bit of a drag. The man born under the sign of the Goat is often a closed person and difficult to get to know. Even if you do get to know him, you may not find him very interesting.

In romance, Capricorn men are a little on the rusty side. You'll probably have to make all the passes.

You may find his plodding manner irritating and his conservative, traditional ways downright maddening. He's not one to take chances on anything. If it was good enough for his father, it's good enough for him. He follows a way that is tried and true.

The Capricorn man is habit-bound. Whenever adventure rears its tantalizing head, the Goat will turn the other way.

He may be just as ambitious as you are—perhaps even more so—but his ways of accomplishing his aims are more subterranean or, at least, seem so. He operates from the background a good deal of the time. At a gathering you may never even notice him, but he's there, taking in everything, sizing everyone up—planning his next careful move.

Although Capricorns may be intellectual to a degree, it is not generally the kind of intelligence you appreciate. He may not be as quick or as bright as you; it may take him ages to understand a simple joke.

If you do decide to take up with a man born under this sign, you ought to be pretty good in the cheering up department. The Capricorn man often acts as though he's constantly being followed by a cloud of gloom.

The Capricorn man is most himself when in the comfort and privacy of his own home. The security possible within four walls can make him a happy man. He'll spend as much time as he can at home. If he is loaded down with extra work, he'll bring it home instead of working overtime at the office.

You'll most likely find yourself frequently confronted by his relatives. Family is very important to the Capricorn—his family, that is. They had better take a pretty important place in your life, too, if you want to keep your home a happy one.

Although his caution in most matters may all but drive the luxury-loving Libra woman up the wall, you'll find that his concerned way with money is justified most of the time. He'll plan everything right down to the last penny.

The Capricorn father is a dutiful parent and takes a lifelong interest in seeing that his children make something of themselves. He may not understand their hopes and dreams because he often tries to put his head on their shoulders. The Capricorn father believes that there are certain goals to be achieved, and there is a traditional path to achieving them. He can be quite a scold if the youngsters break the rules. You will have to balance his sometimes rigid approach and smooth things over for the kids.

LIBRA WOMAN
AQUARIUS MAN

Aquarius individuals love everybody—even their worst enemies sometimes. Through your love relationship with an Aquarius you'll find yourself running into all sorts of people, ranging from near-genius to downright insane—and they're all friends of his.

As a rule, Aquarius are extremely friendly and open. Of all the signs, they are perhaps the most tolerant. In the thinking department, they are often miles ahead of others.

You'll most likely find your relationship with this man a challenging one. Your high respect for intelligence and imagination may be reason enough for you to set your heart on a Water Bearer. You'll find that you can learn a lot from him.

In the holding-hands phase of your romance, you may find that your Water Bearer friend has cold feet. Aquarius take quite a bit of warming up before they are ready to come across with that first goodnight kiss. More than likely, he'll just want to be your pal in the beginning. For him, that's an important first step in any relationship—love included.

The poetry and flowers stage—if it ever comes—will come later. Aquarius is all heart. Still, when it comes to tying himself down to one person and for keeps, he is almost always sure to hesitate. He may even try to get out of it if you breathe down his neck too heavily.

The Aquarius man is no Valentino and wouldn't want to be. The kind of love life he's looking for is one that's made up mainly of companionship. Although he may not be very romantic, the memory of his first romance will always hold an important position in his heart. Some Aquarius wind up marrying their childhood sweethearts.

You won't find it difficult to look up to a man born under the sign of the Water Bearer, but you may find the challenge of trying to keep up with him dizzying. He can pierce through the most complicated problem as if it were simple math. You may find him a little too lofty and high-minded, but don't judge him too harshly if that's the case. He's way ahead of his time—your time, too, most likely.

If you marry this man, he'll stay true to you. Don't think that once the honeymoon is over, you'll be chained to the kitchen sink forever. Your Aquarius husband will encourage you to keep active in your own interests and affairs. You'll most likely have a minor tiff now and again but never anything serious.

The Aquarius father has an almost intuitive understanding of children. He sees them as individuals in their own right, not as extensions of himself or as beings who are supposed to take a certain place in the world. He can talk to the kids on a variety of subjects, and his knowledge can be awe-inspiring. You will sometimes have to bring the youngsters back down to earth, but you will appreciate the lessons of tolerance and fairness your Aquarius mate has transmitted to the children.

LIBRA WOMAN
PISCES MAN

The man born under Pisces is quite a dreamer. Sometimes he's so wrapped up in his dreams that he's difficult to reach. To the average, ambitious woman, he may seem a little passive.

He's easygoing most of the time. He seems to take things in his stride. He'll entertain all kinds of views and opinions from just about anyone, nodding or smiling vaguely, giving the impression that he's with them 100 percent while that may not be the case at all. His attitude may be why bother when he is confronted with someone wrong who thinks he's right. The Pisces man will seldom speak his mind if he thinks he'll be rigidly opposed.

The Pisces man is oversensitive at times—he's afraid of getting his feelings hurt. He'll sometimes imagine a personal affront when none's been made. Chances are you'll find this complex of his maddening. At times, you may feel like giving him a swift kick where it hurts the most. It won't do any good, though. It would just add fuel to the fire of his complex.

One thing you will admire about this man is his concern for people who are sickly or troubled. He'll make his shoulder available to anyone in the mood for a good cry. He can listen to one hard-luck story after another without seeming to tire. When his advice is asked, he is capable of coming across with some pretty important words of wisdom. He often knows what's bothering someone before that person is aware of it. It's almost intuitive with Pisces, it seems.

Still, at the end of the day, your Pisces lover looks forward to some peace and quiet. If you've got a problem on your mind, don't dump it into his lap. If you do, you're apt to find him short-tempered. He's a good listener, but he can only take so much.

Pisces men are not aimless although they may seem so at times. The positive sort of Pisces man is quite often successful in his profession and is likely to wind up rich and influential. Material gain, however, is not a direct goal for a man born under the sign of the Fishes.

The weaker Pisces is usually content to stay put on the level where he happens to find himself. He won't complain too much if the roof leaks or the fence is in need of repair. He'll just shrug it off as a minor inconvenience. He's got more important things to think about, he'll say.

Because of their seemingly laissez-faire manner, Pisces fathers and Pisces men in general are immensely popular with children. For tots, Pisces plays the double role of confidant and playmate. It will never enter his mind to discipline a child, no matter how spoiled or incorrigible that child becomes.

Man—Woman

LIBRA MAN
ARIES WOMAN

Aries and Libra are zodiacal mates or zodiacal opposites, depending how individuals of these signs link up in love. For many a mild Libra man, the Aries woman may be a little too bossy and busy. Aries women are ambitious creatures. They tend to lose their patience with thorough and deliberate people, like Libra, who take a lot of time to complete something.

The Aries woman is a fast worker. Sometimes she's so fast she forgets to look where she's going. When she stumbles or falls, it would be nice if you were there to grab her. But Aries women are very proud. They don't like to be criticized when they err. Tongue-wagging can turn them into blocks of ice.

However, don't think that the Aries woman frequently gets tripped up in her plans. Quite often they are capable of taking aim and hitting the bull's-eye. You'll be flabbergasted at times by their accuracy as well as by their ambition.

You are perhaps somewhat slower than the Aries woman in attaining your goals. Still, you are not apt to make mistakes along the way. Libra is seldom ill-prepared.

The Aries woman is sensitive at times. She likes to be handled with gentleness and respect. Let her know that you love her for her brains as well as for her good looks. Never give her cause to become jealous. When your Aries woman sees green, you'd better forget about sharing a rosy future together. Handle her with tender love and care and she's yours.

The Aries woman can be giving if she feels her partner is deserving. She is no iceberg; she responds to the proper masculine flame. She needs a man she can look up to and feel proud of. If the shoe fits, put it on. If not, better put your sneakers back on and quietly tiptoe out of her sight.

She can cause you plenty of heartache if you've made up your mind about her and she hasn't made up hers about you. Aries women are very demanding at times. Some of them tend to be highstrung. They can be difficult if they feel their independence is being hampered.

The cultivated Aries woman makes a wonderful homemaker and hostess. You'll find that she's very clever in decorating; she knows how to use colors. Your house will be tastefully furnished. Both of you see to it that it radiates harmony. Friends and acquaintances will love your Aries wife. She knows how to make everyone feel at home and welcome.

Although the Aries woman may not be keen on burdensome responsibilities, she is fond of children and the joy they bring. She is skilled at juggling both career and motherhood, so her kids will never feel that she is an absentee parent. In fact, as the youngsters grow older, they might want a little more of the liberation that is so important to her.

LIBRA MAN
TAURUS WOMAN

The woman born under the sign of Taurus may lack a little of the sparkle and bubble you often like to find in a woman. The Taurus woman is generally down to earth and never flighty. It's important to her that she keep both feet flat on the ground. She is not fond of bounding all over the place, especially if she's under the impression that there's no profit in it.

On the other hand, if you hit it off with a Taurus woman, you won't be disappointed in the romance area. The Taurus woman is all woman and proud of it, too. She can be very devoted and loving once she decides that her relationship with you is no fly-by-night romance. Basically, she's a passionate person. In sex, she's direct and to the point. If she really loves you, she'll let you know she's yours—and without reservations.

Better not flirt with other women once you've committed yourself to her. She's capable of being very jealous and possessive.

She'll stick by you through thick and thin. It's almost certain that if the going ever gets rough, she won't go running home to her mother. She can adjust to the hard times just as graciously as she can to the good times.

Taurus are, on the whole, even-tempered. They like to be treated with kindness. Luxurious things and artistic objects win their hearts.

You may find her a little cautious and deliberate. She likes to be safe and sure about everything. Let her plod along if she likes. Don't coax her, but just let her take her own sweet time. Everything she does is done thoroughly and, generally, without mistakes.

Don't deride her caution or shyness. It could lead to an explosive scene. The Taurus woman doesn't anger readily but when prodded often enough, she's capable of letting loose with a cyclone of ill will. If you treat her with kindness and consideration, you'll have no cause for complaint.

The Taurus woman loves doing things for her man. She's a whiz in the kitchen and can whip up feasts fit for a king if she thinks they'll be royally appreciated. She may not fully understand you, but she'll adore you and be faithful to you if she feels you're worthy of it.

The Taurus woman, ruled by lovely planet Venus as you are, will share with you the joys and burdens of parenthood. But the Taurus mother seldom puts up with any nonsense from the youngsters. It is not that she is strict, she is just concerned. She likes the children to be well behaved. She can wield an iron fist in a velvet glove.

Nothing pleases a Taurus mother more than a compliment from a neighbor or teacher about her child's behavior. She may have some difficult times with them when they reach adolescence. And some teenagers may inwardly resent their Taurus mother's tutelage. But in later life they are often thankful they were brought up in such a conscientious fashion.

LIBRA MAN
GEMINI WOMAN
You may find a romance with a woman born under the sign of the Twins a many-splendored thing. In her you can find the intellectual companionship you often look for in a friend or mate. A Gemini partner can appreciate your aims and desires because she travels pretty much the same road as you do intellectually—that is, at least part of the way. She may share your interest, but she will lack your tenacity.

She suffers from itchy feet. She can be here, there, all over the place and at the same time, or so it would seem. Her eagerness to move about may make you dizzy, still you'll enjoy and appreciate her liveliness and mental agility.

Geminis often have sparkling personalities. You'll be attracted by her warmth and grace. While she's on your arm you'll probably notice that many male eyes are drawn to her. She may even return a gaze or two, but don't let that worry you. All women born under this sign have nothing against a harmless flirt once in a while. They enjoy this sort of attention. If she feels she is already spoken for, however, she will never let it get out of hand.

Although she may not be as handy as you'd like in the kitchen, you'll never go hungry for a filling and tasty meal. She's as much in a hurry as you are, and won't feel like she's cheating by breaking out the instant mashed potatoes or the frozen peas. She may not be much of a good cook but she is clever. With a dash of this and a suggestion of that, she can make an uninteresting TV dinner taste like a gourmet meal. Then, again, maybe you've struck it rich and have a Gemini who finds complicated recipes a challenge to her intellect. If so, you'll find every meal a tantalizing and mouth-watering surprise.

When you're beating your brains out over the Sunday crossword puzzle and find yourself stuck, just ask your Gemini mate. She'll give you all the right answers without batting an eyelash.

Like you, she loves all kinds of people. You may even find that you're a bit more particular than she. Often all that a Gemini requires is that her friends be interesting—and stay interesting. One thing she's not able to abide is a dullard.

Leave the party organizing to your Gemini sweetheart or mate, and you'll never have a chance to know what a dull moment is. She'll bring the swinger out in you if you give her half a chance.

A Gemini mother enjoys her children, which can be the truest form of love. Like them, she's often restless, adventurous, and easily bored. She will never complain about their fleeting interests because she understands the changes they will go through as they mature.

LIBRA MAN
CANCER WOMAN

If you fall in love with a Cancer woman, be prepared for anything. They are sometimes difficult to understand when it comes to love. In one hour, she can unravel a whole gamut of emotions. Her moods will leave you in a tizzy. She'll always keep you guessing, that's for sure.

You may find her a little too uncertain and sensitive for your liking. You'll most likely spend a good deal of time encouraging her, helping her to erase her foolish fears. Tell her she's a living doll a dozen times a day, and you'll be well loved in return.

Be careful of the jokes you make when in her company. Don't let any of them revolve around her, her personal interests, or her family.

If you do, you'll most likely reduce her to tears. She can't stand being made fun of. It will take bushels of roses and tons of chocolates—not to mention the apologies—to get her to come back out of her shell.

In matters of money managing, she may not easily come around to your way of thinking. Money will never burn a hole in her pocket. You may get the notion that your Cancer sweetheart or mate is a direct descendant of Scrooge. If she has her way, she'll hang onto the first dollar you earned. She's not only that way with money, but with everything right on up from bakery string to jelly jars. She's a saver. She never throws anything away, no matter how trivial.

Once she returns your love, you'll have an affectionate, self-sacrificing, and devoted woman for keeps. Her love for you will never alter unless you want it to. She'll put you up on a high pedestal and will do everything—even if it's against your will—to keep you there.

Cancer women love home life. For them, marriage is an easy step to make. They're domestic with a capital D. She'll do her best to make your home comfortable and cozy. The Cancer woman is more herself at home than in strange surroundings. She makes an excellent hostess. The best in her comes out when she's in her own environment.

Cancer women are reputed to be the best mothers of all the signs of the Zodiac. She'll make every complaint of her child a major catastrophe. With her, children come first. If you're lucky, you'll run a close second. You'll perhaps see her as too devoted to the children. You may have a hard time convincing her that her apron strings are too long.

LIBRA MAN
LEO WOMAN

If you can manage a partner who likes to kick up her heels every now and again, then the Leo woman was made for you. You'll have to learn to put away jealous fears when you take up with a woman born under this sign, as she's often the kind that makes heads turn and tongues wag. You don't necessarily have to believe any of what you hear. It's most likely just jealous gossip or wishful thinking.

The Leo woman has more than a fair share of grace and glamour. She knows it, generally, and knows how to put it to good use. Needless to say, other women in her vicinity turn green with envy and will try anything to put her out of the running.

If she's captured your heart and fancy, woo her full force if your intention is to eventually win her. Shower her with expensive gifts and promise her the moon if you're in a position to go that far. Then you'll find her resistance beginning to weaken.

It's not that she's such a difficult cookie—she'll probably boast about you once she's decided you're the man for her—but she does enjoy a lot of attention. What's more, she feels she's entitled to it. Her mild arrogance, though, is becoming. The Leo woman knows how to transform the crime of excessive pride into a very charming misdemeanor. It sweeps most men right off their feet. Those who do not succumb to her leonine charm are few and far between.

If you've got an important business deal to clinch and you have doubts as to whether you can bring it off as you should, take your Leo wife along to the business luncheon. It will be a cinch that you'll have that contract—lock, stock, and barrel—in your pocket before the meeting is over. She won't have to say or do anything, just be there at your side. The grouchiest oil magnate can be transformed into a gushing, obedient schoolboy if there's a Leo woman in the room.

If you're rich and want to see to it that you stay that way, don't give your Leo spouse a free hand with the charge accounts and credit cards. When it comes to spending, Leos tend to overdo. If you're poor, you have no worries because the luxury-loving Leo will most likely never recognize your existence let alone consent to marry you.

A Leo mother can be so proud of her children that she is sometimes blind to their faults. Yet when she wants them to learn and take their rightful place in the social scheme of things, the Leo mother can be strict. She is a patient teacher, lovingly explaining the rules the youngsters are expected to follow. Easygoing and friendly, she loves to pal around with the kids and show them off on every occasion.

LIBRA MAN
VIRGO WOMAN

The Virgo woman may be too difficult for you to understand at first. Her waters run deep. Even when you think you know her, don't take any bets on it. She's capable of keeping things hidden in the deep recesses of her womanly soul—things she'll only release when she's sure you're the man she's been looking for.

It may take her some time to come around to this decision. Virgos are finicky about almost everything. Everything has to be letter-perfect before they're satisfied. Many of them have the idea that the only people who can do things correctly are Virgos.

Nothing offends a Virgo woman more than slovenly dress, sloppy character, or a careless display of affection. Make sure your tie is not crooked and your shoes sport a bright shine before you go calling on this lady. Keep your off-color jokes for the locker room; she'll have none of that. Take her arm when crossing the street.

Don't rush the romance. Trying to corner a Virgo woman in the back of a cab may be one way of striking out. Never criticize the way she looks. In fact, the best policy would be to agree with her as much as possible. Still, there's just so much a man can take. All those dos and don'ts you'll have to observe if you want to get to first base with a Virgo may be just a little too much to ask of you.

After a few dates, you may come to the conclusion that she just isn't worth all that trouble. However, the Virgo woman is mysterious enough to keep her men running back for more. Chances are you'll be intrigued by her airs and graces.

If lovemaking means a lot to you, you'll be disappointed at first in the cool ways of your Virgo partner. However, under her glacial facade there lies a hot cauldron of seething excitement. If you're patient and artful in your romantic approach, you'll find that all that caution was well worth the trouble. When Virgos love, they don't stint. It's all or nothing as far as they're concerned. Once they're convinced that they love you, they go all the way, tossing all cares to the wind.

One thing a Virgo woman can't stand in love is hypocrisy. They don't give a hoot about what the neighbors say when their hearts tell them to go ahead. They're very concerned with human truths. So if their hearts stumble upon another fancy, they will be true to that new heartthrob and leave you standing in the rain.

Virgo is honest to her heart and will be as true to you as you are with her. Do her wrong once, though, and it's curtains.

The Virgo mother has high expectations for her children, and she will strive to bring out the very best in them. She is more tender than strict, though, and will nag rather than discipline. But youngsters sense her unconditional love for them, and usually turn out just as she hoped they would.

LIBRA MAN
LIBRA WOMAN

You'll probably find that the woman born under the sign of Libra is worth more than her weight in gold. She's a woman after your own heart, your other half in the astrological scheme of things.

With her, you'll always come first—make no mistake about that. She'll always be behind you 100 percent, no matter what you do. When you ask her advice about almost anything, you'll most likely get a very balanced and realistic opinion. She is good at thinking things out and never lets her emotions run away with her when clear logic is called for.

As a homemaker she is hard to beat. She is very concerned with harmony and balance. You can be sure she'll make your house a joy to live in. She'll see to it that the house is tastefully furnished and decorated. A Libra cannot stand filth or disarray. Anything that does not radiate harmony runs against her orderly grain.

She is chock-full of charm and womanly ways. She can sweep just about any man off his feet with one winning smile. When it comes to using her brains, she can outthink almost anyone and, sometimes, with half the effort. She is diplomatic enough, though, never to let this become glaringly apparent. She may even turn the conversation around so that you think you were the one who did all the brainwork. She couldn't care less, really, just as long as you wind up doing what is right.

The Libra woman will put you on a high pedestal. You are her man and her idol. She will share the decision making—large or small—with you, although you both have trouble in this area. She's not interested in running things, but she will offer her assistance if she feels you need it.

Some find her approach to reason masculine. However, in the areas of love and affection the Libra woman is all woman. She'll literally shower you with love and kisses during your romance with her. She doesn't believe in holding out. You shouldn't either, if you want to hang on to her.

She is the kind of lover who likes to snuggle up to you in front of the fire on chilly autumn nights. She will bring you breakfast in bed Sunday. She'll be very thoughtful about anything that concerns you. If anyone dares suggest you're not the grandest guy in the world, she'll give that person what-for. She'll defend you till her dying breath. The Libra woman will be everything you want her to be.

The Libra mother is well-balanced and moderate, like you, so together you will create a harmonious household in which young family members can grow up in an environment sensitive to their needs. The Libra mother understands that children need both guidance and encouragement. Her youngsters will never lack for anything that could make their lives easier and richer.

LIBRA MAN
SCORPIO WOMAN

The Scorpio woman can be a whirlwind of passion—perhaps too much passion to suit the moderate Libra man. When her temper flies, you'd better lock up the family heirlooms and take cover. When she chooses to be sweet, then she is on your wavelength. But then her mood mysteriously changes, and you don't have a clue.

The Scorpio woman can be as hot as a tamale or as cool as a cucumber, but whatever mood she's in, she's in it for real. She does not believe in posing or putting on airs.

The Scorpio woman is often sultry and seductive. Her femme fatale charm can pierce through the hardest of hearts like a laser ray. She may not look like Mata Hari (quite often Scorpios resemble the tomboy next door), but once she's fixed you with her tantalizing eyes, you're a goner.

Life with the Scorpio woman will not be all smiles and smooth sailing. When prompted, she can unleash a gale of venom. Generally, she'll have the good grace to keep family battles within the walls of your home. When company visits, she's apt to give the impression that married life with you is one great big joyride. It's just one of her ways of expressing her loyalty to you, at least in front of others. She may fight you tooth and nail in the confines of your living room. But during an evening out, she'll hang onto your arm and have stars in her eyes.

Scorpio women are good at keeping secrets. She may even keep a few buried from you if she feels like it.

Never cross her up on on even the smallest thing. When it comes to revenge, she's an eye-for-an-eye woman. She's not too keen on forgiveness, especially if she feels she's been wronged unfairly. You'd be well-advised not to give her any cause to be jealous, either. When the Scorpio woman sees green, your life will be made far from rosy. Once she's put you in the doghouse, you can be sure that you're going to stay there awhile.

You may find life with a Scorpio woman too draining. Although she may be full of the old paprika, it's quite likely that she's not the partner you'd like to spend the rest of your natural life with. You'd prefer someone gentler and not so hot-tempered, someone who can take the highs with the lows and not bellyache, someone who is flexible and understanding. A woman born under Scorpio can be heavenly, but she can also be the very devil when she chooses.

The Scorpio mother is protective yet encouraging. The opposites within her nature mirror the very contradictions of life itself. Under her skillful guidance, the children learn how to cope with extremes and grow up to become many-faceted individuals.

LIBRA MAN
SAGITTARIUS WOMAN

You'll most likely never come across a more good-natured woman than the one born under the sign of Sagittarius. Generally, they're full of bounce and good cheer. Their sunny disposition seems almost permanent and can be relied upon even on the rainiest of days.

Women born under the sign of the Archer are almost never malicious. If ever they seem to be it is only a regrettable mistake. Archers are often a little short on tact and say literally anything that comes into their heads—no matter what the occasion is. Sometimes the words that tumble out of their mouths seem downright cutting and cruel. Still, no matter what she says, she means well. The Sagittarius woman is quite capable of losing some of her friends, and perhaps even some of yours, through a careless slip of the lip.

On the other hand, you will appreciate her honesty and good intentions. To you, qualities of this sort play an important part in life. With a little patience and practice, you can probably help cure your Sagittarius of her loose tongue. In most cases, she'll give in to your better judgment and try to follow your advice to the letter.

Chances are she'll be the outdoors type of date and partner. Long hikes, fishing trips, and white-water canoeing will most likely appeal to her. She's a busy person. No one could ever call her a slouch. She sets great store in mobility. Her feet are itchy, and she won't sit still for a minute if she doesn't have to.

She is great company most of the time and, generally, lots of fun. Even if your buddies drop by for poker and beer, she won't have any trouble fitting in.

The Sagittarius woman is very kind and sympathetic. If she feels she's made a mistake, she'll be the first to call your attention to it. She's not afraid to own up to her faults and shortcomings.

You might lose your patience with her once or twice. After she's seen how upset her shortsightedness or tendency to blab has made you, she'll do her best to straighten up.

The Sagittarius woman is not the kind who will pry into your business affairs. But she'll always be there, ready to offer advice if you need it. If you come home with red stains on your collar and you say it's paint and not lipstick, she'll believe you.

She'll seldom be suspicious. Your word will almost always be good enough for her.

The Sagittarius mother is a wonderful and loving friend to her children. She is not afraid if a youngster learns some street smarts along the way. She will broaden her children's knowledge and see that they get a well-rounded education.

LIBRA MAN
CAPRICORN WOMAN

If you are not a successful businessman or at least on your way to success, it's quite possible that a Capricorn woman will have no interest in entering your life. Generally, the Goat is a very security-minded female. She'll see to it that she invests her time only in sure things.

Men who whittle away their time with one unsuccessful scheme or another seldom attract a Capricorn. But men who are interested in getting somewhere in life and keep their noses close to the grindstone quite often have a Capricorn woman behind them, helping them to get ahead.

Although she can be a social climber, she is not what you could call cruel or hardhearted. Beneath that cool, seemingly calculating exterior there's a warm and desirable woman. She happens to think that it is just as easy to fall in love with a rich or ambitious man as it is with a poor or lazy one. She's practical.

The Capricorn woman may be keenly interested in rising to the top, but she'll never be aggressive about it. She'll seldom step on someone's feet or nudge competitors away with her elbows. She's quiet about her desires. She sits, waits, and watches. When an opening or opportunity does appear, she'll latch onto it. For an on-the-move man, an ambitious Capricorn wife or lover can be quite an asset. She can probably give you some very good advice about business matters. When you invite the boss and his wife for dinner, she'll charm them both.

The Capricorn woman is thorough in whatever she does: cooking, cleaning, making a success out of life. Capricorns are excellent hostesses as well as guests. Generally, they are beautifully mannered and gracious, no matter what their backgrounds are. They seem to have a built-in sense of what is proper. Crude behavior or a careless faux pas can offend them no end.

If you should marry a woman born under Capricorn you need never worry about her going on a wild shopping spree. Capricorns are careful with every cent that comes into their hands. They understand the value of money better than most women and have no room in their lives for careless spending.

Capricorn women are usually very devoted to family—their own, that is. With them, family ties run very deep. Don't make jokes about her relatives; she won't stand for it. You'd better check her family out before you get down on bended knee. After your marriage you'll undoubtedly be seeing lots of her relatives.

The Capricorn mother is very ambitious for her children. She wants them to have every advantage and to benefit from things she perhaps lacked as a child. She will train her youngsters to be polite and kind and to honor traditional codes of conduct.

LIBRA MAN
AQUARIUS WOMAN
If you find that you've fallen head over heels for a woman born under the sign of the Water Bearer, you'd better fasten your safety belt. It may take you quite a while to actually discover what this woman is like. Even then, you may have nothing to go on but a string of vague hunches.

Aquarius is like a rainbow, full of bright and shining hues. She is like no other woman you've ever known. There is something elusive about her, something delightfully mysterious. You'll most likely never be able to put your finger on it. It's nothing calculated, either. Aquarius women don't believe in phony charm.

There will never be a dull moment in your life with this Water Bearer woman. She seems to radiate adventure and magic. She'll most likely be the most open-minded and tolerant woman you've ever met. She has a strong dislike for injustice and prejudice. Narrow-mindedness runs against her grain.

She is very independent by nature and quite capable of shifting for herself if necessary. She may receive many proposals for marriage from all sorts of people without ever really taking them seriously. Marriage is a very big step for her. She wants to be sure she knows what she's getting into. If she thinks that it will seriously curb her independence and love of freedom, she'll turn you down and return your engagement ring—if indeed she's let the romance get that far.

The line between friendship and romance is a pretty fuzzy one for an Aquarius. It's not difficult for her to remain buddy-buddy with an ex-lover. She's tolerant, remember? So, if you should see her on the arm of an old love, don't jump to any hasty conclusions.

She's not a jealous person herself and doesn't expect you to be, either. You'll find her pretty much of a free spirit most of the time. Just when you think you know her inside out, you'll discover that you don't really know her at all.

She's a very sympathetic and warm person. She can be helpful to people in need of assistance and advice.

She'll seldom be suspicious even if she has every right to be. If she loves a man, she'll forgive him just about anything. If he allows himself a little fling, chances are she'll just turn her head the other way. Her tolerance does have its limits, however, and her man should never press his luck at hanky-panky.

The Aquarius mother is bighearted and seldom refuses her children anything. Her open-minded attitude is easily transmitted to her youngsters. They have every chance of growing up as respectful and tolerant individuals who feel at ease anywhere.

LIBRA MAN
PISCES WOMAN

Many a man dreams of an alluring Pisces woman. You're perhaps no exception. She's soft and cuddly and very domestic. She'll let you be the brains of the family; she's contented to play a behind-the-scenes role in order to help you achieve your goals. The illusion that you are the master of the household is the kind of magic that the Pisces woman is adept at creating.

She can be very ladylike and proper. Your business associates and friends will be dazzled by her warmth and femininity. Although she's a charmer, there is a lot more to her than just a pretty exterior. There is a brain ticking away behind that soft, womanly facade. You may never become aware of it—that is, until you're married to her. It's no cause for alarm, however; she'll most likely never use it against you, only to help you and possibly set you on a more successful path.

If she feels you're botching up your married life through careless behavior or if she feels you could be earning more money than you do, she'll tell you about it. But any wife would, really. She will never try to usurp your position as head and breadwinner of the family.

No one had better dare say one uncomplimentary word about you in her presence. It's likely to cause her to break into tears. Pisces women are usually very sensitive beings. Their reaction to adversity, frustration, or anger is just a plain, good, old-fashioned cry. They can weep buckets when inclined.

She can do wonders with a house. She is very fond of dramatic and beautiful things. There will always be plenty of fresh-cut flowers around the house. She will choose charming artwork and antiques, if they are affordable. She'll see to it that the house is decorated in a dazzling yet welcoming style.

She'll have an extra special dinner prepared for you when you come home from an important business meeting. Don't dwell on the boring details of the meeting, though. But if you need that grand vision, the big idea, to seal a contract or make a conquest, your Pisces woman is sure to confide a secret that will guarantee your success. She is canny and shrewd with money, and once you are on her wavelength you can manage the intricacies on your own.

Treat her with tenderness and generosity, and your relationship will be an enjoyable one. She's most likely fond of chocolates. A bunch of beautiful flowers will never fail to make her eyes light up. See to it that you never forget her birthday or your anniversary. These things are very important to her. If you let them slip your mind, you'll send her into a crying fit that could last a considerable length of time.

If you are patient and kind, you can keep a Pisces woman happy for a lifetime. She, however, is not without her faults. Her sensitivity may get on your nerves after a while. You may find her lacking in practicality and good old-fashioned stoicism. You may even feel that she uses her tears as a method of getting her own way.

The Pisces mother has great faith in her children. She makes a strong, self-sacrificing mother. She will teach her children the value of service to the community while not letting them lose their individuality.

LIBRA
LUCKY NUMBERS 2010

Lucky numbers and astrology can be linked through the movements of the Moon. Each phase of the thirteen Moon cycles vibrates with a sequence of numbers for your Sign of the Zodiac over the course of the year. Using your lucky numbers is a fun system that connects you with tradition.

New Moon	First Quarter	Full Moon	Last Quarter
Dec. 15 ('09) 8 3 5 4	Dec. 24 ('09) 3 9 5 5	Dec. 31 ('09) 1 0 7 9	Jan. 7 9 2 4 8
Jan. 15 9 2 4 4	Jan. 23 6 6 2 9	Jan. 30 8 5 1 6	Feb. 5 6 3 4 7
Feb. 13 3 9 0 9	Feb. 21 9 5 3 2	Feb. 28 2 8 4 9	March 7 6 7 1 3
March 15 3 7 9 7	March 23 5 4 1 6	March 29 0 6 2 8	April 6 9 3 5 0
April 14 0 2 7 5	April 21 4 1 7 3	April 28 8 5 6 9	May 5 9 2 0 8
May 13 2 4 2 0	May 20 7 3 2 7	May 27 4 5 8 0	June 4 1 0 7 3
June 12 7 1 9 6	June 18 6 2 7 0	June 26 2 5 7 2	July 4 2 4 9 7
July 11 5 6 3 8	July 18 8 4 1 1	July 25 4 6 0 3	August 3 8 6 5 4
August 9 4 2 7 3	August 16 3 9 1 4	August 24 6 1 5 7	Sept. 1 3 0 9 6
Sept. 8 1 2 7 4	Sept. 15 4 5 8 0	Sept. 23 1 0 8 3	Sept. 30 1 7 3 6
Oct. 7 6 8 5 6	Oct. 14 6 9 2 0	Oct. 22 0 8 7 5	Oct. 30 5 4 1 6
Nov. 6 2 8 9 3	Nov. 13 3 5 0 2	Nov. 21 2 7 8 7	Nov. 28 7 4 5 2
Dec. 5 8 3 6 8	Dec. 13 8 0 5 1	Dec. 21 1 8 3 9	Dec. 27 5 0 7 8

LIBRA
YEARLY FORECAST 2010

*Forecast for 2010 Concerning Business
and Financial Affairs, Job Prospects,
Travel, Health, Romance and Marriage
for Persons Born with the Sun
in the Zodiacal Sign of Libra.
September 23–October 22*

For those born under the zodiacal sign of Libra, ruled by Venus, planet of romance, money, and the good things of life, the year ahead offers the opportunity to get in touch with your true self and start living in harmony with your inner desires. The year 2010 will challenge any outmoded habits and structures, forcing you to reassess what and who you really value. The universe is giving you a chance to restructure your life with a renewed sense of purpose and to start manifesting your hopes and wishes. Although you may have many responsibilities on your plate, your accomplishments will be great.

Saturn, the planet of responsibility and limitation, is touring your sign of Libra at the start of the year and into April, then again from late July into 2011. Saturn in Libra signals personal growth. Your attention will turn inward to discover what it is you really want. Up until now your attention may have been focused on interactions with others, with your social life. While you may be adept at fitting into social life and understanding what other people expect of you, you may be less aware of what is going on inside yourself. Now is the year to find out who you are in your own terms, not in other people's terms. The more you get in touch with yourself, the more successful you will be in the future. The universe has a way of forcing growth. So you might find that many of your social commitments become burdensome, forcing you to cut back on these commitments so that you can spend your time looking after what is important. Counseling can help you exchange old habit patterns that are no longer useful for new and positive habits that suit your new personal needs. These changes extend to all aspects of your life, including relationships and work. As you get more in touch with yourself, you will be less inclined to have people telling you what to do. You will not put up with dull and oppressive routines that deny you some freedom and creativity. As you learn to express yourself appropriately at the right time, you won't have to repress your feelings.

Mars, the planet of energy and action, lingers in Leo, your solar house of friends, associations, and aspirations, for the first half of the year. You can expect to be dealing with a lot of relationships and social expectations. Your actions can be group-oriented in an idealistic frame of reference. So you may give your energies to a worthy cause urging world peace, health reform, or a safe and balanced environment. Mars in Leo poses arguments among colleagues, and you may blame them, and they you, for failures that are really just bumps in a shared road. Remind yourself that friendship is more lasting than a passing storm, and you'll still be close when the weather clears. You will also be making loyal new friends. Because Mars in Leo represents your solar house of hopes and wishes, it is a great time to take action toward manifesting your dreams.

Love and marriage are highlighted this year. As you start to understand what you truly desire, you might find that your needs in a love relationship start to change accordingly. If you are already in a relationship, changes you undergo can arouse fear and insecurity. Change always shakes up the applecart. Some relationships may not be able to withstand this. For some Libras, separation and divorce will bring pain and more self-analysis but will ultimately enable you to follow a more fulfilling path. Counseling will help you to sort through the minefield of issues. If a relationship is strong and based on good foundations, it can be transformed into a truly open and honest union. The period between June and September brings many changes as well as opportunities for growth. If a relationship is on shaky ground during that time, it may end. For some single Libras, this period may bring a love-at-first-sight experience where you meet your soul mate and decide to get married on the spot, taking everybody by surprise. But you probably would be wise to wait through this period before setting a date for tying the knot. If you are still in love in December, your love should last a lifetime. The period from October 9 to November 19 is when Venus, your ruler, is moving retrograde. This is a great time for rethinking your values around relationships to see if what you are projecting is what you want to attract.

For some young single Libras, love and romance might be a thing of dreams and imagination if you are wearing rose-colored glasses. Try to be realistic about potential lovers. Don't fall for a good line—hook, line, and sinker. Keep in mind that the higher on a pedestal you put a person, the farther they have to fall when the light of reality shines upon them. Family matters can figure for some young Libras. You may have to break away from the family home in order to live your life according to your own values, rather than what your parents have mapped out for you. Keep your options open as much as you can by talking to your parents. And stay in touch with siblings, uncles, aunts, and grandparents. Some of you may have to move away from home due to work or marriage commitments. In a new place you will have to make new friends and networks. But you will soon settle in thanks to your Libra charm, diplomacy, and social graces.

Over the last seven years, rebellious and unconventional Uranus has been breaking up the monotony of your daily routines as it moves through Pisces, your work and health sector. Uranus in Pisces poses changes and disruptions and will continue to do so until you find a job that gives you the personal freedom you need and the interesting challenges to keep your mind stimulated. A job loss might lead to a better, more suitable position. You might enjoy working in the areas of information technology, electronics, radio, or television. Jupiter, the planet of expansion and positive influence, will be in Pisces part of this year and will impact this sector also. So you can expect to have opportunities for an improved job and better working conditions. But you must guard against complacency. With Jupiter giving off good vibes in this sector, it is easy to relax and expect good results. If you don't put in the hard yards, you can hurt your chances. If you work with the positive energy, you can set yourself up and reap the benefits for the rest of your life. Maybe the job you feel stuck in might get better and you figure you shouldn't change. But you should because Jupiter will not be in Pisces again for another eleven years. So don't waste this fortunate time. Be prepared; let luck be preparation for opportunity!

In matters of health, Jupiter will give you much protection from illness, and you are likely to be full of vitality. But you may be so optimistic about your health that you put off having a checkup. You also can overdo indulging in food and drink that might be detrimental to your health, causing problems for the future. And Pluto, the planet of hidden things, is in a close aspect to Jupiter. It would be wise to make sure there isn't any unrevealed medical problem. It is often a simple matter to fix something small before it takes hold and affects your whole system. Jupiter can often expand your waistline as well, as the love of good food can lead to excess weight. See a naturopath for options. Start a wholesome diet, one you can enjoy, to maintain your correct weight and well-being with a minimum of fuss. Guard against industrial accidents. If you want to have cosmetic surgery, the period from June 1 to August 15 would be the best time.

Business and financial affairs will be in flux from June through August. Libras involved in a business partnership might seek to end it or to renegotiate the arrangements. Untraditional deals should be checked thoroughly before you invest your hard-earned money. You should also beware any underhanded dealings. If you get involved in any scheme that is not strictly aboveboard, you are likely to lose more than you gain. This period is also not a good time to start a business with your partner or to invest your savings. From September to November your ruler Venus visits Scorpio, your sector of money and values. During this time Venus turns retrograde in motion. Retrograde means that a planet seems to move backward; this is an optical illusion caused by the view from planet Earth. Venus retrograde in Scorpio marks a good time to redo your finances and to create a budget or financial plan, but is not the time for major financial undertakings. Use great care with money because your ruler Venus tempts you to buy lovely things.

Travel is not strongly indicated. Apart from enjoying a vacation, travel may be only for work or for study. You might decide to work abroad as a volunteer for the betterment of humanity or for political reform. Some Libras might join the armed forces to serve a just cause and to demonstrate your idealism or patriotism.

Note when Mercury is retrograde this year: December 26, 2009, to January 15; April 18 to May 11; August 20 to September 12; December 10 to 30. Misunderstanding, delays, and confusion are possible during these retrogrades. Breakdowns in electronic equipment, communication, and transportation also may occur. Avoid binding decisions, signing important paperwork, and purchasing expensive items in these periods. But these retrograde periods are good times to review, rethink, and reconsider situations, choices, and current goals to ensure that you are working toward your main aims.

This year is full of the promise of personal growth for Libra individuals. The result will ultimately be a more balanced and satisfying life. Such a good outcome requires that you put in the effort and be mindful of what it is you really want. By making the most of the wealth of opportunities that come your way, you will have a very successful 2010.

LIBRA
DAILY FORECAST

January–December 2010

JANUARY

1. FRIDAY. Happy New Year! With the emphasis on family and friends, allow yourself to get sidetracked by other issues and you might regret it in the future. Stay clear of secrets and other people's dramas or the repercussions could last all year. This is a good time to focus on family expenses. Work out a practical and conservative budget that will get you through the year to come. Changes are on their way. By preparing in advance, you will be much more able to deal with them. Staying off the roads if possible and being choosy about the type of venue you decide to visit, you will will save unnecessary grief. A sensible approach will lead to many rewards.

2. SATURDAY. Edgy. A restless, impulsive edge to your emotions could intrude on routine and comfort. An invitation to experience some excitement and adventure may disrupt your family's expectations and cause some disgruntled responses. Consider other people before making a decision and you should come out unscathed. Your passion for redecorating combined with some innovative ideas can create a fabulous new ambience in your home. Just be sure to spend time not only at the drawing board but in discussion with the rest of your family before you start tearing down walls. If you aren't feeling one hundred percent, you'll benefit from a quiet day at home and nourishing meals.

3. SUNDAY. Flamboyant. As a Libra you probably love to dress up, and today you should have reason to do so. A new romance may be arousing your spirit and motivating an exploration of life, travel, and fellowship. A group meeting could become heated and test your skill as a mediator. No matter how heated it becomes, the results should be startling, offering a whole new perspective on human relations. If your child is having trouble with a bully, it would be wise to keep them apart to avoid this destructive influence. Work on the youngster's self-esteem, talking out feelings and encouraging development of inner resilience and spirit.

4. MONDAY. Thoughtful. Insight into family dynamics can be very useful, and this will only be gained by listening. Turn your thoughts inward and spend a little time listening to yourself as well; what you're thinking might truly amaze you. No matter the circumstances, harmony should prevail. If someone is causing stress at work, leave them alone. Such people usually are the source of their own undoing. Check your schedule this morning, as you risk missing an appointment or overlooking an important occasion. Don't socialize very much. Keep to yourself and you will do some of your best work and achieve a lot. An old family friend could be helpful to you.

5. TUESDAY. Confronting. Issues of security can cause discomfort, and you may have many worries on the home front. If your problems are outside your control, practicing meditation can help. Start a diary or journal, writing down your thoughts rather than mentally plotting and planning all the time. Relaxation techniques will also be helpful. Changes at work can make you uncomfortable. If fears of the unknown are dominating your thoughts, escape for a while by reading a book or watching television; tomorrow will be a new day. Stay away from caffeine and drugs, and give yourself a rest from stress.

6. WEDNESDAY. Emotional. To improve your self-image, have a facial, schedule a massage, or buy some new clothes to brighten your day. A lovers' quarrel could be upsetting but don't give it any energy; get on with your day, and the rest will take care of itself. Legal matters or the settlement of a contract may be delayed. Not expecting anything to happen for at least ten days will save you useless worry. Be careful what you say to an acquaintance later today. Even a friend is likely to be a gossipmonger and spread your secrets all over town. If you have worries that are causing depression, a counselor can help you deal with them practically and effectively.

7. THURSDAY. Positive. Someone may interfere with your plans and cause setbacks, but you are in a positive frame of mind and will have no shortage of solutions no matter what problems arise. Friends can be of great benefit; don't hesitate to take up their offers of assistance. A romantic interlude may seem like a dream come true, but don't let rose-colored glasses detract from what common sense tells you. A wait-and-see approach would be much more practical right now. Your managerial skills come into play at work, spotlighting your ability to make good decisions in difficult situations. Don't let self-doubt inhibit your actions.

8. FRIDAY. Successful. Feelings of harmony and balance make this a comfortable day. Family relations favor working on problems, or differences of opinion, in a constructive and amiable manner. Libra job seekers are likely to meet with success, especially if looking for work in a creative field. Inhibitions are your only obstacle. You are likely to be worried about your future economic security and may also lack confidence in your own abilities. If you face your fears head-on and don't hold back, your creative talents can lead to a lucrative and satisfying future business venture.

9. SATURDAY. Volatile. One thing can lead to another so quickly that you end up in a situation you never envisioned. Daily chores may turn into major cleaning, only to have you run out of time and energy after you have pulled everything out of the cupboards and closets, leaving your home in a mess. Friends may drop by, leading to an impromptu party but causing you to forget a promise you made to someone close and needy. Pay attention to what is most important today. Write out a timetable if necessary so that you don't get sidetracked. Guard against arguing with a loved one or standing up a well-meaning friend because of impulsiveness.

10. SUNDAY. Expansive. Plans can go awry, but don't be discouraged because new ones should come along to fill the void. Visitors might arrive and interfere with your schedule, but if you are open and honest about prior commitments they will understand. Although you are inclined to take a few risks, be smart and counsel yourself before doing so; keep in mind the wise old saying about looking before you leap. Pay attention to your lifestyle and diet, and make sure you are looking after your own physical and mental well-being. The more comfortable and secure you feel, the better your life will become. Don't overlook the mental, physical, emotional, and spiritual aspects of life.

11. MONDAY. Auspicious. Opportunities are coming your way, either through work or through personal contacts. Keep your ears tuned in and your eyes wide open so that you don't miss the chance of a lifetime. Good relationships are highlighted at this time. You might receive an amorous message from a friend that surprises and bedazzles you, the start of a long and fruitful journey together. Plans to renovate or redecorate your home can get the go-ahead, or some interesting new fashions can catch your eye and give you plenty of creative ideas to work with. Shopping for a new computer or other electrical goods could turn up a bargain, especially if you visit an auction or check online ads.

12. TUESDAY. Productive. Face early-morning stress head-on. Procrastinating or putting off inevitable decisions will only cause more tension in the future. Pay particular attention to any paperwork or an expected report, especially in regard to workplace health and safety. There could be someone watching and evaluating you. You may be offered sponsorship or a scholarship from your workplace to update or expand your skills. This kind of backing will enable you to take a more responsible position with greater opportunities for financial benefits. Trust your good Libra intuition to do the right thing and you won't be let down. A health issue may be aided through a change of diet.

13. WEDNESDAY. Pensive. A certain situation can trigger a flood of memories and put you in a brooding mood for the rest of the day. Find some space to be alone if you can. Writing down memories and the feelings that go along with them might help you gain invaluable insight into your psyche. You are likely to be serious, cautious, and responsible in everything you do, but may underestimate your own worth. Although you may be apprehensive about meeting up with competition, this is a groundless fear. Dress well, get a manicure or anything that will boost your self-image and confidence, and buy something beautiful for your home. Then watch your self-esteem soar.

14. THURSDAY. Refreshing. The New Moon in Capricorn joins the Sun and Venus in your solar sector of home and family, highlighting your relationships and home life. If you are searching for a new home, be on the lookout for one that will accommodate the whole family in comfort and style. Just be sure that it fits in with your budget and won't add too much commuting time. This is an excellent time to start new projects, especially home-based ones. If interested in researching your family tree, begin the process now. Home renovation plans should inspire cooperation from your whole family. Pool your creative talents to both beautify your home and cut costs.

15. FRIDAY. Heartening. Improvements are the order of the day, whether in a difficult relationship, living arrangements, a change of study plans, work opportunities, or a new creative opening. Your self-confidence is high and anything is possible. The day gets off to a slow start, allowing you space to get organized before you leave home. Even if it means setting the alarm an hour early, the extra time will put you on the right foot for whatever is ahead. A budding romance may start to shake off those first-date jitters and begin to feel comfortably exciting. A romantic evening highlighted by a candlelit dinner would be the perfect end to this great day.

16. SATURDAY. Happening. Mercury, the planet of mental pursuits, contracts and agreements, and local travel, has turned direct in the sign of Capricorn. Mercury here will allow holdups and problems with your plans to start moving and clearing away. A conflict of interests might leave you in limbo, wondering which way you should turn. You will be happier in the long term if you stick with your heart and do what inspires you, not what someone else might want you to do. If you become overwhelmed by your feelings, passion, aggression, or anger, confide in a trusted friend who can give you good counsel. Rethink, regroup, and try a new way to attack the challenges that are causing the problem.

17. SUNDAY. Mystical. Your ruling planet Venus is making powerful connections and dancing with the stars, while the Moon meets the romantic and dreamy Neptune to allure and arouse. The potential for romance and illusion are rampant. You may look back on this day and wonder what it was all about, a bit like Alice in Wonderland. Be as practical as you can. Don't allow yourself to be easily led, and you might find someone or something that is very special. While you are outdoors, watch that a child doesn't wander off and become lost. A social gathering can become strained when someone is disagreeable or allows their passion to get the better of them.

18. MONDAY. Creative. Your ruling planet Venus moves into Aquarius and your personal sector of fun, love, and creativity, which gives your artistic and loving flair a powerful boost. In the workplace you might take a new employee under your wing, showing what needs to be done and how best to do it, making a new friend and ally at the same time. A new artistic project could inspire you to accept an organizational role that will take up much of your spare time for a lengthy period. The experience and new skills that you acquire will more than compensate for your dedication. Your family may complain at first about this new commitment, but they are likely to get caught up in your enthusiasm and get over it.

19. TUESDAY. Stressful. After yesterday's highs you now have to knuckle down and work hard to catch up with matters you have let slide. A work issue could be very stressful, with the nervous tension causing you to suffer physically. Breathe deeply in tense moments, and don't try to take charge of what is beyond your control, such as other people's feelings and emotions. Take a reasonably long lunch break. Go for a walk in the fresh air, where you can let the wind blow away the negative energy. Herbal tea is also a good panacea in such a time, helping to calm your mind and soothe your nerves.

20. WEDNESDAY. Excellent. Get up early this morning, organize yourself for the day, and get your chores done. Everything is likely to fall into place like clockwork. An important deal can be finalized, and you are sure to come away with a good profit and a positive boost to your reputation. The Sun now in Aquarius brings warmth and optimism into your creative sector, joining Venus in Aquarius to ensure success and originality in your creative ventures. If you are hoping to start a family, make use of this powerful duo in the sector that also rules children. Parents may reconsider a child's schooling and make plans to visit various educational facilities before making a decision.

21. THURSDAY. Determined. No matter what problems arise today, you can methodically work your way through them. Just beware of inadvertently upsetting people by your actions because they could be quite vindictive toward you. Your good work will not go unnoticed, and you might find that you are in line for a promotion. Try to avoid getting drawn into intense discussions unless you know precisely what you are talking about. Otherwise you could end up being blamed for something that is not your fault. Married Libras may find issues from the past being resurrected. Be prepared to accept responsibility for your own actions and to take positive steps to improve your current relationship.

22. FRIDAY. Problematic. A practical no-nonsense approach will gain you the most ground in work and play. Your creative talents need space to be expressed. Keep to yourself as much as possible and you can achieve a great deal. Don't let anyone push you around. There are likely to be some very hurtful and vindictive remarks floating around, and it will be quite painful if you take these personally. What comes out of a person's mouth is a vibration that emulates their spirit and has nothing to do with you unless you take it on yourself. Your mate or partner's expectations and your family commitments may be in opposition to each other, so be honest and only do what you can do.

23. SATURDAY. Secretive. Conspiracies and innuendos abound, and you might be forgiven for getting a little paranoid at times. Take everything you hear with a grain of salt. Try to ignore the advances of someone who should know better. Single Libras might receive a proposal of marriage that doesn't quite live up to personal fantasies. You may wonder if true love is simply a fairy tale. Gambling is not a good idea because the odds will be stacked against you. Any investments you are considering should be put under the microscope before you make a definite decision. Seek the security and comfort of home this evening, and enjoy the love of family members, adoring pets, and home cooking.

24. SUNDAY. Eventful. If a business partner tries to coerce you into a deal you don't feel comfortable with, trust your instincts. An outside interest could take you away from the love of your life, leaving that person feeling snubbed and jealous. Buy something special to show your affection, and plan a romantic dinner. If that doesn't work, you might need to start learning about codependency. Single Libras could meet an intriguing stranger who oozes sex appeal and romance. But don't rush in where angels fear to tread. Hold off and do some checking in the light of day before putting your heart on the line. A family heirloom might find its way into your possession.

25. MONDAY. Pleasant. This day should be full of all the things a Libra enjoys, such as art, beauty, creativity, and socializing. Parents might drive a child to a function and end up having a great time meeting interesting new people among the other parents. You and your mate or partner may decide to visit an exhibit or gallery and take in the awesome visual art on display. Mental activity is likely to be fast-paced and could knot up your emotions as you plot and plan. Practice deep breathing and relaxation. If possible, get away from your home environment for the day by visiting relatives or going for a long walk or drive to a popular scenic site.

26. TUESDAY. Beneficial. Jupiter, the planet of expansion, has entered Pisces, your sector of work and health, and will stay in Pisces for much of the year. Jupiter here brings many opportunities for advancement at work. Obtaining extra training in your field of choice will give you an edge over competitors. Travel in connection with work is also indicated, suggesting an exciting job offer from a distance. Your health should remain fairly robust if it is already so. However, the urge to overeat might add to your waistline unless you are careful; if you are hungrier than usual, eat lots of salads and vegetables. There is an impatient edge to the day, so take it easy to avoid an argument or accident.

27. WEDNESDAY. Intense. What starts out to be friendly could turn completely unpleasant. To protect yourself from unnecessary emotional pain, do your work and stay out of backbiting and gossip. Some of you may be going for a job interview, and the prospects look favorable as long as you have necessary references and certificates with you to make a professional presentation. A meeting could begin to fall apart, giving you a chance to hone your leadership skills. If you keep the group moving through the agenda and don't let the discussion stray, you will be able to maintain control. By the end of the day you may be feeling emotionally wrung out; a long soak in a hot tub can do wonders.

28. THURSDAY. Enticing. There are a lot of opportunities available for you, but how you react to them will depend on your mood. A family member could be making unreasonable demands on your time and energy, or you may feel a conflict of interest between your home commitments and your need to forge ahead in your career. Instead of allowing your emotions to take over, or your head to think you into a corner, focus on just being in the moment. Thinking or worrying about the past or about the future isn't necessary. If you deal with the now, everything will fall into place satisfactorily. When you have faith in yourself, the natural order of events and of your wishes can come true.

29. FRIDAY. Motivating. High energy and enthusiasm will get you going early today. Make a to-do list before you leave home, and begin to act on it right away so that you aren't left rushing around at the last minute trying to get everything done. A number of invitations for the weekend could overwhelm you, leaving you with the unpleasant task of telling a friend you can't come to their party or function. Tonight's Full Moon in Leo joins Mars in Leo, which could see tempers flare and impatience become rampant. Be extra careful not to take risks, and stay away from using drugs and alcohol in excess. A creative project might get the green light, along with free promotion from an advertising company.

30. SATURDAY. Complex. A new romance can put a blush on your checks and make the routine of work relentless and long. Whatever you do, don't accept an invitation from workmates to go for a long lunch because this will put you in a vulnerable position with your employer. Or you could talk way too much about your personal life to colleagues who don't have your best interests at heart. A meeting can become drawn out with too much discussion regarding side issues that are not important. Basically, people might find it hard to agree on anything right now. Get everybody to focus on the main issues and you will be done earlier. This evening should be quite different from the day, with harmony and love reigning supreme.

31. SUNDAY. Peaceful. The urge to flee from the rat race and find a quiet refuge could be very strong. Plan a getaway for the weekend with that special person in your life. Get away from your local neighborhood; a bed-and-breakfast hideaway in a remote and romantic setting will relax and inspire both of you. Or you may need to stay in bed watching movies and snacking to give yourself a break from the demands of modern life. If you want to gamble, beware of breaking the budget; take it easy on the size and amount of your bets. Libra writers and artists can get some valuable work done and find inspiration. Following your own original ideas should impress even you.

FEBRUARY

1. MONDAY. Caring. A community project can inspire you to volunteer your services. If you have never done this before, you will be surprised how good it makes you feel to selflessly be of help. Spiritual issues could also be on your mind. If you are not a member of a religious group, start to read up on different ideas of kinds of faith and various spiritual beliefs. Take some time today to nurture yourself as well as other people, consciously treating yourself well and enjoying the warm and fuzzy feelings this evokes. An older relative might call on you for some help. While doing so you could have the best conversation ever, discovering personal information about them that means a lot to you.

2. TUESDAY. Fair. Any decisions regarding your future should be put on hold for the day. If you receive a proposition that seems too good to be true, be sure to discuss it first with your family and not give an answer until tomorrow. Any new ventures should be checked out thoroughly; there is a good chance of not getting the whole truth about the situation. A disagreement with your mate or partner could cause you to rethink what you expect from the relationship, but don't get depressed because things could turn out very positively. You have the stamina and perseverance to overcome obstacles, so stick to your guns on the most important issues.

3. WEDNESDAY. Promising. The solar influences are all on your side, highlighting Libra good looks and charm. Make the most of these positive influences and you will have a very remarkable day. Spend a little on pampering yourself; a massage or facial will add to your happy, relaxed glow. Contact that special someone and arrange a romantic outing without worrying about the expense. Go to a concert or the theater, then enjoy a late-night dinner for two. You might spot the perfect art to add a special feel to your home plus potential profitably as an investment. Students may be able to do extra work at home and save on travel.

4. THURSDAY. Useful. Don't get up early in the hope of accomplishing a lot. This morning's influences suggest that nothing much will happen until the afternoon. If you use morning hours to get organized and prepare for a late rush hour, you will come out ahead. Money earned now is likely to give your budget an added boost, making you feel positive about recent decisions. Your employer may ask you to take on additional work, but don't let the promise of extra pay blind you to what you can realistically do. Too much work can make your life drudgery. This is an excellent time to focus on your health. Become active at your local gym and make new friends at the same time.

5. FRIDAY. Frustrating. No matter how hard you try you might not get any reaction or appreciation for your hard work, but don't worry. There is a lot going on, and tomorrow is a new day. Keep doing your best and you will win out in the long run. Someone you normally rely on might seem aloof and let you down significantly, forcing you to personally take care of what's important to you. Your mind is likely to be working overtime and stressing you out. Try to turn your thoughts to the present moment, and get away from the shoulds and what ifs. Work with what you have now and your frustrations will slowly melt away, leaving peace in their wake.

6. SATURDAY. Interactive. The atmosphere this morning is so full of romance and idealism that whatever you do might not match the perfection you expect. A relationship may not be working out, leaving you feeling that you have been led down the garden path. Keep in mind that all's fair in love and war, and know that you will live to love another day. The pace at work is likely to be hectic. But once you get into it, you can forget all your regrets and enjoy the tasks at hand. Interacting with colleagues is likely to have you laughing in no time. If you are invited to go out for a while after work, let your hair down and enjoy being part of the group.

7. SUNDAY. Interesting. Your good Libra insight and understanding can be valuable when dealing with the overinflated ego of people you see occasionally. The desire to cut someone down to size may be strong, but you will be better off being humble and leaving them alone. Be true to yourself and live by your own ideals. Watch your spending if you go shopping. Also watch what you eat or you could suffer a bout of indigestion. Romance is indicated. There are harmonious vibes all over the place, but don't let your kind nature lead to telling someone they are your one and only if they are not. Likewise, there could be plenty of lies floating around, so guard against being taken in by a smooth talker.

8. MONDAY. Diverse. Set patterns of thinking may be challenged by situations that don't fit into the pattern. By being willing to open your mind to new ideas and new concepts, you might experience a life-changing revelation. Travel plans can be disrupted, either through a mechanical failure or when other people reschedule, leaving you to wonder what to do for the rest of the day. Venture out into your neighborhood and experience the local flavor, whether at a mall, library, restaurant, park, museum, or historical site. You are sure to have an enjoyable adventure and meet some interesting people wherever you go.

9. TUESDAY. Sensitive. Family secrets that surface can stir up unconscious resentments among your tribe. There may be some ongoing emotional manipulation, expectations, and jealousies. However, even though it may seem as if the sky is falling in, the upset will serve to clear away some of the baggage that everyone has inherited. Once the storm clouds move on, there will be freshness in the air and strengthened bonds between relatives. A surprise visit from an old family friend might arouse all sorts of emotions, especially if this person wants to stay at your place while in town. Just be sure to set clear boundaries to guard against the chance that your guest will become the visitor that never leaves.

10. WEDNESDAY. Innovative. Mercury, the planet of communication, moves into Aquarius and your solar sector of fun, lovers, and children. This will help cultivate added relating and understanding with those close to you. Libra students who are feeling bored should talk with an adviser about changing classes or your major. Even if doing so sets you back a semester, in the long run you will be doing what you enjoy, learning more, and making life more fun. A sports interest might suddenly become serious when you are offered a professional position. Although this is bound to be very flattering, put plenty of thought into your decision.

11. THURSDAY. Industrious. Venus, your ruling planet, moves into sensitive Pisces and your solar sector of service and health. Your critical faculties are excellent, and you can easily and quickly pick out what is worth saving and what is not. Your natural flair for work that involves diplomacy, beauty, and art should help you take a more independent role in your workplace. Put in for a promotion or a pay raise and you might be pleasantly surprised. Be careful to keep your love life separate from your working life, especially if you are inclined to make a romantic connection with a coworker at this time. Drink plenty of water, and keep alcohol consumption to a minimum over the next month.

12. FRIDAY. Surprising. There is a fine line between an argument and a discussion, and today that line is likely to become very blurry. To sort out disagreements without hurting feelings or losing a friend, step back a little and don't let it become personal. Then you can do your Libra best to mediate between different views. The Aquarius Moon is sending some wacky emotional vibes into your love life, making this a time to withdraw a bit and focus on what you want and feel. The role of group leader might be relegated to you. This will provide a chance to take control and be assertive, something that you might prove surprisingly good at and want to do more of.

13. SATURDAY. Encouraging. Tonight's New Moon in Aquarius falls in your solar sector of lovers, children, and creativity. This is the perfect time to start something new, especially any creative project already initiated and in the pipeline. If you have been secretly admiring someone special, gather the courage to ask for a date. Many ideas and plans are forming in your mind, and you would be wise to take the time to put them down in writing to give yourself something concrete to work from. Don't discuss your problems with anyone because you will only get their biased views and judgments. Instead let your feelings and solutions percolate to the surface in your own unique style.

14. SUNDAY. Enjoyable. Your morning ritual is usually enjoyable, and today may be ever so pleasant. Going out for breakfast could bring local people into your life who will be good friends for many years to come. Markets and local shops might be selling some interesting art to beautify your home and be a potential investment. Or you may be having a garage sale to get rid of what you consider old junk. Be rigid with your prices because some buyers will haggle you down to the ridiculous if you let them. Dieters beware; this is a day for enjoyment, whether it is good friends or lots of your favorite food.

15. MONDAY. Social. The calendar is likely to be full of possible social events. You might particularly enjoy physical exercise, a team sport, a vigorous debate, maybe even a political rally. Take your time while driving because there are bound to be people trying to make up lost time due to a bottleneck that has traffic at a standstill. A romantic encounter with a very alluring and unusual stranger might get your imagination working overtime, but the chances of a real relationship coming from this are very slim. If you can't resist, it might be in your favor to play hard to get, and mysterious, in order to catch their interest. Go to bed early tonight.

16. TUESDAY. Disconcerting. Changes in the workplace can be frustrating, especially if you feel they threaten your security as an employee. Take it easy, however. You are probably not alone in your feelings. Angry workmates may be talking about striking or walking out, but make sure you really want this and aren't just letting your emotional insecurities run riot. Small annoyances can become mammoth problems if you let your mind take over, so be practical. Write down what's upsetting you and look at all options. You might just need a break from everyday monotony to revive your interest and enthusiasm for life. Plan a long weekend away that will give you and your mate or partner time to talk and to make love, not war.

17. WEDNESDAY. Satisfying. Legal matters can become embroiled in messy details and third-party intrusions, but the trick for success is to remain aloof and untouchable. If you are right, you won't lose. Mediation and cooperation will lead to incredible benefits in any relationship crisis. Now is the time for compassion and forgiveness, keeping in mind that great things can grow from humble beginnings. Your challenge is to evolve and move on, leaving behind an old way of life and, if possible, inspiring someone else to do the same. Good communication will be a bonus later today. You might be able to outdo an admirable foe and give yourself a considerable edge over all competition.

18. THURSDAY. Practical. The Sun now moves into Pisces and your solar house of health and service, putting the spotlight on your workplace and daily routine. If you are overweight, you might decide to start dieting and get back into shape. Instead of opting for a fad diet, try eating plenty of whole foods and cutting out fast food, sugar, coffee, and alcohol. You can still eat as much as you want while losing weight and getting healthy at the same time. Drinking lots of water and getting a good night's sleep will make your eyes sparkle and your skin glow. You'll also see the difference in your performance at work and your ability to get along with relatives. Problems disappear when you are feeling good.

19. FRIDAY. Influential. A meeting with remarkable or powerful people could make this day memorable. Connections through your business may open up a whole new perspective on wheeling and dealing, but you will have to keep your wits about you and treat all aspects seriously. In this world some people will be your friends only if you are of value to them. Looking to see who profits will provide insight into what is really going on. If worried about your credit card debt, contact the financial institution and ask about arranging a lower interest rate. It is better for them to get something back rather than nothing, and better for your credit to get out of debt.

20. SATURDAY. Insightful. A lovers' quarrel can cause emotional pain. On the upside, however, this can turn out to be the catalyst for better self-knowledge and understanding. Don't dwell on the negatives or wallow in self-pity. Forgive and forget. This is a perfect time to start learning a martial art or other type of self-empowerment that will also aid in structuring your daily tasks around achieving your life's goals. One day at a time should be your motto for living right now. A dispute over shared resources can be a challenge. If you are dividing up an inheritance with your siblings, try to keep focused on the big picture rather than letting individual desires run rampant.

21. SUNDAY. Rewarding. Ambitions can be realized as a hobby grows into a livelihood or an artistic project gains recognition. Conditions favor working within the community to help people who are worse off than you, perhaps by gaining extra support and funding from a private sponsor. Inspiration to travel and experience lands and cultures different from your own can lead to making plans for your vacation. If you book into the future, you will have plenty of time to pay it off without straining your budget. Make time today to explore the culture in your own area. There may be an interesting play or exhibit worth visiting, or a political forum where you can express your views and hear those of elected officials.

22. MONDAY. Convivial. Enjoy this lovely day, with stimulating conversation and interesting and attractive friends helping to pass the time. A social gathering will be lots of fun, providing you with plenty of opportunities to learn about different points of view. If you are stuck at home you can find plenty of conversation on the Net regarding whatever subject interests you and with people from all over the globe, and you won't even have to dress up. Libra lovers might be wise to take a break from romance, just to get perspective back and be able to digest the implications of where the relationship is heading. If it is true love, a few hours apart won't hurt.

23. TUESDAY. Helpful. Intuitive and sensitive forces hold sway as Mercury and Neptune hook up with the Moon, creating an understanding environment for all things human. You can make decisions based on both your heart and your mind, and you should find plenty of support for your ideas. Although you may be excited about future plans, be careful to stay anchored in the present. Otherwise you could have an accident or forget something important. Take to heart the saying that life is what happens while we are busy making other plans. If you feel an injustice has been done to you, speak to a lawyer rather than trying to right it yourself because you might unwittingly make matters worse. You can count on a lot of support from friends.

24. WEDNESDAY. Harmonious. Goodheartedness and cooperation are the order of the day. Any changes you are trying to implement will advance smoothly. You may have strong ambitions for yourself or a family member. The chances of getting into a world-renowned college are high. If you are strapped for cash, there may be a scholarship available to help cover the cost. Do your homework and you can't fail. Libra writers and artists may gain recognition for your work. An offer from an agent should be considered; if you are not sure about the person's integrity, speak to some of their other clients. Check in with older relatives or neighbors and let them know you are available if they need you.

25. THURSDAY. Opportune. A chance for a promotion could be in the pipeline. There may be praise and support coming from your boss or other superior to give you the courage to apply for an opening. Don't think too hard about it; let your reputation do the talking for you. If a situation necessitates you taking control, don't hesitate. Trust what you know, let experience be your guide, and you won't put a foot wrong. Some workmates could annoy you with their petty squabbles and gossip. Gravitate toward those who prefer more deep and meaningful conversations, and you will discover some interesting facts and information that could be very useful to you in the future.

26. FRIDAY. Heartening. An unexpected invitation to a sports match or group gathering could lead to strong interest and involvement in the club and the start of a new aspect to your life and personality. A leadership role or position on a committee that is offered to you may open up financial or political opportunities as well. Whatever you are planning at the moment, you need to cooperate and coordinate with other people if you want to succeed. Be aware that this can lead to involvement in power plays and secrets that you would rather not know about. Listen and be sympathetic when confidences are revealed, but keep them to yourself and don't offer any personal advice.

27. SATURDAY. Idealistic. You may be drawn to unusual types of people now. On the positive side, they may be artistic and spiritual, or in a negative vein they may be confused and selfish. The lesson for you is to recognize your own special gifts and stop idealizing anyone else's. Put your dreams into practice. Start planning a new project that will manifest your hopes and wishes, and they are likely to come true sooner than you think. An opportunity to go on an adventure with friends should not be missed; you never know where it might lead or who you might meet. The more social connections you make, the better. Your future networking depends on who you get to know now.

28. SUNDAY. Enthusiastic. Today's Full Moon in Virgo highlights your service sectors, not only service to other people but to yourself as well. Aim at finding a workable balance between the two. Take yourself out of the fast lane and go for a walk in nature, soak in a tub and meditate, or do anything that will remove you from the hurly-burly of ego and desire. Think about offering your services in a volunteer setting. Whether you work for the environment, wildlife, the handicapped, or the poor, it will broaden your outlook on life, taking you away from negative self-indulgence while gaining the benefits derived from giving. Most importantly, love yourself.

MARCH

1. MONDAY. Stressful. It is commendable to be industrious and efficient. But if you take on too much all at once, you are just being unkind to yourself. Playing the role of martyr won't get you respected. In fact, appreciation for such effort is apt to be nil. Slow down and look after yourself. Consider what you would like most, then give it to yourself; you've earned it. If you can't afford what you want most, work out a budget so you can afford it in the future, meanwhile allowing yourself to dream. Mercury, the planet of communication, moves into Pisces and your house of health and service. So this a great time to record your daily thoughts and feelings in a diary for later reflection and healing.

2. TUESDAY. Vibrant. The Moon moves into your sign of Libra, imbuing you with vitality and confidence. Your eye for detail is sharp as a tack, making this a great time to do bookwork and to study. You will want to dress to impress today. A trip to the mall might turn up a bargain on a designer label, which will give your image extra interest and allure. A business meeting is likely to be a success. Although you might end up working in an area that you hadn't planned on, it will be exciting and grab your interest. A long-term goal may draw a little closer thanks to your focus and hard work, giving you incentive to keep going and have faith in yourself.

3. WEDNESDAY. Intuitive. Although a restless and excitable feel is in the air, trust your own instincts so that you don't get caught up in wild-goose chases or impulsive behavior. If you are starting a new project, allow plenty of time to get it established; it is always a good idea to provide extra time. A group situation could be stressful, with plenty of disagreement and egocentric opinions flying about that no amount of mediation can assuage. Instead of expending energy with no results, just agree to disagree. A former lover may turn up and ask you to give them another chance. Take a lesson from the past before you decide to let bygones be bygones.

4. THURSDAY. Lucky. Put in for a raise at work and you might get a pleasant surprise. If you have been very dedicated, your hard work will not have gone unnoticed. If you have applied for other jobs, you may now be in the happy position of having hopeful employers vying for your skills. Don't get over confident, however. Be practical and conscious of your goals, not betraying your values even with the offer of big money. A coworker might be trying to undermine your confidence and support. Just ignore what's being said, and your good reputation and kind nature will remain intact. If you buy a lottery ticket or raffle chance, it could be your turn to win.

5. FRIDAY. Productive. Hard work will get you what you want now, while avoidance will only hinder your progress and cause headaches you could do without. Don't procrastinate over decisions. Instead of trying to find a perfect balance, follow your heart on any important matters. Trust that the universe will provide if your intentions are good. Guard against getting caught up in an illegal or underhanded scheme; you are sure to get caught and have to pay the consequences. Moving will be stressful due to basic problems like getting a fridge or a sofa up a narrow stairway. Double-check everything ahead of time to save yourself money and strain.

6. SATURDAY. Creative. Libra writers can do some of your best work now as well as line up a publisher to put it into print. Your circle of friends is bound to be growing, with intellectual and sporting types to stimulate your mind and add fun to your life. Consider taking a course to complement your talents and to further your employment prospects. This will open doors for you and also put you in touch with people who will be invaluable contacts in the future. Expect travel delays. If you go by public transportation, check the Internet for any holdups or accidents, and give yourself plenty of time to get to your destination relaxed and in a good mood.

7. SUNDAY. Problematic. Trials and tribulations are likely. You will either be running around after other people or playing the role of people pleaser. However, you need to start valuing yourself more. You can be kind and understanding without being subservient. Venus, the planet of love and harmony, moves into Aries, your solar sector of partnerships and legal issues. This should help you maneuver through any tricky business agreement or within your relationships. If you are going through a legal struggle, you might encounter resentment this morning. But as the day progresses, this can be smoothed away and agreement worked out, even if it is simply agreeing to disagree.

8. MONDAY. Mixed. No matter how you are feeling this morning, the day is not likely to be your own. You are duty bound to fulfill promises made yesterday. Whether you have to chauffeur the kids, show up at a social event, or catch up on a backlog of work, once you put your mind to it you will become totally involved and enjoy the moment. A loved one may not be feeling well, and you may need to tend to their needs for a while. Take the time to sit and talk, enjoying each other's company. Disagreements with your mate or partner can be worked out later in the day. An evening of domestic chores and loving can stem from honestly and openly sharing your innermost feelings.

9. TUESDAY. Stimulating. Intellectual stimulation and good communication are on the menu. You are likely to be surrounded by friendly, outgoing people who match your mood. Spontaneous activities might stimulate new interests and relationships. If you go shopping, you could find some great bargains on items for your home that are both practical and decorative. An older relative may need some help at home. Arranging someone to help with cleaning, weekly cooking, or grocery shopping will make life easier and provide friendly contact as well. A major reshuffle at work could be causing insecurity, but you are sure to keep your position.

10. WEDNESDAY. Friendly. Hustle and bustle plus an overbooked calendar can contribute to stress that you could do without. Start your day by prioritizing appointments and work. Don't hesitate to cancel or postpone activities that will just set you back. A visit from an old friend might test your diplomacy, which as a Libra normally comes naturally. Today, however, you could end up frazzled by the encounter, especially if you let your guard down and allow this person to take advantage of your good nature. An offer to escape for the weekend might be the best news of the day. Say yes and worry about the consequences later. Nothing is impossible if you just believe it.

11. THURSDAY. Energetic. Fun and romance shouldn't be allowed to take a backseat in your life. Single Libras may experience the first lustful stage of a new relationship, with the excitement that goes along with poetic and loving text messages and snatched phone calls while at work. Mars, the planet of action and energy, goes direct after two and a half months in reverse motion. This ease frustrations and boosts your energy. So it is a positive time to start new projects and to resurrect those that have stalled. Partnered Libras who are experiencing problems communicating with a loved one should consider counseling to help open the channels once again.

12. FRIDAY. Hopeful. The possibility of new beginnings can eliminate a sense of stagnation. New job possibilities could also be on the horizon, but don't rest on your laurels. Start working on your resume, and make sure you do some research and come up with references so that you will make a good impression. If marriage plans are in the pipeline, finding a balance between the celebration you would like and what you can afford might be difficult. Put your own talents into play instead of paying other people for all that must be done. By doing it yourself, you can get exactly what you want. An impromptu party at your place will be raved about for weeks to come.

13. SATURDAY. Active. Take it easy this morning and pamper yourself if you can. The day is likely to become hectic by afternoon. You may be expected in two places at once, or have to cope with a week's work in a few hours. Try not to drink too much caffeine; stick to water or juice to help you stay calm and think straight. With the Moon sailing into Pisces and your sector of work and health, you might experience some physical signs of stress if you allow anyone to treat you like a machine. Be sure to take breaks and eat wholesome food. Smokers should consider joining a self-help group for extra support quitting the habit.

14. SUNDAY. Emotional. As the Moon makes contact with Jupiter, the planet of expansion, you can expect plenty of extravagance and exaggeration. Try not to take on too much. If you already feel fragile, cancel the day's agenda and look after yourself. Vow to make an appointment for a medical checkup, including any shots you need for the workplace or for travel. If the weather permits, get outside for some fresh air and to casually enjoy the sights and sounds of your own neighborhood. Singles might consider purchasing a pet for company, but be realistic about your domestic situation. For the pet's happiness as well as yours, only look for one that suits your environment.

15. MONDAY. Eventful. Today's New Moon in Pisces heralds a promising new beginning for Libra job seekers. Use the Internet to get your resume out to as many potential employers as possible. Don't hesitate applying for jobs that would mean relocating; a change of scenery would do you good right now. An unexpected invitation can surprise and delight you with plenty of mental stimulation and out-of-the-ordinary activity. A friend who is going through a bad time due to a broken relationship would welcome a visit from you. Cheer them up. Let them know that they don't have to be all alone.

16. TUESDAY. Nostalgic. Libras who are away from home are likely to miss the comfort of loved ones and, on a more practical note, the comfort of your own bed. Even if you are not away from home, you may be feeling rather isolated and lonely. The best way to deal with this is to engage in some self-analysis, which should be very effective so long as you are willing to be honest. You are apt to be experiencing anxiety in anticipation of a situation that may have to be faced. If you can calm your mind and your nerves either through relaxation and meditation or by going for a walk, you can get to a point where you accept that whatever will be, will be.

17. WEDNESDAY. Surprising. Today's stellar influences suggest that you can expect the unexpected. Everyday routines may be upset by last-minute changes. Or a strong urge to escape from the daily grind can make you act in surprising ways. Libras who are in business might have to placate an important client or customer, or put up with a disgruntled employee. On the other hand, as an employee you might be annoyed at your working conditions and join in with workmates to demand better pay and conditions. As the day progresses, love and harmony prevail. Libra couples should find a loving space to share, while Libra singles can enjoy an evening of romance with someone very special.

18. THURSDAY. Fair. This is a good time to enter into contracts or negotiations. You can clarify and explain issues clearly and uncritically. If there is a matter that concerns you, consult a specialist for the best advice. A property settlement can be extremely hard if you have to part with any possessions that hold memories from the past. However, if you understand that the other party is also experiencing the same feelings of grief and loss, you might be able to avoid too much conflict. There is a risk of hasty action and the chance of an accident, so think before you act and don't let anger rule your head. Angry friends should also be avoided.

19. FRIDAY. Benevolent. Although good feelings abound, in business dealings be very careful to study the fine print. You feel so good that you might be tempted to take other people at face value, which is not smart business. An element of luck is also in the air. If you are tempted to make a wager or buy a lottery ticket, you might just be a winner. Religion, philosophy, and psychic realms might spark your interest. Or you could visit a fortune-teller for insight into the future. If you are unsure about what to do next, wait until you gain confidence. You will know when the time is right to act.

20. SATURDAY. Upsetting. As a Libra you are normally well equipped to cope with disagreements. However, the conflicts you encounter now might make you want to escape, to simply run away to a peaceful and serene place. If you are unhappy in your present relationship, consider seeing a counselor or going to meetings of a self-help group to gain the strength to act positively. A social event could be fun for a while, but you would be wise to leave early to avoid the unpleasantness that is bound to arise later. The wisdom of somebody older could be your saving grace. Instead of struggling with what's upsetting you, get some well-grounded advice and insight from an elder.

21. SUNDAY. Diverse. The focus shifts from your daily routine to issues relating to other people. You might be more inclined to seek out fun-loving and eccentric types to hang around with in the hope of finding challenging new situations that add spice to your life. Libra couples should plan to do something different, something that is challenging physically, allows healthy competition, and provides new subjects to talk about. Singles who start learning a sport can meet new people who will be like a breath of fresh air. Venture out to get away from what has become boringly familiar.

22. MONDAY. Starred. A holiday atmosphere in a social setting can add enjoyment to the day. Don't be surprised if friends drop by or you receive an invitation for fun and laughter. Or you may be departing on an overseas trip or seeing a friend off with lots of partying and promises for the future. Libra students who have a deadline to meet can accomplish some valuable research and good writing to award you top marks. Start early and you won't miss out on this evening's events. You could discover some dark secret from your family's past, or receive some news that gets you closer to a long-awaited meeting.

23. TUESDAY. Confronting. Intensity and a dog-eat-dog attitude reign supreme at the moment, adding a nasty edge to competition. The opportunity for advancement may come at the expense of an opponent. Ask yourself if you want it that much, aware that if you don't maintain peak performance you will be the next victim. Those of you experiencing any workplace bullying or sexual harassment should consider reporting this to the relevant authority who by law must maintain your anonymity and safety. Your mate or partner may change jobs and have to accept a lower wage, regardless of your budget. Offer emotional support, looking to the future with confidence.

24. WEDNESDAY. Successful. Public relations or sales is right up your alley. Working with groups is a Libra specialty, because you are sensitive and responsive to the general mood. If you are active in a social or sports club, don't be surprised if you are nominated for an elected position or an award. You tend to wear your heart on your sleeve. Even if you have reservations about a public display of emotion, you are likely to indulge in that now. Positive creative aspects can give you an original and unique edge on the competition. Don't be shy about expressing your ideas, which are apt to receive a far better reception than you thought possible.

25. THURSDAY. Interesting. All sorts of influences are forming cross-currents, leaving a strange feeling that there is more to what's happening than meets the eye. You might walk away from a conversation wondering just what the person was getting at. Don't think about it too much, however, because the other person is probably feeling exactly the same. Focus on what you want to get done, and ignore interruptions if you can. This is a very creative time, and you should be well pleased with your day's output. Physical activity is recommended as a stress buster. This is a great time to sign up for lessons or join a club to pursue a sport that captures your interest.

26. FRIDAY. Expansive. If you follow the golden rule and don't discuss politics or religion while out with your peers, you will get along just fine. You may encounter someone itching for a fight and will have to use all your diplomatic tactics to keep the exchange harmonious and friendly. Partnered Libras might want to buy something sentimental to surprise and delight a loved one this evening. Your gift will provide an emotional lift, showing that you care in this way. Spend some time planning for the future. Write down your hopes and wishes, and put them out to the universe. Think big, and have the courage to dream.

27. SATURDAY. Sensitive. Your romantic relationship can be considerably enriched as you are able to get past superficial communication that may have been driving you and your loved one apart. Once again you will feel as one. Karmic encounters are also on the cards. You are likely to experience such an intensity on meeting someone that you feel you have known each other before. This can be exhausting, and you need to monitor your energy level and make sure you don't give too much away to other people, no matter how needy they may be. You will benefit from a time of solitude this evening to reminisce about people and events of the past.

28. SUNDAY. Useful. Your enthusiasm for spring-cleaning or another home project can see you up at the crack of dawn with a long list of chores. Don't push yourself too hard. Be happy to do what you can. If you start to tire, take a break to restore your energy with rest and relaxation. Meditation would be beneficial, giving you the space to digest your thoughts and feelings. Look for an opportunity to do some volunteer work for a community project; the benefits that you receive will far outweigh what you give. Be careful to lock up your home if you go out today. Also be sure to lock car doors if driving after dark.

29. MONDAY. Exciting. All your well-laid plans can change on a whim when unexpected visitors or a wonderful invitation bedazzles you. The Full Moon tonight is in your own sign of Libra, creating a very romantic setting for you and that special person. Reserve a table for two at a top-notch restaurant, and enjoy your meal with a view that money can't buy. Only family worries could upset your day, so check in loved ones before you go anywhere. Make sure there is nothing you need to do on the home front, then you can relax. Any business plan that you have in the pipeline would benefit from networking. While you are socializing, you might find the perfect contact.

30. TUESDAY. Beneficial. Take a break from your workday to do something for yourself. Go for a manicure or a massage or a new haircut or color, something that makes you feel pampered and adds to your sense of self-worth. You may want to check up on your health also. Your immune system could benefit from a change of diet, and this plus some herbal teas might be just what you need to get back in top shape. Dieting along with an exercise routine will get you shipshape and fit for seasonal sports. Whatever feels good will be far better than just mindlessly going through the motions, without a thought for how you are really feeling.

31. WEDNESDAY. Varied. If you are worried about your mate or partner's spending habits, instead of complaining to them try talking about your financial goals and coming up with a better budget. You have an ability to understand your opponents in business and may clinch a deal that will solve all your financial problems with one stroke of a pen. A craft or hobby can also turn into a viable business proposition. Obtain help from a respected financial adviser to set up and enjoy making a living doing what you love. The end of a relationship can lead to fighting over possessions. Let go and enjoy the sense of freedom you will feel, trusting that what is yours will come back.

APRIL

1. THURSDAY. Rewarding. As a Libra you are generous and good-natured, and goodness is likely to come back to you today. Good feelings at work will benefit your output and pump up your feelings of self-confidence. No matter how old you are, you might feel you are just getting to know yourself. This sense of self is very valuable and worth developing further with a counselor or with a self-help group. Introspection you gain with guidance can be significant for your future. Singles could meet someone special, finding an intensity of feeling that has been lacking in life. Partnered

Libras may experience heightened intimacy with that very special someone.

2. FRIDAY. Liberating. A check of your bank balance could seem depressing, but stop worrying and put everything back into perspective. Examine the moment and you will recognize that for now you have enough oxygen to breathe, which will get you through. Add up what you do have and work on the positives. If you have a job, you're lucky; if you have a good friend, you're lucky. If you don't have a job, look at what talents or skills you have and work with those. Mercury, the planet of communication, and Venus, the planet of love, are both in Taurus, your solar house of other people's money. So this is a time to buy a lottery ticket. This transit will also give you plenty of support from other people.

3. SATURDAY. Varied. Pay attention to small details and you will save yourself some grief. If you must be on the job, it can be very tedious and your boss cranky or nitpicking. Spend extra time making sure you have done a thorough job, and you might get some praise. Keep in mind that you aren't the only one the boss has to worry about. A contract or agreement can be finalized to your satisfaction, probably providing an added benefit you hadn't counted on. Partnered Libras might start a business together that will combine talents and encourage more time together. Your e-mails could contain an interesting offer. A brother or sister can be a great help; ask for assistance if you need it.

4. SUNDAY. Interesting. Stress and tension could be taking a toll on you physically. If you have the day off, go for a brisk walk in the fresh air to get your blood pumping. Experience your inner feelings and five senses without your mind continually dominating. A local celebration or cultural event will give you a chance to mix with neighbors and also meet some exciting new people. Libras who are relocating for work are likely to be experiencing lots of different emotions and ideas about the future while letting go of the past. Don't get too caught up in any sense of loss, because you can always come back after going on the current adventure.

5. MONDAY. Reflective. Cosmic consequences can give you the sense that something greater than yourself is afoot in your life. A dream or memories from the past might lead to an understanding of your inner self that is totally new to you. Investment advice should be acted on for your long-term benefit. A tantalizing encounter with an attractive stranger might linger in your mind and drive you to distraction. Before you part, be sure to exchange phone numbers or arrange to meet again. News of an inheritance can touch you deeply, stirring up emotions from the past. By talking these feelings over with another relative who you are close to, you might learn some very interesting family history.

6. TUESDAY. Memorable. Close friends and relatives make this day special. Be careful, however, if your mate or partner seems a bit touchy about your plans. You might want to make some compromises to accommodate their feelings as well. A legal situation may seem to blow up in your face, or you may reach a point where you feel like withdrawing because the costs will outstrip what you hope to win. An old friend could contact you and pull at your heartstrings, rekindling feelings you thought were long gone. Don't agree to get together if you are at all unsure. If you have no doubts, a meeting might be a chance for a new start. Be wary of borrowing money from a friend, who might expect interest.

7. WEDNESDAY. Disconcerting. Creative projects can come to a halt due to a disagreement. If you decide to continue on alone, you may do some of your best work. Don't be frightened of autonomy because the outcome will be all your own and will give you added confidence in your abilities. A child's education may become very expensive. However, if you feel they have talents that warrant the expense, getting some extra work on the side will be worth your effort in the long run. A secret and steamy alliance might be in danger of being discovered, bringing you back to earth with a thud. Seriously consider what you are doing, and be honest; if you stand to hurt someone, stop.

8. THURSDAY. Smooth. Apart from a few early hassles, the day should be smooth sailing and enable you to have some fun and relaxation while you are immersed in your work. A new relationship might be taking up a lot of your thoughts and overworking your imagination, but try not to have too many expectations. When what ifs come to mind, examine them closely because they will be saying a lot about you. Gambling should be avoided due to lack of much luck. You may find that activities and attitudes that used to fit in well in your life no longer do. With Saturn moving back into Virgo, your solar sector of endings, this is a good time to take a project through to its final finishing-up phase.

9. FRIDAY. Sensitive. A friend in need may drop by hoping for some sympathy, but be careful not to condone self-indulgent complaining. Your time is too valuable to waste on anything that is negative. Also be careful not to mix with negative people because their mood can wash off on you and change your whole outlook. Your creativity is highlighted. Libra artists and writers can come up with some very original and professional work. Avoid drugs and alcohol, which your physical body will not be able to tolerate well. Even though you might think they will help your creative process or at least keep you awake, they are more likely to do the opposite. Love is also in the air.

10. SATURDAY. Comfortable. Routine is the name of today's game. Do what comes naturally and you will get far more accomplished than you expected. You have a lot of support at the moment, so don't hesitate to call on family members or friends if you need a hand. If friends try to interrupt your work, be firm and honest with them. Otherwise they might not leave or might end up picking a fight or being resentful, which could lead to starting malicious gossip about you in your neighborhood. A new diet could be starting to show results, and some shopping might be in order so that you have the latest fashions to show off the new you. If you live alone, consider buying a small pet for love and company.

11. SUNDAY. Expansive. Get travel plans under way by applying for a passport, making an appointment for any needed vaccinations, and getting your bags packed. Group activities may suffer as the aims get drowned out by the needs and wants of certain individuals. A strong leader will be necessary to maintain order and to reach an objective or win a game. A quiet day at home with the one you love can be interrupted by visitors; if you value your intimacy, don't answer the door or the phone. Students can do some valuable studying if willing to cancel social activities and focus on future goals. This is the day to concentrate on effective time management.

12. MONDAY. Intriguing. Underneath your diplomatic air you may be plotting and scheming with a slight leaning toward revenge. Instead of focusing on some imagined slight or imperfection, today favors gratitude and forgiveness. If you take the first step in that direction, goodwill will win the day. Your mate or partner may be changing jobs and going through a stressful period, needing extra support from you. Instead of dwelling on the worries and uncertainties ahead, count your blessings. Visiting family members will be beneficial. Your parents might need some help from you, and you can get the benefit of their wisdom and even some financial aid if needed.

13. TUESDAY. Secretive. When it comes to business deals, take nothing at face value. Looking beneath the surface to see who stands to benefit most will provide you with understanding and leverage so that you can negotiate to your advantage. You have valuable contacts and support, and should not hesitate to call upon them. They will be pleased to help, and a new alliance may come out of it. There could be a number of irritations throughout the day. Keep to yourself as much as possible to avoid some of the politics, rumors, and gossip. One of your coworkers may annoy you every chance they get; be upfront and end this situation before it gets out of hand.

14. WEDNESDAY. Focused. Today's New Moon in Aries promises the chance of new partnerships beginning. For Libras who are in a relationship, this is a good time to celebrate your love and life together, reminding both of you of your commitment and love. If you are in a business partnership, this is an excellent opportunity to discuss the bottom line and also to make any changes necessary to maximize profitability. Romance is highlighted. Single Libras might start a new romance, but don't rush in too fast. Allow time to get to know the other person. There may be some hidden problems which, once discovered, make a huge difference to how you feel and what you want from the relationship.

15. THURSDAY. Profitable. Money matters can be put in better order. If you are thinking about obtaining financing for a home or some other large-ticket item, this is the time to do so. Your application is sure to be looked on favorably. Someone close to you might need your support. If you are visiting an elderly relative, make sure you have the time to sit and listen to their stories, which you can then pass on in turn. Libras in need of support for an illness or an addiction can find some very valuable resources online that won't cost a cent. A friend may ask for a loan but probably really mean a donation.

16. FRIDAY. Worrisome. An upsetting issue between you and your mate or partner needs to be discussed thoroughly. If you can't do this, either because you feel threatened or can't help threatening, consider seeing a counselor to get to the heart of your communication difficulty. You will be amazed at the sharing possible with just a few simple tools for effective communication. Libras who are finding it financially hard to make ends meet can get plenty of support from community services if willing to search. If you are dealing with a lawsuit that is emotionally difficult, again there are community services that may be able to help if you ask.

17. SATURDAY. Adventurous. A friend heading overseas may leave you with the travel bug. Drop by your travel agent or surf the

Net for travel bargains, and before you know it you'll be off and away. A new job may test your communication skills, especially if you are working with people from other countries or cultures. It can benefit you to take a short course in another language, broadening your credentials while making your job a lot easier. You may be able to get your employer to pay for the class or to give you time off to attend. A spiritual philosophy could help you through a time of pain and grief. Take advantage if you get the chance to go on a retreat; the gain will far outweigh the pain.

18. SUNDAY. Fulfilling. Libra students will benefit from a study plan. Don't let interruptions and social invitations deter you, or you will fall behind and waste your money and time. And be careful who you mix with; the saying that if you hang with dogs you will get fleas is very true now. Make sure you are eating well and exercising regularly. Your health could suffer if you are living to excess, so try to balance late night and binge meals with rest and wholesome food. You are likely to be in contact with many varied people. If you are working in the importing or exporting industry and have the opportunity to set up your own business, take the offer because it may well turn out to be very profitable.

19. MONDAY. Determined. Emotional rivalry can lead to achieving just to prove something to somebody else. Even though this can be a valuable incentive, don't let it start driving you past being reasonable. The lesson here is self-love. It doesn't matter what other people think. Stop reacting, value your own opinions, care for your own well-being and life will be good. You may have to break ties from the past and move on into an unknown future. With faith in your own abilities you will not be sorry. Seek support from family members and friends where possible, and try not to isolate yourself. A political rally might be interesting; go prepared and you might get the chance to speak.

20. TUESDAY. Opportune. Your popularity on the job is working in your favor, and you may be asked to take on a leadership role. This is a great opportunity for you to get into a managerial position and start working your way up the corporate ladder. Do your homework regarding whatever is necessary to impress higher-ups. A promotion could be offered that requires relocating far from your home and family. If you are unsure about whether to accept, talk it over with your family and you will know in your heart what to do. Libra parents with a sick child may need to take some time off work. Or an older relative may need you to lend a hand due to an emergency.

21. WEDNESDAY. Challenging. Deep desires can become conscious as the result of an encounter with someone close, leading you to do some serious soul-searching. A sport or game can become very intense, allowing you to release anger and frustration through sheer physical activity. If you feel you are going to explode with stress, this would be your best and safest outlet right now. Libras who are going through a divorce or involved in an inheritance battle could be having trouble reaching a property settlement. Letting go is the only way to move on into a new life free from the past. There are various self-help groups that might be beneficial, or individual counseling could help.

22. THURSDAY. Trying. Put off any business negotiations at least until after lunch for the most positive result. Any discussions this morning are likely to end in disagreement and irritation regarding minor details. Turn your mind to perfecting your presentation. Go over all of the details to make sure you understand them fully and that there are no mistakes. An important contact might not be available, and you will have to be innovative to find the next best person for your purposes. Don't put off what you can do right away; you might not get another chance. Back problems can be helped with exercise. Join your local gym and you may be surprised how good you feel in a few weeks.

23. FRIDAY. Dreamy. Unrealistic or impractical thoughts and ideas can blind you to reality. Someone may be lying to you, so trust your good Libra instinct as opposed to what you are being told. You don't have to be unpleasant about it; just say thanks but no thanks and go your own way. A stepchild can be demanding, causing more problems within your relationship than you may care to acknowledge. This is a common situation and there is a lot of help available, so don't feel like a failure. Work on fixing the situation for the child's sake as well as your own. A family reunion can put you in touch with relatives you hardly ever see. Don't miss the opportunity to explore your roots.

24. SATURDAY. Introspective. Problems within your relationship that you thought were insurmountable may now seem minor, so relax and enjoy the intimacy and the chance to talk from the heart. Get away for the weekend to enjoy quiet moments with your lover at a secluded resort. You'll feel like a millionaire, if just for a day. A lot of changes are occurring on a global level, and nobody will remain untouched. Relaxation techniques and meditation are great tools for developing flexibility and calmness that will allow you to deal with change in a positive manner. Someone close who is in the hospital would benefit from a visit as long as you keep the conversation cheerful and positive.

25. SUNDAY. Variable. Stay in bed late this morning watching television or reading the newspaper or a book. Escapism is a fantastic way to take your mind off problems. When worry won't solve anything, give yourself over to your fate and enjoy the ensuing sense of freedom. By this afternoon, with the Moon entering your sign, your mood is likely to be positive and cheery. Venus, the planet of beauty and culture, is moving into Gemini, your solar sector of personal growth and foreign affairs. You may attend a concert or an exhibit that expands your consciousness and opens your mind to new possibilities. This is also a perfect time to plan a vacation to foreign shores. Expect a romantic invitation this evening.

26. MONDAY. Pleasant. The Moon is in your own sign of Libra, which is a time for pampering yourself. Shop for some flattering new clothes, or change your hairstyle or color so that you get a lift every time you look in the mirror. Take the family or go with your lover to an amusement park. Whether you ride the roller coaster and scream to your heart's content or just stroll around, it is important to think about yourself and tend to your needs. Don't let guilt trips or obligations hinder you from doing what is best for you. Romance can be problematic. If you find yourself out on a date with someone you don't really have feelings for, be upfront and don't let them harbor unrealistic expectations for long.

27. TUESDAY. Favorable. The vibes among people are sure to be open and pleasant, making for an easygoing atmosphere. Business matters can be cleared up, with negotiations congenial and useful. Being an active listener will you let gain information that gives you the upper hand in the negotiation process. For the same reason you should guard against talking too much and revealing private details. Make sure you have plenty of time to get where you are going. There may be transportation holdups that cause tension and put your nerves on edge, just when you need to be calm. Libra job seekers can land a plum position based on a last-minute interview; prepare in advance so you don't miss out.

28. WEDNESDAY. Confrontational. Today's Full Moon in Scorpio highlights your financial and business sector. A poor night's sleep can make you feel you got out of bed on the wrong side, sabotaging your natural ability to mediate between different factions and reach an agreement in business deals. Postpone appointments if you are honestly not feeling well. Take the day off rather than blunder through and risk making mistakes. Be wary of a need to impress that might entice you to spend more money than you can afford. Stick to your budget and you will have peace of mind tonight. Your mate or partner may have had a bad day too, so enjoy a good home-cooked meal and then an evening of loving.

29. THURSDAY. Positive. A fun-loving attitude will alleviate the boring routine of the workday. You or a coworker might act the clown and have everybody laughing and joking, leading to a pleasant day at work overall. Spend some time paying bills and getting bookwork up to date. In that way you can be sure you haven't missed a due date and won't incur the extra cost of a late penalty. Turn down an offer to extend your credit limit. If you don't have access to the money, you can't spend it. If you have to buy a gift for a loved one and are strapped for cash, use your creativity. Pot up a plant or compile a home video, something to remind them just how much you care.

30. FRIDAY. Hectic. Stay alert at work or a deadline could catch up with you quicker than you expect. Surfing the Net and talking on the phone can take far more time than you think, so watch the clock. A call from someone overseas might cheer you up and make you even more determined to save for your own adventure abroad, but don't let this take your mind off the job at hand. There is a lot of social activity on the horizon, and you may receive more than a few invitations for the weekend. Be discerning, and make sure to allow time for yourself as well as your friends. A small inheritance could cheer you up and give you a financial cushion.

MAY

1. SATURDAY. Meaningful. Superficial chat will not suit you. You might find yourself buried in deep and meaningful conversation all through the day. A female relative can be very helpful, teaching you something about yourself at the same time. You may be inclined to take on more than is humanly possible and attempt perfection, but be reasonable with yourself. Just doing the best that you can will be enough, and you can then relax this evening without suffering nervous exhaustion. A coworker who starts preaching religion or politics to you could cause irritation, but don't be too dogmatic about your judgments. Something that is said may whet your interest and make you think twice about the subject.

2. SUNDAY. Interesting. The realization that your habits and past conditioning control your life can occur during a confrontation in which you suddenly understand that your words or actions are inappropriate to the situation. This will be of very real value for your personal growth. You may feel possessive and jealous of both possessions and intimate relationships. Try to be aware if and when you let fear start to control your life. Steer clear of intense and angry people who are just venting their inner anxiety; anyone who gets in their way will be subject to their abuse. Home is where the heart is now, so cuddle up this evening and know you are loved.

3. MONDAY. Nurturing. By not answering the phone or the doorbell, you can create your own personal bliss. This is a perfect day for doing whatever pleases you most, whether at home or on the job. A few needy friends may try to feed off your energy and positive vibes, but keep those for your family. Giving too much of yourself when you are away from home will just leave you feeling drained. You and your mate or partner might have an ambition to start a business together. This is the perfect time to begin laying a foundation; before you know it you will have a framework to build on. Enjoy a leisurely evening at home, skipping a meeting unless it is vital.

4. TUESDAY. Inspiring. Plans should go like clockwork. New ideas are flowing, adding excitement and interest to your work. Be sure to jot down ideas that you cannot use right away so you don't forget them. Libras who are planning to retire soon or relocate should tour potential areas, talking with current residents if possible. You could decide that it is better to stay right where you are for now. Children can be a lot of fun later in the day. Count them as the blessings they are, even if at times they get on your nerves or interrupt your own plans.

5. WEDNESDAY. Artistic. Your creative talents won't let you down. You can do some of your best work now. Libra students may even receive honors for an exam or assignment. Libra singles might start a new romance with someone from foreign shores, finding their accent fascinating and their culture totally absorbing. Partnered Libras can enjoy the help and support of an older family member; you may learn some very valuable skills from your mother-in-law. A good friend can break your trust and seem unreliable; talk and find out what is going on in their life before crossing them off your list of friends. It may be that they are in dire need of your support.

6. THURSDAY. Fascinating. Alice in Wonderland's announcement of curious and curiouser fits today's happenings perfectly. Just when you think you know what is going on, something will make you think again. Do not take anyone or anything at face value. There is a lot going on beneath the surface, and you can only hope to uncover some of it. A business deal that sounds too good to be true is probably exactly that. It might even be more appropriately described as a rip-off, so keep your money in the bank and don't be gullible. Set the scene this evening with a candlelit dinner for you and your loved one, then move on to passionate after-dark activities in the comfort of your home.

7. FRIDAY. Caring. Pleasing aspects bless this day with harmony, even though there are a few undercurrents. A family issue that you want to keep private, or an uncertain situation that sustains a level of fear about the unknown, may be nagging at your thoughts. Overall, however, your daily grind will be pleasant and familiar. Extra household duties such as washing the dog can be done with pleasure. Going for a walk might put you in touch with a neighbor you would like to get to know better. A health checkup is likely to come back with the all-clear, or you might get a check in the mail from an investment long forgotten about. This is not a good day to start a diet.

8. SATURDAY. Sentimental. Memories from the past can resurface, giving you reason to pause. You may feel very close to people you knew long ago. A family argument can stem from possessiveness and spark the need to seek help overcoming anger issues or financial problems. Make a start by calling a local group or counselor. There is a strong influence toward overindulgence, so take heed and practice restraint so you do not fall back on bad habits. A friend could repay some money that you had written off, renewing your faith in the friendship as well as boosting your bank balance. If you owe money borrowed from a friend or relative, pay it back or at least stay in touch.

9. SUNDAY. Fair. Trust your own judgment, no matter what anyone is telling you. Right now you know intuitively what is best for you. A deadline might create so much pressure that you can't get the work done. Don't keep trying. Instead take a break outside in the fresh air, breathe deeply, then make yourself a nutritious snack.

Then you'll be feeling fresh, ready to get back to work. A woman in your neighborhood or workplace might be annoying you with her impatience and intolerance. If you can speak to her without getting angry, see if you can compromise in some way. Meeting new people can broaden your views and begin an interest in a topic you never knew about before or even considered.

10. MONDAY. Productive. Interesting gossip might occupy your mind and take up much of the morning, with numerous phone calls from family members all wanting to talk about it. Whatever you do, don't judge too harshly without knowing the full story. Your plans for the afternoon should go off well as everybody cooperates and lends a helping hand. This is a good time to finalize any group arrangements. If you are attending a meeting there are sure to be some favorable decisions made. An older relative would appreciate all the help you can provide. Don't begrudge giving your time and effort.

11. TUESDAY. Rewarding. You may get the chance to take on a leadership position that would really suit you, so don't be shy. Step up to the challenge and you will be stretched, becoming better than you thought you could be. Frustrations may arise due to a holdup in a contract or agreement. You might have to deal with an annoyed associate, but if it is not your fault don't accept the blame; just be polite and retreat. Hard work and a vigorous exercise regime will be a good outlet for extra energy. If you often just sit all day, stop by a gym or sports field on your way home. Intimacy can be a real turn-on tonight, and you could learn something new.

12. WEDNESDAY. Expressive. With Mercury, the planet of communication, moving forward after three weeks of holdups, expect all sorts of information and ideas to start flowing once again. This can also mean that some pent-up emotion might burst forth within the family or between you and your lover, causing a few upsets to start with. Be very conscious of what you do, what you hear, and what you say. Agreements and contracts can get the green light and clear the air among business associates. A check might finally arrive and restore your trust or your creditor's. Deep thinking and reflection can be very insightful. It would be valuable to you in the future if you write down some of your insights.

13. THURSDAY. Revealing. Today's New Moon in Taurus highlights your solar house of sex, death, and transformation. It may also herald a new understanding of your unconscious desires regarding possessive love and unconditional love. If your energy level is low, proceed slowly and let your energy build up to set the scene for the rest of the lunar cycle. Take extra precautions with your health, and if possible avoid surgery at this time on throat, neck, lower ears, and the lower part of your head and brain. Also avoid alcohol and drugs, which will sap your energy. Learning about natural therapies and healthy food choices might be beneficial. Just be sure to avoid fads.

14. FRIDAY. Restless. It is said that change is as good as a vacation. If your everyday life is getting a bit stale and boring, take your mind on a journey by studying a topic of interest, or go to different places and meet interesting new people. Tension in your love life can be eased with more consideration and understanding, hopefully not only on your part but also from your partner. Have faith that if you are meant to be together you will work it out. Retail therapy could be fun, with lots of bargains to be found. However, if at the end of the day you might have more problems paying your bills, leave your credit card at home.

15. SATURDAY. Energetic. Organization is the key to how much you manage to get done. Be diligent or you will feel you have been all over town with nothing to show for it. Plan your precise route if traveling in a city, and tune in to all the road reports that might warn of major holdups. If you are journeying overseas, your trip to the airport could be frustrating and you might even arrive late, so allow plenty of commuting time. The Internet will be heaven-sent for students; even if all needed information isn't online, you can find out where to get it. Before making any evening plans, check the Net for where to go, what restaurants are recommended, and whether you will need an umbrella.

16. SUNDAY. Trying. Intense encounters are the order of the day. A certain amount of rebelliousness adds impatience to the mix, suggesting that socializing might be better postponed to another time. A family member may be suffering from a medical condition and need to seek professional help if home remedies haven't helped. Anything you say could just make things worse, although love and understanding never hurt. Spend extra time with your loved one and enjoy each other's company. Talk about your ambitions and desires, in a relaxing environment without anybody else's drama to contend with. If you are staying with a friend, give them some extra space as well.

17. MONDAY. Tense. A need to finalize an important project will leave no time for interruptions, so hang a Do Not Disturb sign on your door or simply ignore the bell. Don't back down, only to get annoyed later and take it out on your family. A close friend might be leaving town, and the separation won't be as easy as you thought. Make sure you have their e-mail address and phone number so you can keep in touch. You may not be feeling well, and being unable to do what you want can be very frustrating. Take this time to catch up on your backlog of work. Contact people you always intend to call but never do; talking to them will break the monotony.

18. TUESDAY. Helpful. Identify what you are feeling and what you really want before you have to deal with the everyday world. If you are clear, you will be able to navigate through the continuous demands being made of you without selling yourself short. An important assignment will be helped along if you delegate some of the work to coworkers who have a talent for that particular job. Instead of running yourself ragged trying to prove you are the best, you will simply be successful. A new romantic attachment can be taking up a lot of your head space. There could be strings attached to this liaison that are bothering you, so once gain be clear about what you want.

19. WEDNESDAY. Complex. With so much going on beneath the surface, you need to use your basic Libra instincts to navigate through all the subconscious phenomena. Inspiration and creativity are abundant. Any project that you are working on could be held up by necessary adjustments that will actually add originality and pizzazz. Any sort of illegal activities or secret financial agreements should be avoided; if you allow yourself to get drawn in, you will pay the price. This is not a good time to discuss any issues that are critical to your welfare and happiness. You will find it hard to stay calm and not fly off the handle, just as you may find it hard to discern what's important and what's trivial.

20. THURSDAY. Favorable. Venus, your ruling planet, moves into Cancer, your career sector, and will stay there for the next month. This creates favorable circumstances in your business and professional life, attracting persons and circumstances that facilitate your work. A career in the arts, design, layout work, office decorating, or public relations should be profitable for school graduates and those of you looking to make a career change. A new love relationship with someone older, or a guide, can help you learn how to get ahead in life. You might even start a romance with your employer, but beware of underlying emotions that can ruin the relationship.

21. FRIDAY. Expansive. The Sun has just moved into Gemini and your solar sector of long-distance travel and higher learning. This suggests that you should broaden your horizons through study, new and unfamiliar experiences, travel, or by meeting people from totally different backgrounds who can reveal another aspect of the world. Study, hobbies, and intellectual disciplines will be a positive influence in your life, stimulating your intellect and broadening your perspectives. You may become involved or be interested in the law, not necessarily in a legal case but in connection with your business or daily activities. You will also be more receptive to spiritual values.

22. SATURDAY. Subdued. A sense of loneliness or isolation can permeate the day with a pessimistic flavor, but try to recognize that the negativity is your mood rather than the true state of things and shouldn't be taken seriously. Take a break and give yourself a rest from the humdrum of normal life. Be kind to number one; eat your favorite food, lie around watching movies or listening to music, plan a quiet weekend away, or have a massage. Going on a guilt trip will only bring you down further. Live in the moment, not worrying about the next, and the world won't look so bad. A certain relationship can take on a romantic feel, so give it a nudge by enjoying a dinner for two at your favorite restaurant.

23. SUNDAY. Testing. Balancing work and play could be too hard. You need to beware taking work home to do when it should be your leisure time. If you are cranky and irritable and the family starts to complain, take a long, hard look at your life and make some changes. The work always gets done, so make sure you enjoy life as well as work. There could be a few blame games or guilt trips going around, but don't be the instigator. Try to maintain objectivity. Spend some time brightening your environment, perhaps painting paint a room a different color or adding artwork. You will be surprised by the mood change you create.

24. MONDAY. Bright. No matter what problems reality throws at you, your will and discipline are working in your favor. Decision making, which can always be trying for a Libra, will come naturally. Family worries shouldn't be ignored; confront the problem collectively and a solution is sure to be found. Romantic influence is strong. Singles could be starting a relationship that is thrilling and all-encompassing, taking up every second of life. Partnered Libras can enjoy the comfort and love of your mate, as if you were just starting out. Artistic creations and hobbies will be a genuine source of inspiration, even offering an opportunity for a stunning and lucrative new career.

25. TUESDAY. Successful. Concentrate on your finances and make sure no bills are outstanding. If you are tight for cash, contact creditors and make arrangements to pay a little at a time, giving you a breather. You may be in line for a promotion at work. With the aspects indicating that you occupy a favorable position in your employer's mind, this is a good time to talk about your opportunities for advancement. Recognize that there is a lot of competition around, but think positively. Quietly work on achieving your own goals, avoiding backbiting, and you should come shining through. Treat yourself to a little luxury tonight despite the expense.

26. WEDNESDAY. Challenging. Money matters may have reached a point where you need to reevaluate what you are spending it on. A club's fees may have gone up and put you out of its price range, but there are a lot of other group activities that you can afford. It's just a matter of accepting the change, which can sometimes be the hardest thing to do. Tightening your belt may not be that difficult, so take a good look at your positives and you'll realize life isn't that bad. A relative or friend in a powerful situation will be happy to help you out of a difficult situation if you just ask. Negotiations concerning joint finances or investments will be very productive.

27. THURSDAY. Auspicious. A karmic connection is on the cards, and there is a strong influence around a love union, maybe even the meeting of soul mates. An old family friend might bring you news of your home and childhood friends. They may stay a few days, which should be a positive visit although an emotional one. The Full Moon in Sagittarius highlights your communication with family and friends. Libras who are currently traveling overseas should make contact with home because there might be some important news. A job in the import and export business or with foreigners is indicated, and you might start studying a second language at this time.

28. FRIDAY. Positive. A quick mind can work with you or against you. Be mindful of what you say and what you feel, especially refraining from sarcasm. With many things on your mind, the best approach is to deal with each of them one at a time. Turn off the television and you will be on top of everything by the end of the day. This is an excellent time to focus on your own feelings. Try to quiet your mind and let your emotions surface. No matter how painful they may be, you can get to know yourself intimately instead of always being too busy to notice. Tension in a relationship is best talked out rather than bottled up only to explode at a later time.

29. SATURDAY. Demanding. Business negotiations demand some quick talking on your part. You might have to fall back on a family contact or find a guarantor to help you clinch a deal. Independent Uranus has moved into Aries and your partnership house, where it will reside over the next seven years. Uranus urges freedom, which will put pressure on all of your relationships. You may be keeping a marriage going for the sake of the children, or because of finances or emotional dependence. If so, this transit of Uranus will make it extremely difficult to maintain the deception within your relationship. Although a reasonably secure partnership is likely to weather the storm, counseling will help.

30. SUNDAY. Comforting. You will seek and need comfort from the demands of the outside world. A pleasant, relaxing time at home is probably the best way to accomplish this. If you are house hunting, you could be lucky enough to find just what you want within your price range. Don't procrastinate because there are likely to be other people looking as well. A family home may have to be sold. The influences are favorable for a quick and profitable sale. Be sure to give yourself and the rest of your family time to first let go of the memories and emotions, which are priceless and need to be savored.

31. MONDAY. Profitable. You may need to make a decision that affects your whole family. Trust your feelings and be willing to finalize the matter. You are very popular at the moment, and will get agreement on most aspects of what you want and do. An invitation to speak at a large gathering can cause you to be anxious. But make notes about what you wish to say and you should be very happy with the reception you get. If a large backlog of work is preying on your mind, this is the perfect day for getting down to the job and removing the cause of concern. Business deals will be favorable for you. A family gathering could be the breeding ground for financial success.

JUNE

1. TUESDAY. Tricky. Do not attempt any form of deception because other people will be able to read you like a book. Libra salespeople may not do well today, but don't be disheartened. There will always be some bad days, and the current mood is transitory. Libra parents may be a little too overprotective of children. Watch that a desire to protect them is not depriving them of their freedom; otherwise you might have to deal with teenage rebellion. Communication is the key to resolving any problems that occur. If you are involved in a major business deal, don't be shy about asking questions. You might win a promotion for your astuteness at uncovering important facts.

2. WEDNESDAY. Stimulating. If vacation plans are your focus of the day, visit a travel agent to explore various trips designed for adventure and fun. A new romance can take you to places you have never been before, sparking new dreams for your future. Libras who are in a loving relationship might decide to start a family or add to the family circle, acquiring the gleam of all prospective parents. An emotional mood can invoke a touchy response, to the point where an innocent remark will be rebutted with an angry reception. If you get your buttons pushed, try to remember that the comment probably wasn't meant personally, and let it go so it doesn't ruin an otherwise fine day.

3. THURSDAY. Distracting. The concentration needed to keep your mind focused could elude you. Instead of making headway with your work, you may find yourself miles away in dreamland. A new relationship, a late night, or plans for the future could be occupying your thoughts, but try to also stay on top of your work for your health's sake. Mental stress is one of the biggest health threats, and life might not be so rosy without money in the bank. If your health has not been good, don't wait any longer to see if it improves. A visit to your health provider could lead to simply changing your diet, with no need for drugs or expensive treatments. Also get plenty of physical exercise.

4. FRIDAY. Caring. Good feelings abound, and this workday should be one of the better ones. A long lunch could tempt you to indulge in too much food and drink, so dieters beware. There is also a lazy feel to the day, which could tempt you to cut corners on the job. This might be all right on small matters, but on anything else it is sure to be discovered and won't do your reputation any good. An opportunity to volunteer your help and support to someone in need will be so rewarding that you may decide to focus on this kind of work in the future. Take care of your own health. Drugs and alcohol should be avoided like the plague because your attention may get foggy and lead to an accident.

5. SATURDAY. Sentimental. News from someone far away can create tears of joy, making you feel on top of the world for the rest of the day. Normal routine housecleaning could turn into a major effort that gives you the impetus to get rid of junk you have been stowing away in the attic, basement, or closets. A certain piece of junk is apt to rekindle such feelings from the past that you decide to restore it to a place in your home. The birth of a baby today is sure to be joyful and memorable. If you go out tonight, steer clear of dark and disreputable haunts for safety's sake. This is a good night to get in touch with a friend or family member who is going through tough times.

6. SUNDAY. Beneficial. Partnerships of all kinds will be harmonious and productive. If you have been going through a divorce or inheritance squabble, you can now settle any disputes attached to the property settlement. A chance meeting with an extraordinary person is bound to bring unexpected delights into your life, with new experiences and interests sure to follow. Although the universe may appear to be overflowing with special abundance, exercise a certain amount of moderation whatever your situation may be. Basically, don't get greedy. If you are preparing to travel, double-check what you have packed because there is the chance that you overlooked something small but important.

7. MONDAY. Renewing. Mars, the planet of action and energy, moves into Virgo, your house of solitude and retreat. This is a good time to focus on your inner world rather than filling up every moment of your time and taking your mind away from your actual life. By dwelling on the past and the future it's all too easy to miss what is happening in the here and now. Act upon a desire to work for the collective good rather than just for yourself, perhaps joining an environmental or caring group and giving your services free. If you learn to paint, play a musical instrument, or meditate, you will gain benefits that last for the rest of your life. As the saying goes: Go within or go without.

8. TUESDAY. Encouraging. Be resolute and determined. Do your homework and you will reach your goals. If you feel that you are getting stale in any area, change a few of your ingrained habits. Be diligent about the change for at least two to three weeks, until you have new habits that work and are becoming ingrained. Get some advice from a professional to help choose the replacement habits that will work best for you. Your business outlook is promising. If you are short of cash to get started, consider joining forces with someone who will be happy to be your silent partner at least until you can buy them out once you are in a position to do so.

9. WEDNESDAY. Excellent. Change is in the air here, there, and everywhere. New ideas and challenges are likely to have an optimistic slant. Legal matters can be settled in your favor. A matter that has had you on edge will be resolved, letting you breathe a sigh of relief. You are apt to be looking for more freedom. Partnered Libras may start to make changes to the relationship. If your partner isn't as enthusiastic as you, working with a marriage counselor could help you both be able to enjoy your romance with an added spark. Don't take on too much alone over the next year. As Jupiter moves through your house of partnership, you will benefit from the help and support of those around you.

10. THURSDAY. Expansive. With Mercury, the planet of communication and the mind, gliding into Gemini and your solar sector of travel and the higher mind, a more philosophical outlook is likely to color your thinking. Travel arrangements should fall into place after you decide to change your itinerary so as not to miss any of the cultural icons of your destination. Contact with foreigners is also indicated, and you may start a new relationship with someone from a distant shore. This is also an excellent time to check out further education to see if there is any course that will help you advance in your current work or in an area that stimulates and interests you more.

11. FRIDAY. Studious. This is an excellent time to do research. If you are a student, are involved in litigation, planning a vacation trip, or involved in anything else that requires an informed decision, get on the phone or check the Internet for all the necessary information. An assignment done now should earn a top mark, and a local study group could be invaluable. Steer clear of irritable people; they may not be feeling well, and nothing you say or do will make any difference. If it is you who feels irritable, some extra vitamins and minerals could give you a lift. Smokers who want to stop should find a local support group and get with the program.

12. SATURDAY. Pleasing. A helping hand from someone higher up than you at work will aid your popularity and success. Just be careful how deeply indebted you become to this person. He or she may be attracted to you. So if you cannot reciprocate, it is probably better to be upfront from the start, avoiding any future resentment. This morning's New Moon in Gemini signals the start of a new lunar monthly cycle, auguring the time for starting new projects. Get out your tools and begin laying the foundation for something you have dreamed about. No matter how outlandish you think it is, anything can happen if you do the groundwork. Luck often comes from simply preparing for opportunity.

13. SUNDAY. Opportune. If you take action rather than letting matters slide, you will win respect and recognition. Family issues can become strained, with unconscious motives likely to be driving behavior and creating a diversion from the real problem. Try calling a family meeting and letting everybody get to talk for a certain time. Nobody is permitted to interrupt the speaker. You might be surprised how this technique can help. Solitude would be beneficial for you today. Going for a walk or sail will give you a chance to be with yourself to consider some of your own ideas, please yourself, and appreciate the spiritual aspects of your existence. Heed your nagging conscience.

14. MONDAY. Promising. Arranging today's social activities might fall to you, but don't complain. You will do an exceptional job, and everybody will thank you for it. A friend in need might confide in you, and pulling a few strings to help them out will be greatly appreciated. Sexy Venus, your ruling planet, glides into Leo and your social sector, suggesting a broadening of your friendship circle and of group participation. The opportunity to combine socializing and networking should work out well if you are aiming to market your talents. Romance among friends is also indicated, and the possibility of falling in love with a friend tops the day off nicely.

15. TUESDAY. Heartening. Good feelings in love and work make this a very promising day. Your interest in a civic organization can result in being nominated for a leadership position or to be on a committee. Accept readily; you will enjoy the experience. A new relationship might put you in the role of stepparent. Although there is bound to be a time of uncertainty and adjustment as a family group, this can be a very rewarding and fulfilling role for you. There is a lot of support available for blended families, and it can help to some of the literature that will give you useful suggestions and insights. Plans can come together for a long-term goal, but instead of resting on your laurels start planning the next step.

16. WEDNESDAY. Ambitious. Examine your overall goals in life. It is important that they be a real expression of yourself, not simply the product of emotional attitudes and unconscious drives from an earlier time that no longer apply to your present situation. Understanding your motivations can help lay the framework for a creative transformation and the birth of a new you. Concentrate on your hopes and wishes, and look forward to a great future. Emotional contact with friends is also indicated. You could even become jealous if a friend seems to be showing more interest in somebody else. Pamper yourself this evening with a nourishing meal and an early night.

17. THURSDAY. Energetic. Start the day by prioritizing your activities, and you will have a very productive and rewarding time. Do not discuss any issues that are critical to you because you can find it difficult to maintain your cool and not fly off the handle. Instead, write them down and put them out to the universe for an answer. You might be feeling quite differently about a certain matter by this evening. Be extra careful to lock up before going out. To be on the safe side, and especially if you have been worried lately, look into getting a security system so that you can rest easy. A younger family member may need some help with a job search. Any support you provide will be greatly appreciated.

18. FRIDAY. Unsettled. Change is in the air, and you may feel quite insecure about the unknown. Don't worry, however. As a Libra you are very resilient at this time and are likely to end up in a better position than at present. Just be sure about what you really want so that the universe can help you manifest it. Indecision over an important matter can cause you grief, which could be due to your feelings and thoughts being at odds. If you take some time to sit quietly and analyze why this is so, you will be much wiser for it. Prepare now for an overseas trip; make sure you get all necessary shots to avoid an illness that might otherwise be with you forever.

19. SATURDAY. Motivating. With the Moon swinging through your own sign, you will feel an added surge of vitality and optimism about yourself and what you are doing. An urge to splurge on beauty products, a massage, or a body wrap could be a bit painful when you review your bank balance, but at least do something special for yourself today. Libras who are in the throes of house hunting may feel that finding the right property at the right price is starting to look impossible. However, don't give up. Your family may be able to put you up until the right place becomes available. If you are offered a promotion, consider all that it will entail before accepting.

20. SUNDAY. Expressive. You are likely to be feeling good and looking even better. Social activities should keep you busy most of the day. You could meet some interesting new people who open you up to ideas and opportunities you had never thought about before. Single Libras may meet someone fascinating; the chance is good that this person hails from a foreign shore. Partnered Libras may together experience a new spark of love and friendship, finding an intimacy that hadn't seemed possible at this stage of life. If a friend or family member is hospitalized and if you have the time, drop in and cheer them up. Give them a call first to see if they need anything.

21. MONDAY. Creative. The Sun rolling into Cancer turns the spotlight on your career and long-term goals. If you haven't been happy with your direction lately, this is a great time to start looking into other career options. Check the Internet to see what might be posted. Libras who are considering starting a family should make sure they are doing it for the right reason, not to strengthen a shaky relationship. Problems between you and your mate or partner may stem from financial insecurity. Discuss ways to overcome this rather than fight about inconsequential matters. Artistic talents that come to the fore now could be developed into a career providing a good source of income.

22. TUESDAY. Vexing. Consider what you value most, then ask yourself if you are staying true to that. A close friend or associate may be trying to influence your decisions, but don't let this happen. Be upfront in stating what you can and can't do. If this person is worth knowing, they will understand; otherwise you are better off without them in your life. Your mate or partner's spending may be giving you cause to worry. If you are unable to address these concerns, it might be smart to open an account of your own to allay your worries. You are quite justified in keeping this a secret if being open and honest will only inflame matters more.

23. WEDNESDAY. Useful. Plans and expectations for the day may have to be put on hold for reasons out of your control, but don't fret. Instead get involved in whatever is happening and make the most of it. If you are not feeling up to par, see a doctor or healer. There may be a condition underlying your symptoms that you need to be aware of in order to get better permanently. Don't be afraid to have whatever tests are necessary or to get a second opinion; the cause may not be what is obvious. A legal matter can work out in your favor and cost less than expected. A property settlement can be resolved amicably now.

24. THURSDAY. Friendly. You will not wish to be on your own, and all joint activities are likely to be productive and pleasant. Guard against a tendency toward extravagance. You might buy an item because of a passing fancy but then question your own taste later. Objects and machinery can break down, forcing you to stop what you're doing in order to repair them. A power struggle at work might test your skill and patience. However, if you don't fall into the habit of gossiping in retaliation, you will come out with lots of support from associates and possibly a promotion as well. A friend may seek your love and support. Being compassionate and allowing them to vent their frustrations is probably all that is needed.

25. FRIDAY. Favorable. This is a good time for new studies that might help your career. Or you could speak to the boss or other superior about your work and how to advance in your job. This will give you an idea of what you need to do. Mercury, the planet of communication, is now visiting Cancer, your career sector. Communication on the job will assume greater importance. You may become involved with advertising or contract negotiations, which will give you plenty of scope for your natural Libra talents. Don't be afraid of a challenge. You will do well in any undertaking that you start now. Avoid an argumentative neighbor for your peace of mind.

26. SATURDAY. Challenging. Balancing home and work can be extremely hard. If your child is not well but your employer is unsympathetic, maybe you should consider changing to a job where you can be a responsible parent as well as a good employee. Look into options for working from home. Or you might be able to persuade your boss that you can do at least some of your work on your home computer. A disagreement in a romantic relationship shouldn't be allowed to escalate out of control. Focus on the relationship and see if you can agree to a truce so that you have time to put matters in perspective. There is a romantic and caring atmosphere, so make the most of it.

27. SUNDAY. Comforting. Enjoy the relaxing and soothing comforts of home. Instead of going out, catch up with friends and family members by e-mail or phone. Give yourself a break from nerve-racking, time-consuming highway traffic. A shopping trip might turn up some great new items for your home. You might decide to renovate and update your bathroom, going from practical to luxurious. Aspects favor buying and selling, so you could decide to hold a garage sale to get rid of some accumulated junk and make quite a significant sum. If there is a community affair at a local park, go along. You'll meet your neighbors and are bound to make new friends and contacts.

28. MONDAY. Social. There should be plenty of social affairs and functions to keep you occupied. If not, expect visitors. Libra parents may have to drive kids to various activities. If this is inconvenient, call some of the other parents and see if they will give your kids a lift this time, and you can reciprocate another time. A love affair may be blooming. If a decision has been made to move in together, look for a new place rather than one person moving into the other's home. That way you will have a fresh start without any telltale signs of the past to get in the way. Creative Libras performing or exhibiting at a public function should get positive feedback.

29. TUESDAY. Positive. Libra students may be off on summer break but can still keep up via a study group on the Internet. You will be amazed how well you do next semester if you make the effort now. A secret romance might be causing you to lose sleep worrying about someone finding out. It is time to rethink the situation. If you truly love each other, why keep it a secret? If you are going behind someone's back, it is probably best to be honest or end the affair. You may simply want out of a relationship because you are not able to be yourself and do what you really love. If you are true to yourself and take a stand, life is bound to get better.

30. WEDNESDAY. Dreamy. A late start to the day can be colored by a persistent dream, leaving all sorts of fantasies and ideas in your mind. Don't push yourself too hard because you may not be able to make much use of the operational side of your brain. This is a great time to take the day off and enjoy a creative hobby, start a hobby class, or engage in some other pursuit for pleasure. You may be putting too much pressure on yourself trying to keep up with the Joneses. Be original. Surprise yourself and other people with how much talent you really have. As a Libra you are renowned for beauty and artistic ability, so you can impress others by simply doing what comes naturally.

JULY

1. THURSDAY. Mixed. Career prospects look good as long as you guard against taking on too much in an attempt to prove what you're worth. You know your stuff, so relax and let everything take its course. If you are on the ball, you will be able to see what needs to be done at the appropriate time. Work at valuing your own skills and gaining greater self-confidence. Hasty, impulsive action can cause an accident, so be mindful of what you are doing. Domestic bliss may be lacking at home today. It might be better to turn off the television, leave the dishes in the sink, and call a family meeting so that you can work out the problem together.

2. FRIDAY. Good. Catch up on odds and ends of jobs and put your house in good order. If you don't overbook your schedule, you'll have plenty of time for each job and should have a relaxing, productive day. Libras who are looking for work are likely to meet with success. You may be offered a leadership role that is sure to stretch your talents; you never know what you are capable of doing until you try. Research a health concern. You may be able to heal yourself simply by adjusting your diet, adapting an exercise routine, and drinking plenty of water. If you do not already exercise regularly, check out what is available at the local gym that will suit your schedule and benefit your body.

3. SATURDAY. Exciting. The cosmic atmosphere has Libras on edge, which should turn out to be a positive experience. Relating is one of your natural strengths, and today you should be in your element. Whether it is your relationship with friends or human relations work on a broad scale, the challenge that confronts you now is apt to get you fired up and will demand the best you can give. A legal matter could be touch-and-go. Be guided by your good instincts, and it is bound to turn out in your favor. Don't sell yourself short in any matters. Believe in yourself and you'll succeed despite obstacles. A lovers' quarrel can be very upsetting, but then produce insight and honest communication.

4. SUNDAY. Controversial. Collusion and deceit make it hard to understand what is really going on. Your natural instinct is to cooperate, but you might be wise to stay aloof until the facts of the matter surface. Be noncommittal and supportive and you will come through unscathed. Relatives from out of town may be due for a visit. If your perfectionism is driving you or your partner wild, take a few deep breaths and relax and let go. The company will be happy to see you and catch up, which will be difficult if you are too busy trying to impress them instead of enjoying their visit. If you are asked to speak at a public function or meeting, prepare early. You are likely to find an ease and confidence you didn't know you had.

5. MONDAY. Mystical. A spiritual meeting might leave you with a new understanding of what you want and appreciation of what you have. This is the perfect day to get away with your lover to enjoy the love and intimacy that is uniquely yours. A dream might convey a message that you later find to be right. Or you may experience a powerful feeling of déjà vu that sends tingles up your spine. You can use this special day to your advantage if you don't allow yourself to get caught up in gossip and trivial pursuits. Your sympathy and compassion for those who are in need can make you a willing helper, either personally as you encounter a situation or through volunteering with a charitable group.

6. TUESDAY. Heartening. A fortuitous turn of events can steer a confidential contract or business deal your way, with results far beyond what you anticipated. You are likely to make an important contact but would be wise to keep this to yourself. Whatever transpires between you will be what you want, without anyone else's influence. If a certain matter has been weighing on your mind and disturbing your sleep, now is the time for decisive action. Don't procrastinate and don't ask for advice. Rely on your good Libra instincts and you won't go wrong. A family matter can be resolved satisfactorily, with an outcome that is beneficial for all and that heals wounds from long ago.

7. WEDNESDAY. Constructive. The Taurus Moon makes this a perfect day to organize your finances, look into ways to reduce debt, and begin a savings plan. Sort through all of your bills and your bank and credit card statements to guard against an overdue account and stay informed about your financial situation. You may have misunderstood terms and conditions on one of your accounts but now be able to straighten it out. This is not a good time to go into a partnership business deal. If you have been offered an opportunity that looks too good to be true, check it out thoroughly before signing anything. A visit to an elderly relative might be far more enjoyable and informative than you expect.

8. THURSDAY. Tricky. An obsessive attitude can mark this morning as difficult. Try to maintain objectivity even if it means slowing down and broadening your horizons. This is a perfect time to start planning a trip. The farther the destination from home, the more chance you have of letting go and relaxing. If you are having difficulty finding romance and a loving relationship, you may need to free yourself from the web of fantasies and romantic illusions that are all of your own making. Find a creative outlet for your own imagination so that it doesn't have to manifest itself in your love life. Start by loving yourself and good times will follow.

9. FRIDAY. Disconcerting. Mercury, the planet of communication and short-distance travel, moves into Leo and your solar sector of friends, hopes, and wishes. Today you are apt to be out and about visiting friends and discussing topics of mutual interest. Be careful not to let the conversation deteriorate into gossip. If someone irritates you, bite your tongue before you say something you will regret. Impulsive actions will be all too frequent unless you restrain yourself. The traffic could be horrendous; it can take less time to travel overseas by plane than a few blocks away by car. This is also a time for adventure, so check out travel prices and look for a last-minute bargain.

10. SATURDAY. Difficult. Power struggles and stressful situations are indicated. Although your instinctive Libra approach may be to give in, if you feel strongly you should say what's on your mind. At the end of the day your ideas might be the ones that are accepted. A female relative, possibly your mother, may be playing martyr and putting a guilt trip on you. Talking with love and understanding about the reasons could take a great weight off her shoulders and yours. Expect frequent ups and downs in your relationships. Also practice caution if making any long-term decisions. It would be better to put off deciding until tomorrow, and be sure. A job offer might take you away from home; assess what is right for you, not what other people say.

11. SUNDAY. Encouraging. Heightened sensitivity is foreseen for the next month regarding your standing in society and your long-term goals for constructive progress. With the New Moon starting a new cycle in Cancer and your solar house of career, this is a good time to develop new business plans and goals that offer the potential for renewal and reinvigoration. This is also a time to assess the outward aspects of your life, such as your career and your role and reputation in the larger society. Analyze whether you are making good progress. Be wary of creating public displays of emotion. These can make it difficult to hide certain personal facts, especially if you have a public argument with your mate or partner.

12. MONDAY. Sociable. Good vibes, good friends, and good food are on the menu today. A social occasion will be a good opportunity to leave all your troubles at home and enjoy conversation and interacting with the world at large. If you have just gone through a relationship breakup or are simply taking a temporary break, a social outing will reduce the sense of loneliness and pain that could drive you back into a relationship that is not positive. Let go and enjoy yourself. If there isn't a gathering to attend, go to the local shopping plaza or attend a political rally or a concert. You will be surprised how much better you feel thanks to the mental stimulation of a crowd.

13. TUESDAY. Emotional. Innuendo and unfinished sentences can hit a raw nerve and set you off on all sorts of imaginings. Just remember that it is all your perception. The people around you might be feeling exactly the same as you, with everyone feeding off each other. A friend might need help, support, and a shoulder to cry on. Invite them to your home for the evening and let them vent their feelings in a neutral and safe environment. Networking can be frustrating. If you allow yourself to get sucked in by word-of-mouth advertising you might end up very disappointed. Don't send money without knowing exactly what you are paying for and obtaining a guarantee.

14. WEDNESDAY. Harmonious. The outside world won't bother you as a new relationship consumes your thoughts and keeps you from dwelling on your routine existence. A secret affair with a coworker could become very difficult to hide. You both may have to confront your situation and decide whether to come out in the open or to call it quits. Libra students can do some invaluable studying at the library. If you are suffering from a stressful career, meditation will help you relax and rejuvenate. Be sure to set priorities so you have some time to yourself. If working on a creative project you may be so engrossed that mealtimes pass you by.

15. THURSDAY. Active. If you start to become bogged down with work, go out for a walk and free up your mind. When working against a deadline, delegate some tasks so that you can concentrate on areas of major concern, simplifying your own workload. A job in a caring profession such as nursing or senior assistance would suit you and also offer employment security in these shaky times. Check out what training and credentials are necessary, then find out how to get involved. Time spent on self-analysis will be beneficial. You might want to start a journal or diary to provide the tools for examining your thoughts and feelings in a private and secure way.

16. FRIDAY. Eventful. Nothing will be quite as you expect it. Any impulsive actions are likely to cause upsets and arguments. You might decide to alter your image by getting the latest hairstyle, or spend some of your savings on a new wardrobe. When shopping be very careful not to give yourself the option of overspending, which can make your outing disastrous. Libra people like art and beauty. An item to beautify your home might be too good to resist, but still you can regret the decision when the bill comes in. Watch your speed while driving to avoid an accident and possible fine. Nor should you get involved in road rage, even if you were disrespected.

17. SATURDAY. Manageable. Family issues can get the day off to a rough start, perhaps due to a phone call containing subtle emotional blackmail. Or you might have to deal with sibling rivalry that involves yelling, screaming, and door slamming. Put it behind you when you step out the front door and the rest of the day should go well. Good communication will facilitate the success of a meeting, and you are apt to learn a new trick or two regarding how to present yourself and your opinions. A friend or associate might ask you to join their sports team or club. You will find that to be the perfect way to eliminate stress, to exercise, and to relax after a hard day. Competition can keep you fit and mentally alert.

18. SUNDAY. Agreeable. Let the day unfurl with its own momentum, and relax as much as possible. Romance from last night might linger on, transporting you to additional realms of desire. An important social occasion may be scheduled for this evening. Allow yourself the whole day to prepare. If you have to go shopping for something to wear, a designer label will ensure buying something of quality and substance. You may be asked to give a speech or a toast in a friend's honor. The more time you spend on reflection, the more memories you will be able to recall of their prouder moments, which will do them justice. Libra homebodies will enjoy gardening or going for a stroll with a friend or neighbor.

19. MONDAY. Zany. Unexpected outcomes and wacky misunderstandings add a slapstick flavor to the day and will give rise to laughter. Don't get too serious or you will miss out on the fun. Visitors may arrive all at once, creating an impromptu party. Get everyone mingling and interacting and you will only have to provide food and drinks while fun is had by all. A day out with the family can end up costing far more than you expected, but it will be enjoyable. Just remind yourself not to do it again, unless you win the lottery. If you have to purchase a gift, remember it is not the price tag that makes it meaningful. An original creation by a local artist might be a good choice.

20. TUESDAY. Complex. In order to impress someone in a powerful position, make sure you know what you are talking about before you open your mouth. Your mate or partner may want to invest joint savings in a deal you don't have any confidence in. Don't agree until you have thoroughly investigated what is involved and feel it is promising. Research is the key to any business deal right now. You might discover a very lucrative idea if you do your homework thoroughly. If you are frantically organizing a big welcome-home party for a brother or sister returning from overseas, you may have trouble finding most of their longtime friends and will have to settle for a small gathering.

21. WEDNESDAY. Major. Saturn, the planet of responsibility and limitations, moves back into your sign of Libra today, where it will stay for about the next two and one-half years. During this time you can expect a new spurt of personal growth. Turn your attention inward. This is a time to learn about yourself, what you really want and need. You will come to understand yourself on your own terms, not anybody else's. This is also an excellent time for any kind of psychotherapy, human potential work, or consciousness-raising. You need to unlearn incorrect and inaccurate ways of thinking about yourself so that you can start to lay the foundation for the real you.

22. THURSDAY. Receptive. Creative thinking is the ace up your sleeve. In any form of communication, whether study, exams, meetings, or business dealings, you should be able to come up with the answers every time. A difficult coworker may confide in you, giving you an understanding of what's really going on. Instead of seeing this person as a thorn in your side, you might now want to help them and alleviate their suffering. Libra artists and writers will have a very productive day. Put out the do-not-disturb sign, so that visitors who are likely to drop by don't interrupt your flow of creativity. Take loved ones out for dinner tonight and celebrate being alive.

23. FRIDAY. Intense. This is a great day to delve into your past. Energies from the deepest part of your psyche may surface, giving you amazing insights into your emotional self. In everyday life this may manifest as some kind of analytic interaction with another person, possibly a family member. Events that take place now will allow you to learn about your real feelings as long as you are paying attention.

The Sun has moved into Leo and shines its light on your associations, hopes, and desires. This is a great time to start wishing for something; it may come true when the Sun moves into your sign of Libra in approximately two months. Be especially mindful about feelings of possessiveness and jealousy.

24. SATURDAY. Fulfilling. Warmth and affection are in abundance, making this the perfect day to plan a weekend getaway with your loved one. Spend some time on the Internet looking for a hotel overlooking the ocean or a lake, a virgin mountain range, or perhaps the spectacular desert. Take this time for loving intimacy. A large celebration could be on this weekend, so get all the finishing touches done early in the day. Don't let anybody get lazy, assuming you'll do the work. You may be very concerned for the environment or the population of the world. Join a volunteer group to add your energy and vitality to a worthy cause. You might want to check out volunteer opportunities or jobs abroad and get to travel the world.

25. SUNDAY. Stimulating. Today's Full Moon in Aquarius highlights your fun-loving, romantic, and creative sides and bodes well for any social activities you have planned. Budding Libra artists should consider taking classes to learn more about all the different media that could be used to display original style. Sports and games will be a lot of fun. A little gambling might pay off for you, but don't go too far. Betting could become very expensive if you don't know when to stop. Also be careful when it comes to drugs and alcohol because it will be easy to overindulge. Romance is a definite possibility, and an encounter with an alluring stranger is possible.

26. MONDAY. Puzzling. Emotional sensitivity can make the people around you very touchy, and you may experience self-doubts from time to time because of the mixed messages coming from them. Do not get caught up in gossip. Half of what you hear won't be true, and you could end up taking sides with the wrong people. Also be awake to any deceit or underhandedness so that you avoid being used and abused. A hobby can consume your thoughts and time; the more adept you become with it, the more creativity you will be able to express. With personal planets Venus and Mars clustered in Virgo, your house of confinement, you will benefit from whatever solitude you can get.

27. TUESDAY. Sensitive. A sympathetic understanding of other people will be a major plus for you. You are likely to find yourself among upset or confused people. Someone could fool you and take you for a ride unless you stay on your toes. If a coworker is harassing you and making you uncomfortable, consider reporting this person. Harassment is a serious matter, not a joke. An intensely vivid dream may have disrupted your sleep, making it hard to concentrate on your work. Start by writing down your dreams; there might be a message in them. A dream book could lead you to the subtle meaning or warning.

28. WEDNESDAY. Nurturing. Give extra attention to your body. To start an exercise regime, contact a personal trainer at your local gym or health club. Have them give you a program suited to your body type and special needs. Extra attention to your diet would also be valuable. A naturopath or dietician can tell you exactly what type of diet you should be following and may also suggest vitamin and mineral supplements if needed. Check your pet for grooming needs, especially a good brushing for a hairy companion. If you don't have a pet, you might want to look into what type would suit you and be a wonderful addition to your life.

29. THURSDAY. Useful. This is a perfect time for getting odd jobs out of the way and organizing for the remainder of the week. Coworkers may be more emotional than usual. You might have to give one of them a shoulder to cry on, which could set you back in your work but create a friend for life. If you are dieting, be particularly vigilant at lunch, when the desire for rich food can become very difficult to deny. Actually you would be wise to stay away from a restaurant that specializes in dessert goodies. A secret rendezvous can be fun. Even if you don't have a secret lover, plan a romantic night that will surprise your mate or partner.

30. FRIDAY. Frustrating. Energetic Mars catches up to restrictive Saturn in your sign of Libra, lowering your energy level and putting a brake on some of your plans. Other people may come across as unusually irritating and may even seem to work against your best interests, but this is probably just your perception. If you find yourself seething over some injustice, try to let go of this destructive energy because it will only eat away inside you. If starting a new project your concentration should be better than usual. In addition, your self-discipline, training, and experience will get you off to a flying start. Plans for an exciting evening could be canceled unexpectedly.

31. SATURDAY. Compassionate. Communications with other people can be serious and profound, and you may be transformed by something that you learn today. Focus on what is occurring beneath the surface. You could spend part of the day reading a mystery or horror story or else looking for something you have lost. A contract or agreement may be on-again, off-again at the moment. The best you can do is make sure you have covered all your bases to avoid any more disruptions to the deal. You may be on the edge of your seat waiting for a legal verdict or mystery solution that doesn't come until the very end. You can breathe a sign of relief as all such situations turn out all right.

AUGUST

1. SUNDAY. Spirited. An enterprising spirit imbues you with abundant energy and optimism. However, think twice about what you might take on, and make sure it is humanly possible. Marriage difficulties can start affecting other aspects of your life. If you fit that category, seek some help and support so that life isn't way too hard. A fortunate business deal or settlement may boost your confidence and allow you to buy a large-ticket item you have desired for a long while. Although you might not feel like mixing with a lot of people now, you need to find a constructive outlet for your energy along with time to think. A round of golf or a hike through the woods could be a good option.

2. MONDAY. Lively. Restlessness and desire could be the driving force behind all of your actions. You have plenty of support from other people, even if you are not aware of it. If you have had a project on the drawing board for a long time because its size is very daunting, this is the perfect time to focus on getting it done. Support will come when you need it. Your creative juices are powerful and you can convince anyone, anywhere, about anything at the moment. If relationship issues are preying on your mind, talk honestly to your mate or partner. At the end of the day you will know the answer in your own heart. Your loved one might earn some extra cash that helps alleviate your joint money worries.

3. TUESDAY. Tricky. Steer clear of any type of unwanted publicity or exposure. Don't allow a journalist to put any details about you in the newspaper unless you want the information known. Even your age or address should be withheld. You may receive a demand for money that is so outrageous you need to go through the court system. check out the help available. You may be able to represent yourself and save extra dollars. Proposed surgery or other medical treatment may seem quite dangerous, although positive aspects today suggest it will be a success. Make sure your home is insured for the maximum amount. Check with an insurance broker to compare deals so that you get the best one.

4. WEDNESDAY. Favorable. A strong dream can stay with you all day. Or a situation that arises may seem dreamlike, leaving you with a spiritual sensitivity to life as a whole. This is an excellent time to turn your thoughts to a more philosophical frame of reference. You can enjoy conversation with like-minded people and learn about concepts you never thought about before. Good friends will be good company. A long lunch accompanied by frequent outbursts of hilarity should put a smile on your face. An interesting foreigner might talk to you about experiences you find hard to imagine. Finance for a major purchase, such as a house, may be approved.

5. THURSDAY. Invigorating. Libra students attending a discussion group may learn totally new aspects of the course. If you go to a seminar or meeting in a distant city, look up a relative or former friend who lives there. Your world is getting larger, and your enthusiasm is growing along with your mind. Politics or religion could be of interest. You might enjoy debating and learning about interesting topics so much that you never want to do anything else. Research available venues for a large ceremony or party you are planning. You are bound to find one that is not only perfect but less costly than the others. If you want anything badly enough you will get it, so be careful what you wish for.

6. FRIDAY. Powerful. Your popularity is at an all-time high. Lots of invitations to different functions and parties can make picking and choosing almost impossible. Be honest with yourself and select those that your heart tells you. An outstanding job offer might come your way, but your self-confidence may not be high. Go for the interview anyway and you might be surprised when this turns out to be your lucky break. A relative or friend may be jealous, making life hard for you on the home front. Talk to them. They may actually have relevant points to make, which can change you into a better person once you know the facts.

7. SATURDAY. Surprising. Your ruling planet Venus moves into your own sign of Libra, adding a touch of class to your whole persona. Although you may not feel like dressing to impress, the universe is likely to have other ideas. Do what you know is expected of you and you will be rewarded. If you feel down in the dumps, seek some help to brighten up your world. You will be amazed how different the world looks if you meet it with a cheery attitude. Love can walk into your life and knock you over. If you have never believed in love at first sight, you might change your mind. In fact, you might change your mind about a lot of things and make some innovative decisions.

8. SUNDAY. Mixed. Your sense of duty will dominate the inclinations of your heart and override any suggestions that aren't strictly aboveboard. A love union with someone significantly older can introduce you to a deeper and more committed intimacy than you have previously experienced. Or you may decide to walk away from a relationship, preferring your freedom to the expectations and judgments that your lover has been heaping upon you. A surprise invitation this evening might lead to running into people from the distant past and exploring possible new directions in life. A fabulous play or performance can open your heart and mind to the experience of theater and hook you for life.

9. MONDAY. Refreshing. The New Moon culminates in Leo late tonight, opening doors for new friendships and associations. You may be nominated to be on a committee for a social or sports group you have belonged to for a while; accept wholeheartedly. The skills and contacts you make in this position can lead to new opportunities in the workplace as well. Physical exercise can be lots of fun and get you mixing with some new people. An invitation to a social function this evening will introduce you to different social activities as well as useful business connections. There is a lot being offered to you today, so don't waste precious time hiding out.

10. TUESDAY. Dynamic. Forceful and ambitious people can make it hard to maintain a cooperative feel in the workplace. Sit back a little, and you will learn a few techniques for achieving prestige and success in the business world. Trust your good Libra instincts regarding the people around you. Give yourself time for private introspection before going public in any arena. This is a day of excesses, so watch your blood pressure if you get into a physical workout. If you are just starting an exercise routine, begin slowly. Allow your body to limber up and get used to using different muscles in a gentle fashion. Romance and fantasy are indicated this evening; keep them private.

11. WEDNESDAY. Reflective. The Virgo Moon conjoins Mercury in Virgo today, making for changeable moods and wild imaginings.

If you keep a diary or journal, let out your emotions. It's better to put them on paper for future reflection rather than forcing them on innocent bystanders. An acute sense of detail can work in your favor if you are doing any studying, research, or other mental work. You are likely to discover an aspect that has been missed by everyone else. Trust could be an issue with a loved one, but try not to let this get out of proportion. You are probably only imagining a certain scenario, with mistrust emanating from your own self-doubt. An evening at the movies or a play might be fun.

12. THURSDAY. Cloistered. Keeping to yourself and working behind the scenes can be invaluable in your quest for success. A high level of stress can interrupt your thought patterns and create frustration and anger in you as well as in those around you. Try to remove yourself a little from the situation. Bite your tongue and count to ten if someone starts pressing your buttons; otherwise you may do something you regret. If you have to go into the hospital for treatment, be sure to take plenty of reading material with you to help pass the time. A child may be sick and have to go to the doctor or clinic, causing a problem for you if you must go to work. Your mother or another family member who is at home during the day may be willing to help out.

13. FRIDAY. Upbeat. Remain objective and you can rapidly overcome any hurdle to happiness. No matter what you are doing today, don't hurry. If you feel that you don't have time to consult a map, think about the time you will lose driving around in circles. This relates to all actions, not just driving. You will achieve more and achieve faster if you know what you are doing. Sex appeal is yours in abundance at the moment, with lots of glances coming your way from the opposite sex. Dress up and go out partying or dancing; you're on fire tonight. A creative project might be stalled by a problem, and you will need advice from an expert in order to work it out.

14. SATURDAY. Positive. The best approach to getting your own way is to be mature and responsible, not to raise your voice. You will be surprised how powerful softly spoken words can be when everyone around you is yelling. Stress and deadlines can create discomfort and nervous exhaustion. However, if you go quietly amid the noise and scurrying, you will meet deadlines without raising a sweat. Love is in the air for Libras. Romance is a huge possibility. Even if you have been married for years, a night of passion is definitely yours for the doing. Plan to get home fairly early this evening. You will enjoy intimacy with your mate or partner more than advances from assorted strangers.

15. SUNDAY. Happy. Spend the day repairing and renovating at home. Any effort put in now will add to your investment for the future. If you are saving to buy your own home, take a look at what's being offered not only on the Internet but in real terms. By actually visiting places you will get a better idea of what you can get for your money: the type of street, the area, curb appeal, and overall atmosphere. Relatives or old friends may drop by and turn your evening into a social event. If you don't feel like hosting at home, suggest a barbecue at the beach or some other welcoming spot, especially one offering a place to play sports and games.

16. MONDAY. Stressful. It will be hard to keep your cool as the people around you continue to press your buttons and take advantage of your goodwill. Be assertive, eliminating any opportunities to be walked over, and you can have a good day. If a friend owes you a substantial amount of money, you may realize they don't have the ability to pay you back at the moment. It's wise not to loan what you can't afford to give away. Gambling could be a problem today. If you can't afford to bet, stay away from any type of gambling because you are almost guaranteed to walk away penniless. Stay home and nurture yourself, and keep your money in your wallet.

17. TUESDAY. Eventful. Intellectual talents and special interests combine to give you an edge over the competition and to ensure social successes. You have a certain business ability and generosity of spirit that will leave a good impression wherever you go. Be wise and don't waste today's good fortune on worthless pursuits. You can tend to overdo today. In addition to overindulging in pleasure and rich living, beware of overworking. Your intense pursuit of objectives can overstrain your nervous system, which can lead to domestic disputes and differences. While your objectives may be important, so is love and happiness.

18. WEDNESDAY. Helpful. Take time this morning to consider what's best for you. No matter how busy your schedule and how many people want some of your time, take the phone off the hook and do a personal inventory of what you really need. Evaluate your health also. There is a higher than usual chance of catching a viral infection going around. Libra smokers should respect your lungs. If you can't give up cigarettes, at least cut down and start doing some breathing exercises to get added oxygen into your bloodstream. Desire and lust are driving forces right now, so think twice before acting on impulse.

19. THURSDAY. Guarded. Emotional games and power plays are likely to be the order of the day. You can expect to encounter some obsessive behavior either in yourself or in other people. Sexual overtones will be rife, and you might be tempted to stray from the fold with the influences that are percolating in the cosmos. Keep in mind that what seems like a really good idea today might seem like the worst thing you have ever done tomorrow. Subconscious phenomena is close to the surface, making this an opportune time to gain some insight into what makes you tick. Check out the security around your home to be sure everything is working properly.

20. FRIDAY. Innovative. Annoyances and irritations may fuel your desire for change. You are ready to start implementing ideas that have been swirling around in your mind for the past week or so. Group decision making is a great idea for problem solving. In a group you can also pass motions that might otherwise be rebuked by individuals. You are fairly popular at the moment. If nominated to represent your coworkers, don't be shy; take it as a complement, and do your best. This might be the start of a whole new career in public or human relations, which is a Libra's forte. Domestic bliss may seem unobtainable, but take note of everything good and you might be surprised.

21. SATURDAY. Thoughtful. Mercury turns retrograde in Virgo today, meaning it appears to be moving backward through the sky from the perspective on Earth. Mercury will be retrograde for the next three weeks. During this time you may feel you are waiting for things to come together but not really know what those things are. Events are being restructured behind the scenes, and you will be in for some surprises when it is all resolved. Your best course of action now is to make as few assumptions as possible, and don't bet on the same old horses. Be open to your own intuition and ready to jump aboard a new bandwagon when it suddenly materializes. Contracts and agreements can fall through or be delayed.

22. SUNDAY. Varied. For young Libras thinking of leaving the nest and moving out, this is a good idea as long as a job and income will keep you off the streets. Talk to your parents and let them in on your plans gently; there can be a lot of grief when a child leaves home. Partnered Libra may be feeling that you have no time for yourself and are grieving the loss of independence. In a healthy relationship you should be able to discuss this with your mate or partner. If you feel you can't do so, you might want to see a counselor for advice.

A social engagement may be canceled, leaving you and your loved one at loose ends; have a romantic candlelit dinner instead.

23. MONDAY. Quiet. The Sun moves into Virgo, your solar sector of solitude and the subconscious, and will visit Virgo for the next month. This heralds the perfect time to join a meditation class, go on a spiritual retreat, or enter into self-analysis. You will prefer your own company or quiet intimacy with one other person, rather than people-packed nightclubs and parties. Libra students can get into your subject matter and earn top marks on an important assignment. A local study group might provide extra insight to aid research. Work in the healing professions, hospitals, or other institutions is also indicated. You might gain a position that will offer room for advancement.

24. TUESDAY. Healing. Today's Full Moon in Virgo will give you insight into any health issues that you need to address. You may have to look after a loved one who is not well, and you could suffer yourself as you watch them suffer. Alternative therapies are a possibility to consider. Look for a healer whose reputation is well established. It is important to stay quiet and go about your normal daily routine without drama and fuss. Stress will only compound ill health. Drink plenty of water and eat good wholesome home cooking for nourishment. Spend extra time with the people who are most important to you. Listen, laugh, and learn together, and your connections will strengthen and endure.

25. WEDNESDAY. Steady. Your normal routine should flow along steadily, promising to be productive and insightful. In your current mood for reflection, a quicker and easier way to do a certain task might dawn on you, perhaps making you somewhat of a hero among your peers. Enjoy the compliments because you deserve them. A large assignment might best be tackled behind the scenes, so that you have the time and space to figure out how to proceed without any questions or too many suggestions from other people. This is a good time to start a new diet or exercise regime. Just stay away from fads and make sure you are getting balanced nutrition and a holistic workout.

26. THURSDAY. Exciting. The pace will start to pick up a bit and you may have to work to a deadline, enjoying the adrenaline hit that comes with being under pressure. Infatuation with a coworker can give you lots to think about, leading your mind to many different scenarios of altered reality. At the same time stay safe. It is easy to have an accident while daydreaming, especially if you work with machinery, high-powered tools, or electricity. A dinner invitation can come from an unexpected person and put you in a frenzy wondering whether you should go or not. When it comes to new romance, if you have to think about it you aren't in love. But if you like the person, love can grow.

27. FRIDAY. Tense. Caring for somebody else and compromising some of your values can be acceptable to a certain extent. Sometimes, however, you have to draw the line that makes for a healthy relationship. Speak up for yourself and don't let the fear of losing someone lead to betraying your basic values. Stay home if possible and catch up on your backlog of work. This will take an enormous amount of pressure off you so you can relax and enjoy your family. A family friend might drop by and keep you up till all hours reminiscing about the old times and telling tales from way back when. Get out the photo albums and keep the memories flowing.

28. SATURDAY. Rewarding. The morning starts off in the fast lane, so it might be a good idea to get up earlier than usual. Go for a walk or jog around the neighborhood to get your blood moving before you have to race off to begin your daily grind. As the day progresses, peace descends along with a feeling of being rewarded for having achieved the unachievable. Your home life shouldn't be disrupted by this energy, and you can look forward to an evening of love and harmony. A massage, or some other health treatment such as shiatsu or acupuncture, can be very invigorating, leaving you feeling like a new person. You can count on a friend coming through for you.

29. SUNDAY. Harmonious. Good feelings between family members and friends make for a relaxing and harmonizing day. Business discussions on a personal level can be productive, with agreement on fundamental principles and financial backing. This is also a good time to focus on your accounts and tax records so that you will find if anything is amiss. Single Libras are likely to meet someone new and enjoy a flirtatious evening, a lovely start to a new romance. You might decide to make a commitment and move in together or to tie the knot and start a family. Married Libras find can new intimacy as the relationship deepens through understanding and love.

30. MONDAY. Resourceful. A relaxing day at home is indicated. You may decide to go on a massive cleaning spree. As you bring out old and forgotten items you'll probably come across interesting things you can reinvent or recycle into something new and useful. Not only will you clear out your rubbish, but you will enjoy inspiration and creative flair. Visitors are likely to come by and add to your enjoyment of the day, as good conversation brings added enjoyment. If worried about an elderly parent or other relatives this is a good day to cook an impromptu family dinner. Being together can be good medicine.

31. TUESDAY. Imaginative. Libra beauty and magnetism are heightened, and you are likely to be part of all the activity, with plenty of invitations and attention. You might want to treat yourself to a new outfit or hairdo so that you feel pampered. You could easily overspend, so be realistic when buying anything expensive, and don't let a salesperson talk you into purchasing something you don't need. Perhaps you should only visit the stores on your shopping list and avoid all other diversions. A romantic evening could turn into an embarrassment if you allow yourself to drink more than your share. Stay sharp, aware that someone might be trying to blot out your common sense.

SEPTEMBER

1. WEDNESDAY. Encouraging. The adventure bug can strike and set you off on mental travels to far-distant lands with enticing sights, smells, and sounds. Youthful Libras might start to dream of leaving home and heading off to another town or state. You might even set your sights on stardom. If you feel that everything seems to be going wrong and a change in someone else, in the weather, or in the scenery will make all the difference, think again. You will only be fooling yourself unless you start making a few personal changes. Life will remain pretty much the same anywhere you go. Libra musicians and artists can become fascinated with cultural material and decide to study with a teacher in a foreign land.

2. THURSDAY. Fortunate. Dreams can come together now, and a long-desired goal may appear to be almost within your grasp. You should be exuding plenty of charisma, which will help you persuade other people to go along with you. Use this time to your advantage. An interview for admission to a college or university or for a diplomatic post somewhere exotic is likely to be successful. Even if you don't have a lot of credentials, you can sell yourself. You might be searching for spiritual enlightenment. Instead of reading about different paths, you could set off on a trip to experience some of these belief systems firsthand. With the key of willingness, the door will open.

3. FRIDAY. Problematic. All sorts of issues can nag at you and bring you down such as feeling like you are living in the wrong century or in the wrong locale. Or you may feel your clothes don't fit and you need to go on a diet or to the gym for personal training but can't afford it, and on it goes. Start thinking positively and doing something practical. If you are body conscious, changing your diet to raw and whole foods won't cost you any extra and in fact could cost a lot less. Drink lots of water and watch your skin clear up. Don't pick on your mate or partner for perceived bad habits. Change your own life, and as your direction changes your loved ones will probably decide to go along.

4. SATURDAY. Promising. Take control of your own situation. If someone is trying to usurp your authority or push you out, bring the problem out in the open before they succeed. A superior's comments can put you in the hot seat and rankle your nerves. Instead of getting hot under the collar, practice deep breathing to keep cool. Everything points to you eventually coming out on top. A child might be in line for an award. No matter how much work you have on your agenda, be sure to attend the celebration, which will be one you want to savor in your memories. Romance is starred, and the start of a hot and steamy new affair will tantalize.

5. SUNDAY. Irritating. Rashes and allergies can be a possibility for Libras now. If you have been suffering from a health problem that has gone undiagnosed, an allergy test will tell you if it's something you are eating or in your environment that is the cause of your discomfort. Patience and perseverance are fine attributes, but sometimes the struggle becomes a habit. It might be time for you to accept what you cannot change and find something else to focus on. Happiness is attainable, but stop trying so hard. Put your thoughts on hold, and allow your heart to take the lead. A social get-together will be fun and informative, but don't lose track of the time. If someone is waiting for you, give them a call.

6. MONDAY. Friendly. Budding artists should look into a local workshop in order to meet some interesting like-minded people and perhaps discover an untapped personal talent. Sports-minded Libras might be a bit disappointed with today's performance, but you will be very entertaining and the life of the party after the game is over. A family picnic can be fun, and a certain magic might be obvious with one of your relative's friends. If you decide to go off on a walk together, be careful and make sure you don't get lost. Likewise, keep tabs on the kids if you are out in the wilds or there is the possibility of poison ivy. Drugs and alcohol should be avoided no matter where you are.

7. TUESDAY. Arousing. It will be hard not to take sides in any altercation, even for diplomatic Libra peace lovers. Walk away if you think you might lose your cool. It could be useful to write down your thoughts as an aid to clarity. Working behind the scenes to help someone worse off than you or for a charitable cause will be very satisfying. You may want to join a worldwide organization striving for peace and universal well-being. Set up a quiet space in your home where you can shut the door and get valuable work done. Make a do-not-disturb sign for when you really need it. Let the family know you will repay them later for the respect they show when you are occupied.

8. WEDNESDAY. Extravagant. This morning's New Moon forms in Virgo, your solar house of solitude and reflection. With your ruling planet Venus moving into Scorpio, your house of possessions, you might work behind the scenes on a plan for making your fortune. Whatever you do today, you are bound to overdo. A shopping spree might turn up some fantastic bargains but break your budget. Try to think before you act, although that might be hard. The aspects are perfect for starting a class in meditation or tai chi, where you will gain abundance within your inner self, which means the less tangible assets of love, peace, and freedom of spirit.

9. THURSDAY. Pressured. A merry-go-round of emotions can make it hard to reach any type of decision regarding what you are going to do today. Stick to your daily routine and take one thing at a time. If you can stop your mind from plotting and planning about whatever is distressing you, you will instinctively know what to do. Call or visit a family member who is going through a bad time or is suffering from ill health. The time you share with them will be well worth it, and you may hear some great gems of wisdom to help you succeed in your life. If your energy level is down, try going for a walk during your lunch break; the exercise and scenery are apt to reinvigorate you.

10. FRIDAY. Adventurous. The grass might look greener on the other side of the fence, and you may spend a lot of valuable working time surfing the Net looking at real estate in out-of-the-way places and at job opportunities anywhere but where you are. Call a relative who lives somewhere exciting and ask if they will put you up for a few days while you check out local opportunities. You may learn that your mate or partner is going to have to accept a wage decrease, which will affect your budget. Get out the calculator and see what spending cuts you will need to make. A well-researched new investment might pay off.

11. SATURDAY. Amorous. The sign of Libra often bestows beauty upon its subjects. As your ruling planet Venus combines with the softness of the Moon, the alluring perfection of Neptune, and the powerful attraction of Pluto, your charm and magnetism are sure to impress everyone and anyone. You might even feel that you are beating suitors off with a stick. The other side of the coin might see you infatuated by some untouchable who doesn't even know you exist, at least not until today. Anything can happen now. Libras who are in new relationships should beware idealizing a partner. The higher up they are on the pedestal, the farther they have to fall.

12. SUNDAY. Supportive. Your cash flow problems can melt away with a gift from a relative. You may receive word that you are to receive a share of an estate, or receive a winning lottery ticket as a present. Or you may discover that you have inherited a talent that you hadn't known about. A letter from a secret admirer can surprise and delight you, giving you plenty to fantasize about. If out in traffic, watch for a sudden change of road conditions that can catch you by surprise and cause an accident. Be sure to bring along your cell phone in case you get stuck in an area you don't know or the car breaks down. Don't venture into any part of town known to be unsavory.

13. MONDAY. Expressive. Communication starts to flow again as Mercury, the planet of communication, begins to move forward. You might finally receive news you have been waiting for, or a contract or agreement will get the go-ahead. Libra students may once again enjoy studying; appreciating the subject will increase as the topic becomes comprehensible. Travel plans can start to take shape, and some Libras might even be leaving for distant shores. Baggage insurance is highly recommended because there could be a mix-up. Also make sure you have your accommodation arrangements finalized before you arrive. A brother or sister might need your support as well as a bed for the night.

14. TUESDAY. Hectic. Paperwork and phone calls may inundate your working day, making it hard to catch up with what is important. You might benefit from a book about time management. Your employer may expect you to intuit what they want, and won't be clear with their instructions to you. Don't get confused; simply ask for an explanation of exactly what is wanted. A coworker might be spreading gossip, which you would be wise to stay out of because there are bound to be negative reactions from those who matter. Libra students will benefit from extra study time. After class spend a couple of hours in the library and read up on any aspects that are unclear.

15. WEDNESDAY. Tricky. Be willing to work to establish and defend your values and to make other people understand them. Just be careful not to get up on a soapbox and start preaching. Mars, the planet of energy and action, is now in Scorpio, your house of values and possessions. So you might become very attached to certain items and inclined to make unwise and impulsive purchases. Be careful if buying a large-ticket item on credit because you could decide at a later date it is not what you want. However, the depreciation may leave you owing more than it is then worth. Partnership disputes can arise over ownership of property.

16. THURSDAY. Contented. Home is where the heart is. If you spend the day puttering around at home you will be perfectly happy. Taking time for reflection can give rise to all sorts of creative projects. An inspired start today can become an important project in your life. Green-thumb Libras will enjoy getting outside in the garden, perhaps starting winter beds for flowers and vegetables and also preserving some of the recent fall harvest. An old friend or neighbor may drop by to discuss a business proposition. The hours will pass by quickly as you enthusiastically discuss the logistics of such an enterprise. Your application for home improvements may finally be approved.

17. FRIDAY. Challenging. No matter how disheartened you may feel regarding your workplace, this is not a good day to quit. Bite your tongue and wait until next week to make a final decision. If a child's extracurricular activities are costing you too much, explain your financial position and the budget you have to work with, then leave it up to them to decide which ones to keep and which to drop. Some luck in speculation is indicated as long as you make sure that what is written is truthful; there is also a chance of a rip-off. Property owners could receive some good news regarding the sale of a house; although some minor matters may need to be negotiated, the price will be right.

18. SATURDAY. Agitating. Rash or hasty action can result in harm or inconvenience later. Be especially careful this morning with sharp objects in domestic situations as an accident may occur. The mood will pick up later in the day. Arguments will dissolve as harmony prevails. A tendency to eat or drink too much could be the result of upset emotions or simply feeling unloved. Instead of breaking your diet, try doing something for yourself that you would be pleased to do for someone you love. Be kind and caring to yourself and discover how much better it makes you feel. You can make headway on a large project and finally begin seeing the results of all your hard work. Creative Libras can gain public exposure.

19. SUNDAY. Upsetting. Romance can become tiring if you have to constantly explain where you have been and feel you have to report in every hour or so. This isn't love, it's control. It would be better to stop it now before you get too caught up. To keep a bad dream from setting you on edge all day, try to focus on creative projects and supportive friends rather than isolating yourself. Volunteer work would also be a great way for you to get out, feel valued, and not have to think too much. A shopping trip should be highly successful. A local market may offer some great antique furniture or art objects, or real bargains on fresh local fruit and vegetables.

20. MONDAY. Healing. A sensitive and compassionate mood is likely this morning. Go out of your way to please yourself. Love and imagination should reign supreme. Libra artists and other creative types can do some very exceptional work. Young and old lovers alike can enjoy a special intimacy that sets this morning apart from the usual. A simple walk in the park or ride to work can take on romantic aspects never before thought of. As the day progresses, your energy level will pick up. Domestic chores can then be undertaken with gusto. You might tackle a job you would normally leave for a paid professional. Go out for dinner and save on the cooking and dishwashing.

21. TUESDAY. Inventive. Your good intellectual grasp of a situation will allow you to think laterally and come up with some original ideas that are sure to be impressive. Problem-solving abilities turned toward money matters can produce solutions for increasing your cash flow, which will have positive long-term benefits on your bank balance. People around you may seem argumentative later in the day. No matter how much you try to please, you might come away disappointed. The lesson is to let go and don't expect to be able to control other people's moods. You are the only person you can control, and the best way out of any unpleasantness would be to turn and walk away.

22. WEDNESDAY. Playful. Life is full of possibilities and fun. Travel plans for your next vacation can start to take shape after you listen to a coworker's tales of adventure. When making a promise, be sure that you can follow through. Your good intentions might not take your own commitments into account. Tension involving an evening engagement can put you on edge all day and, unless you are careful, can build up so much in your mind that it will be impossible for any human or event to live up to your expectations. Be kind to your liver; cutting out fats can help keep you healthy.

23. THURSDAY. Fortunate. The Sun is now visiting your own sign of Libra. And with the Full Moon in Aries reflecting your will, it might be a matter of let's all cooperate and do it my way. However, try not to be too dictatorial or you will encounter some rebellion. Otherwise you should get what you want today. Although Lady Luck is on your side, this is not a good time to initiate any legal matters. Your emotions could be clouding your judgment, and instead of facts you could be relying on hearsay. An older relative or neighbor might be able to stay in their home if you commit a few hours a week to lending a hand, perhaps by shopping, doing laundry, or working in their yard.

24. FRIDAY. Distracting. Power struggles and frustrated plans make this a day of changing propositions. Your work schedule could cause problems at home and stymie your own plans for getting some personal space. If you work long hours, make one day a week an early finish so that you can be with your family. So long as they are getting some of your attention they won't begrudge your other commitments and interests. Be alert to fine print on a business agreement or contract because there is a good possibility you haven't been given the full story. Any attempt at meaningful communication will be handicapped, especially if somebody feels their personal security is being threatened.

25. SATURDAY. Supportive. Support from other people can be a lifesaver. A difficult situation may dissolve through no action of your own. Disagreements with a relative are foreseen over your ability to be a responsible, independent, self-sufficient person. The onus is on you to come up with the right approach to justify having faith in you.

Self-confidence is a big issue now. A lot of the problems you come up against will be due to self-doubt, which will be obvious to people interacting with you. Start focusing on your physical and emotional well-being because you may be more vulnerable than normal to a virus or stress-related illness. Be sure to eat three nutritious meals and to get ample deep sleep.

26. SUNDAY. Passionate. Romantic liaisons are likely for Libras. Although you might like to think you are falling in love, it is probably more a case of lust. Don't commit yourself because this type of a situation can threaten your personal emotional stability. Secret deals and entanglements full of intrigue can incite a sense of adventure but will be downright dangerous. Keep out of them for your own sanity and because you will not come out a winner in the long run. You may undergo an almost spiritual awakening regarding the passage of life and the importance of making every day count to the fullest.

27. MONDAY. Insightful. The opportunity to enjoy a spiritual experience continues today. You may have a strong feeling of reliving a prior time or of digesting a powerful dream that carries you through a day of unexplainable coincidences. If you mull over possibilities and identify the most likely, you might not like it but at least you will have some direction. Talk of the long-term future might start you worrying about your finances and savings. Also check out insurance coverage and long-term health care. A failed romance or a serious dispute with a coworker might make it hard to face going to work, but it isn't worth losing your job. Put on a good front and at least pretend that the matter has been settled and forgotten.

28. TUESDAY. Instructive. No matter your age, you are never too old to learn something new. The lure of knowledge might hit you now. Inspiration in a certain area of your work can encourage you to further your education and finally end up with the job of your dreams, even if it will be only later in your working life. If you choose well, you might be able to stay in the workforce for a long period because you will not be doing physically strenuous work. Libras who run a small company or a family-owned business should think about more advertising, especially within the local area. You might offer discounts for locals and expand your customer base overnight. Listen to the advice of a wise elder.

29. WEDNESDAY. Demanding. Nagging thoughts and prickly emotions can give you a critical tongue. Be aware of what comes out of your mouth. Try to maintain sensitivity toward your fellow human beings, even if you feel that the whole world is against you. People or issues from the past can come back to haunt you, giving rise to old fears and doubts. If you have been running away from a fear or a fact, now might be the best time to face up to it and finally free yourself. Responsibilities can weigh heavily on your shoulders, especially if you have elderly parents or other relatives who are trying to continue living independently. Explore help available in their area, and develop a plan of action.

30. THURSDAY. Interesting. A promotion might be in the pipeline because your good work and popularity haven't gone unnoticed. Libra parents with a sick child may find it hard to focus on work. What's most important is nurturing the youngster back to health. The cause might simply be an allergy to something in the environment rather than a disease. An interest in politics might lead you to be a candidate for public office or to get involved in campaigning for a politician you admire. Doing this is likely to lead to an interesting new career or at least will bring new people into your sphere. Don't shy away from making your views known.

OCTOBER

1. FRIDAY. Good. Challenging situations will bring out the best in you, and you should feel good about the authoritative way in which you handle whatever occurs. Even though you are a diplomatic and tactful Libra, you will not stand for childish or foolish behavior. An anticipated pay raise might start to seem like a fanciful dream, making you even more determined to be noticed as a valuable employee. You may have unrealistic and fantastic plans, which need to be brought into the realm of reality so that you express your true artistic and creative flair in a way that will be appreciated by other people. Beware of false pride. You might be popular, but if you come to expect it, someone will cut you down to size.

2. SATURDAY. Lively. Get up early and you will be able to do some of your best work. With your quick and intuitive mind you can come up with unique and novel approaches that grab your employer's or client's interest. As the day progresses, you are likely to get caught up in social situations and spend a lot of time talking about not very much at all. An irresistible attraction to an associate can interfere with any hope of engaging in rational conversation on the job. Ask them out for dinner at an exotic restaurant that will tantalize your taste buds, and make it an evening to remember. Libra musicians can get involved in an impromptu jam session, a mind-blowing experience.

3. SUNDAY. Opportune. Make good use of today's uncanny ability to earn money. Even a short sojourn at a casino might fill your wallet with unexpected dollars. Love is definitely in the air. As a lucky Libra you might find yourself in the company of big-time movers and shakers, with attention paid to you by a millionaire. Your mind should be in fine form, and your ability to amuse and entertain will put your name on everyone's lips and give your self-confidence an added boost. A large-ticket household item such as a refrigerator or washing machine might go on the blink. If you are looking into buying a new one, check out all the deals currently being offered.

4. MONDAY. Lovely. Enjoy a day at home. If you are enjoying a new romance, you might be happy together on the couch without other entertainment. If you are single, fantasy will take your mind off problems and act as a panacea. An early morning sport or workout at the gym will be good for your physical well-being and may inspire you to get into a project that's been on the drawing board for quite a while. Otherwise you might laze around all day and get nothing done. Mercury is in your own sign of Libra now and will speed up your thought processes. Keep focused and you can achieve a great deal over the next three weeks. This is also a good time to purchase a new car.

5. TUESDAY. Nurturing. Drop by a health spa and pamper yourself with a massage, sauna, and meditation. Time for reflection will be invaluable to you. Your mind is quick to understand your own main issues, needs, and addictions. If you have trouble with food and dieting, now is the perfect time to start a practical and effective program to combat health and weight problems. A self-help group would also be beneficial, giving you guidelines for a healthy and spiritual life into the future as well as solving problems of the moment. Relationships with women can be problematic. Communication is the only answer; you stand to learn something.

6. WEDNESDAY. Stressful. There's too much to do today and not enough time to do it. Try not to take on extra work in an effort to impress. If you fall behind, you will do everything but impress. A coworker could be overly critical, picking on everything you do and making you so nervous you make more mistakes. Talk to your supervisor and explain the problem without running this other person down too much. You may be given some very useful advice to help you cope and also to put your nemesis in their place. Remember that you are not alone. As the day progresses you are likely to find yourself in a circle of caring friends eager to hear about your latest escapade.

7. THURSDAY. Helpful. You are apt to be conscious of the most minor matters, making it hard to see the forest for the trees. Or you might focus on the negative traits of those around you and miss their positive virtues. If you have to say good-bye to someone, you are apt to suffer feelings of grief and loss, which will stay with you for some time. You can do exceptional work at the moment thanks to your acute precision. Libra students will find research very enjoyable and should be able to unearth interesting and relevant facts to back up any point of view. The New Moon in Libra gives you a chance to change negative personal traits into positive and attractive attributes.

8. FRIDAY. Introspective. Venus, your ruling planet, turns retrograde, which means it will seem to be moving backward from Earth's perspective. This has the effect of slowing down the Venus attributes of dress sense, visual sensibilities, and decorative abilities. As a result the next month is not a favorable time to buy clothes, start redecorating the house, or change your hairstyle. It is also not the best time to get married or to host a big party. Since Venus rules diplomacy, slowdowns in all sorts of negotiations can be expected, including industrial disputes, legal issues, and diplomatic endeavors. You may be forced to deal with deep issues that have their origins in past events and also to settle unfinished business.

9. SATURDAY. Volatile. Strong emotional impulses warn against making long-term decisions such as marriage or investments. Although you may not be feeling up to par, money worries may keep you from taking a day off work. Be mindful of your condition. If you are working with machinery be very careful because you won't be as alert as you should be. You might also be more inclined to snap at the people around you and upset them. Usually retail therapy can be very effective at lifting your mood, but today you are more likely to waste your money on items that will only gather dust. Instead of going to the mall, go out with a friend for a nourishing lunch and some good conversation.

10. SUNDAY. Optimistic. A job offer might provide a chance to make more than your normal wage due to the opportunity to work overtime. Before making a decision, consider your working hours and the leisure time you will have to give up, not just the money you can earn. An inclination to study psychic or supernatural phenomena could turn your mind to the mystical. Visit a New Age bookshop and pick up a book that catches your eye; there is probably a message in it for you. Food and alcohol can become a problem, so be very careful if invited on a business lunch. If you drink too much you could end up sealing a deal that you would be better off without. Keep your clarity and you'll come out on top.

11. MONDAY. Informative. Focus on paperwork this morning. Sort out bills to get an overview of what needs to be paid and what you can put off. A cell phone bill could be exorbitant. Spend some time checking various other plans and you should be able to find one that will suit your budget and still allow you to make a lot of calls. A conversation with someone older might be very insightful, giving you an answer to a problem without actually discussing it. The universe works in mysterious ways, and you may feel very grateful for the answer you get. An offer to teach something you love could give you an opening to get out of your usual employment.

12. TUESDAY. Uneven. Making a decision on an important issue could be stressing you out. On one hand you want this but on the other hand you want that. Having a foot in both camps means you are playing it safe but aren't getting anywhere. Be patient, and in your own good time the choice will become clear. Anxiety over an engagement later today might have you on edge and unable to think straight, which can color your whole day. If you can't allay this stress, put off anything else that is important until you are once again able to think straight. Be sure to check all your e-mail and snail mail so you don't miss something important. Electrical equipment can go on the blink; be extra careful.

13. WEDNESDAY. Uneasy. Turning your back on a problem won't make it disappear. It might seem easier to ignore rather than confront and resolve a certain situation. However, that means living with the problem for a lot longer, and it might just get bigger and more serious. Money problems can make your home life stress city. If you are not earning enough to make ends meet, consider getting an extra job or obtaining some training to improve your prospects. A self-awareness workshop might be helpful if you tend to balance a busy life by putting loved ones first and relegating your own wants to the back burner. With awareness and training you might be able to please yourself too.

14. THURSDAY. Energetic. Positive emotions can get you off to a great start. A new exercise program may be starting to show results. You may have to move and be in the middle of packing, or be trying to live out of a suitcase. Such conditions make it extra hard to know where anything is, so write the contents of each box in bold letters. A desired object may seem out of reach as your bills pile up. Consider purchasing it on layaway, a little at a time. You could be fooling yourself regarding a new infatuation. Be realistic if possible. Make a list of the pros and cons, and believe what you see. Someone could be lying to you. Even if you can't prove anything, trust your own instincts.

15. FRIDAY. Contented. Use the opportunity of today's emotional calm to freely express yourself. Your creative and artistic talents should help you produce some great work. If a plan for a party or some other celebration is getting out of your price range, bring it back within reason to ensure that it will be enjoyable for you as well as the guests. A romance can be inspiring grand plans for the future, and with a positive approach they are attainable. If you are planning to start a family or add to your family, make sure you have a secure and committed base. A desire for excitement can fuel the urge to speculate. Get into competition games rather than putting your hard-earned cash on the line.

16. SATURDAY. Discordant. What looks really great may not ring true. Don't blindly believe what you are told; do your own detective work and find your own truth. A salary increase could be in the cards and will give you an opportunity to start planning your next vacation. Before you decide on a destination, check the Internet for cheap deals. A class in a spiritual discipline might attract you and be just what you need to add more meaning and satisfaction to your life. Don't worry about what anyone else might say; follow your heart. If you have fallen in love with a person your family doesn't like, again you should listen to your heart.

17. SUNDAY. Stimulating. Heightened senses can produce information overload. Don't try to do too many things at once because you won't succeed. A friend might need your sympathy and understanding, free from interruptions. If you really care, turn off your phone and give them a couple of quality hours. Do something different today. Change is as good as a vacation, and it will renew your interest and inspiration. Go to the beach, an interactive museum, or a theme park and just have fun. Creativity is high. If you have always fantasized about being an artist, now is a great time to start a course in whatever medium inspires you. You might discover a latent talent and amaze your friends and family.

18. MONDAY. Imaginative. Larger-than-life goals can make it hard for you to achieve anything unless you moderate them. Your storytelling talents are strong, and you may attract warm and friendly people with your interesting conversation. If you feel the urge to start writing, you might find that your stories are worthy of being published. Fortune may seem to fall from the sky. Your energy level may be subpar, and it could be beneficial to find a healthy supplement to restore your system to optimum efficiency. Be especially careful of drugs and alcohol, which can negatively affect your energy level for a long time.

19. TUESDAY. Successful. Good feelings and generosity toward other people will hold sway for you and those around you today. You will get back what you give by way of kindness, friendship, and nurturing support. Group effort and public speaking are especially starred due to your good understanding on a deeply intuitive level. A workplace promotion and pay raise can reward you for your hard work and give you the positive energy to work even harder. Home renovations or redecoration can be started now. Utilize the flair of your own individual talents, which you will be proud to show off for years to come. A class in relaxation techniques will benefit you for the rest of your life.

20. WEDNESDAY. Beneficial. You are able to operate with the big picture in mind, making you far more successful and lucky than usual. You can plan with greater foresight and avoid the pitfalls that characterize bad luck. Business activity is highlighted. Today's gift of insight will help you succeed through balanced and considered decision making. It is also important to avoid risky ventures. Emotional manipulation might be underlying a disagreement with your mate or partner. Only open and honest communication can work this issue out in a fair and equitable way, so don't get drawn into anything that isn't going to be productive. Better to walk away and deal with it later when emotions are calm and you both feel loving.

21. THURSDAY. Profitable. Mercury, the planet of communication and the mind, has just moved into Scorpio and your solar sector of personal values and possessions. Turn your thoughts to plans for attaining what you value. You may also have to define your values to another person involved with you in a business or romantic relationship. Property negotiations or a business deal can be long-winded, with the transaction more important and elaborate than usual. A relationship issue can nag at you and make it hard to keep your mind on the job. Guard against an accident, and be especially careful when dealing with anything electric.

22. FRIDAY. Sensitive. Tonight's Full Moon in Aries will highlight your partnership and business sector. You might encounter disagreement regarding your decision-making processes. Be sure to consider other people's values and opinions in order to avoid an argument, although this might be very difficult for you right now. You are working hard and expect the same from those around you, but try not to be insensitive. Practice patience. Harmony between your home and professional life, your conscious and unconscious personality, and your mind and feelings may be hard to maintain, leading to discordant moods. A passing attraction this evening will be a pleasant distraction.

23. SATURDAY. Significant. The Sun moves into Scorpio, your solar sector of personal values and possessions, and joins Mercury, Venus, and Mars also in Scorpio. This adds to your focus on what is important to you and how you can attain your goals. Don't try to ignore problems in this area, or they are apt to get considerably worse until you finally decide to act. Once you do get into gear, you will be amazed how quickly and smoothly you can solve the problem. During this monthlong transit of Sun in Scorpio, you might want to examine your relationship to the resources of your life, and consider whether they serve your needs or if you serve theirs. Your freedom is of more value to you than anything else, so don't let it slip away.

24. SUNDAY. Smooth. Your business instinct is especially good. You may have to take control of a family matter that is a bone of contention between relatives. You are noted for a balanced approach and for keeping the peace. Although you may have to act in a secret and confidential manner, you will succeed in resolving the problem harmoniously. There are unusually strong bonds between you and another family member, and you can benefit from each other's business experience and knowledge. You might have more cash in your wallet after you run into an old friend who owes you money. Don't let your kind nature take away their enjoyment of giving back.

25. MONDAY. Uplifting. Your gift at oratory can be startling today, giving you the ability to sway even the most stubborn opponent to see your side. This will be a heaven-sent skill in business matters. You may be volunteering for a charity and enjoy talking to the public about the needs and good works of the group, which is sure to lead to donations. A spiritual or philosophical debate might inspire your thoughts and spur you on to change some of your attitudes and habits. Or a political rally could be a good outlet for you. If you are at loose ends, go to a cultural event with an open mind. To avoid becoming obsessive and losing your objectivity, slow down and broaden your horizons.

26. TUESDAY. Satisfying. This should be a mainly positive day as long as you don't allow distractions to take your mind away from what is important. Libra students facing an upcoming exam could sit and cram in the hours leading up to it. It would be better, however, to go out and relax your mind. What you don't know now isn't going to be absorbed in a few hours. The more relaxed you are, the better you will be at recalling what you do know and understand. This is true for a business function also; arrive calm and relaxed, and the world is your oyster. A weight may be lifted off your shoulders as something you have been worrying about for a while is resolved without much trouble.

27. WEDNESDAY. Strategic. Do not undervalue the abilities of your opponents. You will have to use every trick in the book to win an argument or clinch a deal. Not everybody will put their cards on the table. On some issues you could be working with only some of the facts. Consciously refer to your instincts, which will keep you alert to underhanded possibilities. If you neglect to do this, you can fall under the spell of someone's crafty plan. Intense emotions can heighten loving moments with your mate or partner and put lust back in the equation. Single Libras might find yourselves in a passionate embrace. However, if you are looking for a serious commitment, maybe you should look elsewhere.

28. THURSDAY. Productive. Your positive, loving approach will be a valuable asset. In business deals and career moves your success looks assured. A bargain can be gained through a property deal or an auction. If you like to haggle over purchases you should come out on top. Your eye for artistic beauty and value is sharp, and the purchase of a piece of art will be an investment for your future. A powerful friend or family member might pull a few strings in your favor and help you advance on your career path. Talk to them about your future possibilities and they will be able to give you some valuable advice from their experience. A parent or other relative could need your help.

29. FRIDAY. Busy. Mars is now in Sagittarius, your house of communication and short-distance travel. So you might be out and about a lot over the next month. If you have to take a driving test, wait until mid-November if you don't feel confident. Meanwhile, keep taking driving lessons to hone your skills. Pointless arguments might arise, and you should consider why you are even bothering to be involved in them. Libra students will benefit from the extra energy for homework and studying that comes with this Mars transit. Any chance to enter into active discussion on your favorite topic will sharpen your mind and strengthen your knowledge and understanding.

30. SATURDAY. Expressive. Being out and about with other people will be enjoyable, opening up lots of possibilities to have fun and learn something new. A female friend might put you in an uncomfortable position by asking more of you than you care to give. It might be better to find a believable excuse rather than hurt her feelings with your honesty at this time. You could accept a local elected or appointed position and enjoy being part of keeping the integrity of the democratic process intact. Your hopes and wishes should be given top priority and can bear fruit within a week if you believe in them strongly enough. A child can bring joy and happiness into your life regardless of any problems.

31. SUNDAY. Manageable. Examine your overall goals in life and make sure that they are a realistic expression of who you are now, not a carryover from a younger you. Libra singles might consider joining an interest group. This could expand your circle of friends and possible suitors. If a local civic group is organizing a social event in your neighborhood, get involved and you will learn new skills as well as make friends. A romance could feel more like hard work than fun as intense feelings get caught up with unresolved resentments and jealousies. If you can't decide to move on, counseling might be the best course of action.

NOVEMBER

1. MONDAY. Serene. The call of the outdoors is likely to be in your system. If you get a chance to go horseback riding, hiking, or hang gliding, you will gain a pastime that gives you a lot of enjoyment as well as a strong love for nature. With your mind clear and sharp, you will enjoy focusing on a project that is close to your heart. No matter how wild it is, you can make it happen. A meditation and relaxation class will provide the tools you need to rejuvenate body and soul, and you are apt to be surprised by the spiritual life that develops with this practice. Spend as much time as possible at home, enjoying your family, catching up on odd jobs, and relishing the simple peace.

2. TUESDAY. Reclusive. Your need to stay out of the rat race may be stronger than your need to go to work. Call in sick, and only make contact with the outside world through the Internet or by phone. You can do your shopping and meet people with your computer, so you don't really need a car. Some Libras may be courting a person from a foreign shore while saving up for the ultimate one-on-one encounter. Secret sorrows could find you mired down with self-obsession. To escape this never-ending cycle, let go and give your mind a break from the continual plotting and planning. The furrows will disappear from your brow as a smile spreads across your face.

3. WEDNESDAY. Fluctuating. A sleepless night won't help your mood, which you can expect to consist of highs and lows throughout the day. Try to be understanding even as you grumble and find fault with everyone. Help youngsters make up a list of their chores, and perhaps include a star system that will reward them for not slacking off. If nothing else, it will give them something practical to think about. Be mindful of your own thoughts. If you look upon a certain job as a chore, it will be hard or not enjoyable; if you are thankful for the ability to perform the task, it might become pleasant. Self-control is available. You can get a lot of work done as the day progresses, so stop procrastinating and get started.

4. THURSDAY. Pleasant. Shopping will be enjoyable. You should come up with many bargains, perhaps even getting some of your holiday shopping done and saving yourself last-minute stress. Your creative flair will influence your clothes choices. Don't be surprised if you purchase a few outfits that are a bit zany and out there compared to your usual. If your employment situation is not satisfactory, brush up your resume a bit before sending it out to prospective employers. This is a time for new beginnings, and that is what you are entitled to. Your creative ability can bring in extra cash on the side, but be sure to keep good financial records for tax time.

5. FRIDAY. Starred. Your Libra diplomatic talents will be on display today. You are likely to be surrounded by some very rich and powerful people, so dress to look your best among them. Libra singles may get to work closely with a fellow worker who adds romance to the air, but take things slow. Savor the romance before becoming too involved. Partnered couples might go into business together and start mixing business with pleasure. An art exhibit can give you some ideas for your own work, sending you off for hours of inspired creativity. Track the hours you devote to creativity so that you have a realistic idea of the time you spend on your creations and what you earn per hour.

6. SATURDAY. Exciting. Your lively mind will come up with a quick answer to anything. Libra salespeople might amaze everyone with a smooth sales pitch and success in earning a large commission. Write out a to-do list for today, and don't forget to take it along when you leave home because your memory may not be as sharp as usual and you are apt to overlook something important. If you have had a lovers' quarrel, write a letter to your mate or partner but don't send it. Read it to yourself later on and you might gain insight into the real issues as well as some insight into how much or how little you really know about yourself.

7. SUNDAY. Energized. Your neighborhood might be offering some interesting entertainment this weekend. If there is a local festival, consider signing up as a volunteer, which will help you get to know people close to home. One of your neighbors might have a domestic problem, but if they try to involve you in this be very careful. You can become involved in a way that puts you in some danger. If you want to help, find out what self-help and counseling is available in the area and offer to provide a lift if needed. An unforeseen bonus might come your way, boosting your bank balance considerably. Rather than spend the money, pay off a credit card debt and eliminate those interest payments.

8. MONDAY. Upbeat. Optimism and positive thinking give the day a golden glow and encourage you to undertake a project you would normally back out of due to lack of confidence. Taking on this work will allow you to stretch your abilities and talents and also bolster your confidence. Intellectual pursuits will appeal. You might begin to study a subject of special interest, or you might even get involved in local politics and start campaigning. Venus, your ruling planet, has slipped back into Libra, urging you to reflect on who you really are and what you really want. Reassess your personal values. This is an excellent time to write thoughts and feelings in a journal for later reflection and insight.

9. TUESDAY. Unsettled. Dissatisfaction with your living arrangements may have more to do with a lack of independence being afforded to you than with the actual dwelling itself. Libras who are on a strict diet may find it impossible to resist temptation when someone else at home eats whatever whenever. Start looking for a place of your own where it will be easier to stick to your diet. If you are suffering from insomnia, examine your diet for answers. Too much caffeine or sugar can keep you awake, and overeating can also upset your sleep patterns. Try drinking plenty of fresh, pure water and eating smaller meals. Also be sure to consume fruit and vegetables in place of snack foods with no nutritional value.

10. WEDNESDAY. Eventful. Money and your personal security may be on your mind. You might decide to take on extra work to ensure your income meets the cost of your preferred lifestyle. However, if your health suffers and you feel continually tired, rethink what you're doing. Looked at from another angle, your quest for money might be the cause of your problems, not the cure. Romance can make problems seem to vanish. A new infatuation can take your mind off your worries and transport you to a blissful haven. A business deal is likely to be lucrative. Make sure that what you are about to risk is affordable and you can't go wrong. A new hobby could pleasantly fill your time, guaranteeing hours of fun and relaxation with friends or your family.

11. THURSDAY. Stimulating. A pleasant restlessness can energize you and send you out in search of something new and interesting. A recently hired coworker might stimulate conversation and add some fun and laughter to the workplace. A proposition to work out of your own home might be fantastic, especially for Libra parents who want to be home more. However, examine what will be demanded of you, and make sure you will feel comfortable with those demands. House hunting might take you on an exhaustive round of open houses. Just when you start to think you will never find the right place, one will perfectly fit the bill. If you have a pet, find out about neighborhood leash laws and available dog parks.

12. FRIDAY. Industrious. An attraction to an older person might bring stability into your life and also open doors thanks to their experience and knowledge. Libra businesspeople should shop around for the best interest rate before signing on the dotted line. A natural talent can become a moneymaker if you are willing to teach what you know. Put an ad in the local paper and start off with a small group to help build your confidence. If you have been feeling argumentative lately, join a debating or public-speaking group and use your talent in a safe environment. You can sharpen your mind and improve your rhetoric, which will be of benefit to you forever.

13. SATURDAY. Buoyant. An attraction to folks who are out of the ordinary and eccentric can stimulate your artistic and creative side and enable you to produce something quite unique. However, be careful of the people you mix with at the moment. You could be easily led, and end up in a situation not of your choosing or liking. As a Libra you are inventive and can come up with some great ideas. At work these ideas can put you in line for a promotion and extra pay. A secret love affair that you or somebody close to you is involved in could be adding stress and complications to life. It might be time to take off the rose-colored glasses and have a good hard look at the situation.

14. SUNDAY. Encouraging. Your thoughts and feelings may be at odds. Continually weighing the pros and cons will get you nowhere. Give full weight to your feelings. They are the part of you that you live with day in and day out, whereas your mind uses information that is often conjecture and perhaps fear-based. Libra job seekers should focus on presentation. Research the type of people who get the positions you are after, and model yourself on them. Ask someone you know and admire for some pointers. Taking steps to improve your fitness level will reap rewards not only in your sense of well-being but also in the looks department. Dress for the part you intend to play.

15. MONDAY. Opportune. Arguments can cloud the early morning, but someone who does you a good turn will change the look and attitude of the day. With a smile on your face, your feelings will be contagious. You may notice that the people around you are in a joking, lighthearted mood. You might decide to clean your home from top to bottom. A friend or neighbor may give you a hand and take some of your excess off your hands, giving you extra space. Don't be afraid to let go of sentimental possessions if they have passed their usefulness; let them bring joy to someone else. Take the family out for dinner and leave the kitchen clean.

16. TUESDAY. Spirited. Put your best foot forward on the job. Someone is apt to be watching your every move, ready to jump on you for the smallest mistake. You're very adaptable and witty now. If the day takes a turn for the worst, you might surprise yourself with your quick comeback and ability to keep on the go. A lovers' quarrel that has persisted may be on your mind. With your natural Libra talent for harmony and diplomacy you can find a way to heal perceived hurts and renew trust and the passion of love. Inner restlessness will not allow you to get much relaxation. A workout in the gym might be beneficial, followed by some quiet reading time.

17. WEDNESDAY. Cooperative. Thought-provoking discussion can encourage helpful and cooperative actions. Look into signing up for a class either locally or on the Internet. If you are going through relationship problems, a self-help group can bring up insights and issues that provide the basis on which to start understanding and rebuilding love and interdependence. Singles might consider making a lasting commitment and finally set a date for a wedding. A surprising turn of events can lead to happiness and insight that opens the door to exciting future opportunities. Don't reject any possibility without first learning more about it.

18. THURSDAY. Profitable. Success may come from what looked like a dire situation. Keep a positive attitude and anything can happen. An investment made as a compromise can turn out to be very fortunate. Marriage plans might have to be deferred, but don't despair; the timing will turn out to be right in the end. Legal matters might seem too expensive, but with some advice you may be able to deal with it yourself and save a fortune in fees. In fact you might be so successful it encourages you to start planning a whole new career in the legal field. Don't let other people influence you to do what you know isn't right for you.

19. FRIDAY. Constructive. What seems like drastic changes can turn out to be the best thing you have ever done in your life. As a Libra you are represented by the Scales, and are always trying to find a balance. Sometimes, however, you need to follow your heart. Do what is best to maintain balance into the future. Always trust your instincts. Impending surgery could be on your mind, making it hard to sleep. If it is necessary for your health you have no choice. On the other hand, if it is simply cosmetic surgery you might be wise to postpone it until you have more information that puts your mind at rest. A relative may have some business advice that will benefit you. If they offer you a job, accept without arguing.

20. SATURDAY. Irritable. Nervous tension that makes it hard for you to be reasonable could be the result of having too much on your mind at the moment. Slow down and delegate some of your work. The need for control might be your single worst enemy; let go and relax. Your mate or partner's income might be reduced. If you have been relying on this for your lifestyle, take stock now and cut back before the bills pile up and resentment takes over. A good honest look at your lifestyle is sure to turn up expenses that you can do without, or items that you can purchase cheaper, without affecting either of you very much at all. You might even get healthier.

21. SUNDAY. Enjoyable. Today's Full Moon in Taurus is all about give-and-take. What makes you feel comfortable and secure needs to be balanced with attention to other people's needs and comfort. This is a good time to settle some of your debts, financial or otherwise. You may be in a position where you are forced to make a financial settlement or large outlay of cash. Or you may find that you are relied upon for some type of support. A budding romance can blossom under the light of this Taurus Moon. If you are thinking about buying a gift such as a ring as a token of your love, orchestrate the best setting to magnify the magic and heighten the romance.

22. MONDAY. Expressive. The Sun is now in Sagittarius, shining its light in your solar sector of communication. Relationships with people from distant lands can come through the Internet. You could become involved in charitable or political actions in far-flung corners of the Earth, all from the comfort of your home. You can expect to be out and about a lot. Keep alert on the road because an instance of road rage may be hard to avoid. A promotion at work might lead to moving into a new office, having far better hours, and being given more stimulating work. With Venus, your ruling planet, moving forward, a stalled relationship may start racing ahead once again.

23. TUESDAY. Emotional. Tempers can flare, and someone that you have to deal with could be exceptionally quarrelsome. Think twice or count to ten before you react to any remarks that get your hackles up. The outburst will have a lot more to do with the person feeling irritable rather than anything you did or said. This is a great day for tackling correspondence and writing the letters or e-mails you have been thinking about for a while. Your ability to write in an entertaining style will make for great reading; you might even decide to write a book. Libras who have submitted a manuscript should get a positive response from a publishing house. Be kind to your nerves and practice relaxation.

24. WEDNESDAY. Ambitious. Self-control and the determination to achieve put you in a promising situation with any work. Your popularity has increased and you will be recognized as reliable and hardworking. You could be discontent in love and give someone the heave-ho because you decide their future prospects are not good enough for you. There is nothing wrong with that; better to do so in advance rather than a few years from now when kids and property may be added to the mix. If you are at odds with your parents over your life's direction, listen to what they have to say before deciding on your next moves.

25. THURSDAY. Varied. You should finally feel your self-esteem rising, especially if you are spending the day with older relatives. Being independent and adaptable can give you a broader view of life and expand your horizons. Make sure you bring along a map if you are venturing out of your local area; there is a chance that you could get lost or get caught in a traffic detour. If you do a lot of traveling for work or pleasure, invest in the latest satellite navigational system so you won't have to worry. Mull over an offer received from your workplace to pay for a managerial training course or for language lessons. Use this holiday to consider the pros and cons, perhaps with family input.

26. FRIDAY. Supportive. On this pleasant day you should find yourself surrounded by friendly, loving people. Discussions and debates can be very interesting. You will actually enjoy having your ideas tested by an intelligent person who believes somewhat differently from you. Don't let dogmatism close your mind to varied possibilities. If an old friend needs your support, get together for coffee or lunch and listen to their doubts and worries. Before you know it, you'll be laughing together over life, love, and future aspirations. Start getting some holiday shopping done now before crowds take away the enjoyment.

27. SATURDAY. Reassuring. An optimistic and compassionate turn of mind will create a passionate aura. However, romantic vibes might be the result of the rose-colored glasses that you have chosen to wear. This is an excellent time to give to a charity or to join a volunteer organization and work for the collective good rather than for purely selfish reasons. Spiritual issues and quests can lead to some deep thinking. You might run into a friend who sparks your interest in that area of life, perhaps even going with them to a discussion group or a class. Drugs and alcohol should be avoided. Libras who are grappling with an addiction of any sort may be able to join a useful organization for support and encouragement.

28. SUNDAY. Sentimental. Nostalgia over the past can lead to reflection. Writing in a journal could be a wonderful outlet at the moment. As you go through this period of your life, reflecting on your previous thoughts can help you see the progress you are making. Memories from your childhood may surface. Instead of trying to quell this tide of awareness, it might be worth seeing a counselor to learn how to deal with these memories and emotions in a positive and healing fashion. Although you like social contact, work behind the scenes today and get some pressing obligations and chores out of the way. You will then sleep well tonight.

29. MONDAY. Cautious. What looks like the opportunity of a lifetime might be anything but. Consider your course of action seriously before jumping into anything new and untried. Likewise, be careful of the company you keep; don't take people at face value for your safety's sake. An argument with a friend can leave you high and dry, without a lift home if you're not careful. Consider your situation before you fly off the handle or go off on your own. Libras walking down the aisle today should be very happy, although there may be a touch of sorrow over leaving independence behind forever. Don't say yes or I do unless you mean it.

30. TUESDAY. Quiet. The Moon glides into your sign of Libra this morning and makes many aspects to other planets. Your moods may be up and down all day. Learn to let go and have no attachment to your emotions; watch them as they change in different circumstances. Underneath you will notice that you remain the same. You may be pressed for time, and find yourself rushing from place to place in an effort to get everything on your list done. A former friend might turn up on your doorstep and have some exciting stories to tell, not to mention the excitement of seeing each other again. Enjoy reminiscing about what was and imagining what might have been.

DECEMBER

1. WEDNESDAY. Beneficial. As a Libra you are quite resourceful and energetic in your ability to make money, but you also love spending it on objects that appeal to your Venus-inspired sense of harmony and balance. A massage or manicure can make you feel like a million dollars. A skin condition may start to clear up, which will do wonders for your self-esteem. Relationships with your family members should be good even if strained earlier in the year. Plans for a large get-together over the Christmas break could be in the pipeline. You may have to take a younger relative under your wing and offer help getting them into the workforce or putting a roof over their head. Your efforts will produce a positive move.

2. THURSDAY. Loving. The Moon dances with Venus, the goddess of love, in the deep commitment sign of Scorpio. This signals romance that touches the instinctual and powerful realm of the subconscious. An overpowering attraction might make it impossible to ignore this person's advances. However, if you are already in a relationship, consider making a quick exit and saving yourself any further tantalization. An accident could occur if you don't keep your mind on the job. Be especially careful when using electricity or operating temperamental machinery. A change of home is possible. Libras who have one or more roommates may be on the lookout for a more like-minded person to share the rent.

3. FRIDAY. Erratic. Plans and inspiration may be swirling around in your mind, but your ability to follow through on them is probably nil. This difficulty can spill over into your spending habits also. Monitor your credit card debt. You may already be having trouble making your monthly payments, so don't add to this debt. A new household appliance might be unnecessary, your urge to buy due to the success of an advertising campaign. If you are shopping for a gift for someone special, you don't have to spend a lot to show your feelings; it is the thought that counts. Be careful while driving, keeping your mind solely on the road.

4. SATURDAY. Buoyant. An early morning disturbance could get you up a lot sooner than usual, which will give you a chance to catch up on some housework. Renovations or a redecorating project can progress well, especially if you have help from friends. Your energy level is soaring. An argumentative neighbor might be particularly annoying. But if you ignore them completely, you might be surprised to see their attitude start to change. Although you can achieve a lot, be careful that you don't set your goals too high, creating emotional tension that could cause an outburst of frustration. Keep tabs on your spending and guard against blowing the budget.

5. SUNDAY. Diverse. This is a favorable time to start learning something new, take a test, fill out forms, sign up for a course, write letters, make phone calls, and carry out daily tasks with gusto. An interest in a broad array of subjects and good rapport with other people suggest that you should get out and mix with current friends and newcomers. Plans to travel can take shape, and a visit to the travel agent can confirm your itinerary. Get away for the weekend if possible; visit a friend or relative in the country to enjoy the open spaces and a break from your usual routine. If you feel reclusive and prefer to hide away indoors, travel via the Internet to escape the commonplace.

6. MONDAY. Surprising. Keep in mind that anything can happen and probably will. Discard preset plans and enjoy a refreshing spontaneity. Let your heart dictate what happens rather than what your mind has mapped out for you. A household appliance may need to be replaced for the family's safety as well as to save on energy. Uninvited guests can disrupt your quiet, but their upbeat attitude and extra help might more than compensate for the inconvenience. A large community meeting can be a great outing, giving you a chance to meet new neighbors and find out what's going on locally. If possible, don't drive anywhere. Use public transportation if your destination is too far to walk.

7. TUESDAY. Disconcerting. A feeling that you can't express yourself freely might create all sorts of frustrations. If you are living with one or more roommates and find that they don't agree with you, consider moving. Affordable housing can be hard to come by; put out to the universe exactly what sort of a home you would like, then see what happens. Results are unlikely overnight, but they will happen. You might be in a faultfinding frame of mind and wonder why people keep reacting negatively to you or acting overly sensitive. Be aware of the type of judgments you form regarding other people, and you will gain some insight into what is causing stress at the moment.

8. WEDNESDAY. Constructive. A bonus from work might help you reach your savings goal quicker than you thought possible. A plan to redecorate your home can come together, boosting your pride and self-esteem. If you take on a large-scale project, you can be assured of success. A tendency toward compulsive behavior could be your downfall with friends and family members. You may find yourself arguing over something you don't even understand or care about. For Libras living with a parent, this is the perfect time to start looking for a place of your own. You will benefit from making your own way in the world, which will give you the space to grow and experiment with your desires.

9. THURSDAY. Varied. Watch your urge to splurge when shopping. You won't be able to accept an invitation to a special social event without some cash in your wallet. If an opportunity to showcase your talents materializes, be prepared to take full advantage. A close friend can ask you for a loan and get quite upset if you say no. Unfortunately you will then have found out how shallow the friendship really is. Your communication skills shine at the moment, and you might be asked to become a trainer in an area of your expertise. Jump at this offer, which you will find to be a wonderful way to earn a living and become your own boss, doing what you love.

10. FRIDAY. Informative. A colleague might offer some very valuable advice. If they have walked in your path, you can be sure they know what they are talking about. A romance may start in the workplace, but be extra careful to keep it low-key during work hours in order to save yourselves a lot of trouble and avoid untrue gossip. Libras involved in the theater could be offered a starring role. If this suits you perfectly, you can't go wrong. Although it may only be a start, there is the promise of a great and long career ahead. Mercury, the planet of communication, moves retrograde now, causing problems and delays in business dealings, agreements, and contracts.

11. SATURDAY. Demanding. Quarreling with the family can try your patience and stir up all sorts of emotions that you find hard to control let alone understand. If you write down your thoughts you might gain some insight. However, while you remain at home it will be impossible to disentangle yourself from the arguments. The chance to learn to play a musical instrument can be the beginning of a lifetime pursuit that brings pleasure and peace of mind. Work is apt to become busy, offering you the chance to work overtime and earn some extra money. The longer and harder you work, the more benefits you will accrue. A relative might pass on a family heirloom that you will value for life.

12. SUNDAY. Testing. A difficult situation can test your diplomatic skills. As a Libra you are valued for your tact and compromise. But sometimes no amount of these talents can sway an excessive and determined individual. Your work might take you out into the community, giving you a change of pace that you will enjoy. If you are out on the road traveling, get a satellite navigation system to eliminate the stress of finding your way around in unknown areas. No matter how much you are doing on the job, don't slack off. Your employer is bound to be watching and may even be on the lookout for an up-and-coming employee to take over an impending vacancy.

13. MONDAY. Expansive. Opportunities to broaden your horizons are becoming available. Don't let small details deter you. Look at the big picture and opt to be a part of it. A position in a different division of your company might seem out of your league, but your reputation is likely to precede you. Or your good results may impress a superior so much that they create a new position just for you. The sky is the limit; be adventurous and ready to try anything. This is a time to take extra care with your diet, especially steering clear of foods high in cholesterol. Impulse buying can set you back and put you in the red for months to come. Shop with a list, and stick to it.

14. TUESDAY. Tricky. As a Libra you excel at compromise. Even if your own thoughts and feelings are at odds, you can gain understanding and insight into a personal matter. Business negotiations can be tricky. If you are dealing with a customer who is very aware of all the legal innuendos, obtain legal advice of your own to protect your interests. Allow plenty of time to arrive at an appointment because there could be unusual delays on the roads. Your mate or partner might make what you consider unreasonable demands or an ultimatum. If you are prepared to talk, listen, and be open to new ideas, you can work through the problem and come out feeling closer than ever before.

15. WEDNESDAY. Mixed. You may feel an odd disharmony within yourself. Or you may feel that the people around you don't care for you in the way you desire and that you are alone. This might be a signal that you need to value and love yourself more, which will build your own self-esteem. On this day of consolidation you need to just settle down and do your work. A shopping trip could be disappointing. If something you wanted to purchase is too expensive, check the Internet and also ask around; somebody may want to sell what you want, and in hardly used condition. A toothache should be taken care of before it gets any worse; as it is, the pain could be limiting your enjoyment of life.

16. THURSDAY. Supportive. Shrewd money management will help you get ahead and stay there. Open communication with your loved one or partner can ensure reaching an agreement on money matters. A joint goal can now seem closer than you previously thought. Lay plans for your mutual future and together you should have no trouble reaching them. The organization of a family get-together could be a logistical nightmare, but don't stress; leave it up to the individuals to organize themselves. So long as the venue is set it will all come together. There is a compassionate note to the day, and social events should be lots of fun. If you are dreading a business meeting, you might get a pleasant surprise.

17. FRIDAY. Variable. The morning hours could be fraught with frustrations and unexpected delays. A coworker can cause all sorts of problems between management and workers. If this upset involves a health and safety issue, you might have to go home and lose half a day's pay. The afternoon should be much better, especially if a love affair consumes most of your thoughts. News of an inheritance can cheer you up and help you feel more confident. Some much needed help is available from family members, so don't try to do everything alone. If you get bogged down and need assistance, just ask and let someone get the pleasure of doing a good turn.

18. SATURDAY. Challenging. With the holiday season in full swing, it will be hard not to get frazzled trying to find a parking place or just coping with the stress. Be prepared for things to go wrong this morning. Continually do an inventory of important items to avoid losing something of value. Problems with government officials are also indicated. Stick to the speed limit while driving and follow all rules and regulations of the road. An insurance claim can be more trouble than it is worth, with many forms to fill out. However, if you persevere you will be happy with the outcome. A romantic evening is assured if you get out of your local neighborhood and dine at a restaurant offering different cuisine and surroundings.

19. SUNDAY. Stimulating. No matter what other people tell you, stick with your own personal values and beliefs, and keep life simple. Go for relaxation when making plans. Steer clear of situations where you will encounter too many cooks in the kitchen. Be independent in all your plans. If you can get around on foot, so much the better. A musical performance or an interesting play would make for fantastic entertainment this evening. If you have kids, a pantomime would weave its magic and inspire them. A local crafts market might have some great offerings that allow you to finish off your gift shopping with some original local treasures rather than standard mall fare.

20. MONDAY. Successful. A lot can be achieved if you take one step at a time and avoid excess. A philosophical attitude is best: win some, lose some. Self-employed Libras might find it hard to divide time between work and family. Try not to let some important work slip by due to extra pressure at home; set some time aside this evening to catch up. Take care to avoid communication mix-ups. If your computer is not performing at its best, have it repaired and restored before you lose some important data. Don't let upsets ruffle your calm exterior. Drinks after work could become an all-night session, so take a rain check. Keep your name out of office gossip.

21. TUESDAY. Interesting. This is a good time not only to think outside the box but to consider tossing the box in the garbage. A feeling of vitality and openness makes it easier to meet new people, share ideas, and find the humor in life. Passions can become a little excessive. If you don't consciously practice your Libra tact and diplomacy, you could come to loggerheads with a member of the family. Traditions seem important to you right now. But if someone doesn't want to fit in with it, then you are going to have to compromise. Holiday shopping can be fun, and you might come up with unforgettable and imaginative gift ideas. Get the whole family involved in some over-the-top home decorating.

22. WEDNESDAY. Fulfilling. Your reserved, responsible side takes the lead, and you will be out to get what's best for you and yours. You are popular with friends and associates. Your employer might pick you to handle a situation. Whether it is sealing a business deal or a human relations matter, you are bound to show competency that will put you in line for a promotion. When accepting tasks, be mindful not to overload yourself with so much that you can't give your best and also enjoy the day. If a relative asks for a favor that is not reasonable, you should have no qualms about telling them so. Compromise is a two-sided proposition.

23. THURSDAY. Hectic. Impulsive action could put you in the hot seat. Also be prepared for the unexpected as a way to guard against accidents and maintain safety. Phone calls, correspondence, and e-mails may take half the day to deal with, along with people knocking on your door. If you are serious about getting work done, hang a do-not-disturb sign on the door. Family matters take priority today. Your plans for the festive season may have to be revised due to an unforeseen problem. Don't let the stress and overload frazzle you. If you sit down and work through each situation one at a time, you will find the perfect solution.

24. FRIDAY. Positive. Your home and family are especially important to you at this time of the year. You might be busy organizing a large social event in your home. You are likely to go over the top with anything and everything at the moment, so get other people involved and delegate for the sake of your back. Good entertainment should be at the top of your list. If you are not getting tickets to a mainline event, you might have performers come to your home to make your party one to remember. An elderly relative may need some of your time. You can pick up great information listening to their tales of tradition and family. A business deal could be causing frustration, and your best bet is to postpone settlement until the New Year.

25. SATURDAY. Merry Christmas! Close family ties are important today. You may have a family member away overseas whose absence is felt by all. Or it may be that you are away and are feeling the distance between you and your roots on this important day. Some Libras will have traveled many miles to be with loved ones and share in the festive tradition. Also celebrate memories from past holiday gatherings. Whatever your activities on this day, you are likely to be in a reflective mood. Think about those who are less fortunate than you. Getting involved in charity work can help ease some of the suffering in the world. Be sure to express thanks for all gifts, even those you plan to secretly return.

26. SUNDAY. Caring. A relative who is in the hospital or confined at home would appreciate a visit from you. If they are not very well, just sitting with them will be good for what ails them. There may be a communication breakdown via the Internet or phone line that keeps you from talking with loved ones who are at a distance. At least put your thoughts in a letter, especially thanks for a gift, and send it snail mail. There is a lot of energy in the air as the Moon makes friendly contact with Mars and Venus, and the harmonious vibes will be all pervasive. Sales might entice you to part with some of your cash, but be prepared for crowds. You actually might prefer peace and quiet, even solitude now.

27. MONDAY. Exuberant. Extra work can get you up before dawn, and the knowledge of the extra cash can be invigorating, making for fun and friendliness on the job. By lunchtime the Moon moves into your own sign of Libra and highlights your emotional side, putting you in the mood for a little pampering and self-nurturing. Make yourself number one on your gift list and go get what you want. Creativity and art can inspire you. If you are starting to feel down and are getting caught up in petty obsessions, later in the day treat yourself to a concert or art exhibit to take your mind off negatives. Stock up the kitchen because you are likely to have unexpected visitors.

28. TUESDAY. Excellent. With the Moon rising in your sign of Libra, you are at your best, full of charm, friendliness, and hospitality. However, you won't put up with fools. If someone tries your patience, you will stop them short. This might upset some friends who aren't used to you being assertive, but you have every right to expect respect. A new association can introduce you to a different crowd of people with new and fascinating interests. Look your best going out on the town because the chance of meeting someone who arouses passion and romance is high tonight. You might be attracted to your boss or another higher-up, then happily discover that the feeling is mutual. But make sure this person is free and available before you become involved.

29. WEDNESDAY. Fair. Your laid-back, detached attitude might make it so hard to keep up with your busy schedule that you wish you could take the day off and watch movies from the couch. The boss could be in a slave-driving mood and really get you annoyed, making it hard to keep your mind on doing a good job. However, sitting around and complaining with other coworkers could cost you your job or a promotion. The occult might interest you. A tarot or psychic reading could be very informative, giving you a glimpse of future portents. A pet might slip away and lead you a merry chase around the neighborhood, but you will manage to bring it home again. Get to bed early tonight.

30. THURSDAY. Helpful. Pay attention to your bills and catch up with any that will soon be due. If you are having trouble paying, call to try to arrange an extension so that you avoid late penalties. A credit card debt can be accruing more interest than you can stay up with; again, try to negotiate a reduced interest rate. From the company's view, some return is better than none. Dissatisfaction with your job could lead to checking out training courses to see if there is one that will get you into a career that you would enjoy. If it is low pay that rankles you, start looking for a new job by putting your resume in the hands of a good employment agency.

31. FRIDAY. Social. Art, beauty, nature, and spiritual pursuits will attract your attention. An outing to the mall can turn up something special to decorate your home and also add to your investments. Friends should be in abundance. You might drop in on one of them who is having a hard time, just to let them know you care and to cheer them up by listening. You are bound to be invited to a socially significant and exciting New Year's celebration and will want to wear something that highlights your best attributes. Being moderate with what you eat and drink will lead to a great night and to meeting interesting people, with no regrets in the morning.

LIBRA
NOVEMBER–DECEMBER 2009

November 2009

1. SUNDAY. Taxing. Life could be a little stressful but only if you allow problems to weigh you down. You might think it is best to say exactly what you think, but this isn't the case. It would be wiser to choose your words carefully. If there is a concern about money, it is pointless worrying about how you are going to pay upcoming expenses. Instead, take a proactive approach by recording all income and expenditure to see where cost cutting can be most effective. If planning an outing with friends, make sure everyone knows beforehand about entertainment expenses to avoid objections regarding their fair share.

2. MONDAY. Upsetting. Disruption arrives today, although it isn't all bad news. Your ruler Venus is wearing rose-colored glasses, awakening your emotional side as she showers love and romance in her wake. This is a good time to pop that all-important question. Or you may receive a special ring as a token of love. The Taurus Full Moon can bring you back to earth with a thud as financial problems have to be sorted out. Libras employed in the field of finances, including debt collection, should be prepared to listen to rude and cranky customers sound off. Promises of any kind are not reliable.

3. TUESDAY. Demanding. Money is again the main priority. There may be a pressing need to complete a tax return or other financial paperwork. If this task is outstanding, take action now to lessen the chance of a fine. A relationship could have you highly emotional, but this isn't the time to make any concrete decision or choices. If your energy is drained due to the pressure of too many obligations, duties, or demands of loved ones, consider taking frequent breaks to clear your head. An unexpected gift or compliment should restore your good humor this evening.

4. WEDNESDAY. Expansive. Consider learning a foreign language if this will help you move up the career ladder. Libras who are involved in overseas trading, political interests, or public relations should make excellent progress. A legal decision could be in your favor. However, don't refuse to accept an out-of-court settlement if this would save you or a family member a lot of stress and strain. Meeting a romantic potential from another country could be a highlight for singles, and love on the high seas is possible for the traveling Libra. Exotic fare might appeal to your taste buds this evening, so book a table at an ethnic restaurant and savor tantalizing flavors from another country or culture.

5. THURSDAY. Excellent. Libra folks will be on the financial ball as the Sun meets up with alert Mercury. Your ability for organization and to get everyone working together enhances your profile. Very little will escapes your eagle eye. One problem could be nonstop interruptions from visitors or phone calls, reducing your productivity unless you lock the office and hide away. You have what it takes to excel in an individual sport or a team event, earning better than expected results. Seriously consider an offer to go into business with a relative, which may provide the independence you currently seek.

6. FRIDAY. Satisfactory. Advice, whether solicited or not, from those closest to you might not be what you want to hear but is nevertheless worth listening to. You don't have to rush ahead with a decision. First weigh all your options, which is something Libra folks are very good at doing. At last pressure is easing and creative juices should again flow freely now that Neptune, planet of inspiration, is moving forward again in Aquarius, your house of artistic expression and talents. A sponsorship deal that has been held up, news relating to exhibiting or publishing your work, or a romance that has been stalled could benefit and advance thanks to this cosmic change.

7. SATURDAY. Fine. Be discerning if shopping for electronic products or communication equipment. Check out warranties thoroughly, and compare prices to get the best deal. Libras who are at work should enjoy being singled out for special mention by the boss or another supervisor. There might even be mention of a pay increase or extra benefits coming your way. Luscious Venus joins the Sun to grace your Scorpio sector of material assets and finances. Venus in Scorpio enhances your ability to attract more money as well as the beautiful things of life. Desiring additional comfort, pleasure, and goodies has a downside, however, because spending more than you can afford is likely.

8. SUNDAY. Manageable. Look before you leap, and beware of promising more than you may be able to comfortably deliver. Minor irritations could grow into large annoyances unless you maintain a calm, cool demeanor. Restrictions abound, with energy slightly under par. This suggests a rest rather than running all over would be of benefit. Prudence is in order. Putting money in a savings account could be the best way to begin managing the future instead of heading off to the boutiques or music store. A speech or public address could be enlightening when it comes to trouble in your community or the wider world.

9. MONDAY. Exciting. Love and romance permeate the air as sexy Venus ignites passionate Pluto. The next few days is a perfect period to make romantic plans, arrange a honeymoon, or plan a sensuous candlelight dinner for two. Splurging on fancy luxury items could be difficult to avoid unless you exercise extra willpower. Friends or associates may let you down, so if plans depend on them be prepared to be left to your own devices. Self-employed Libras or contractors who haven't increased fees for their services for some time should consider doing so now. The currently single can expect a dynamic new attraction.

10. TUESDAY. Moderate. Find a quiet place so you can spend some time in solitude. Although as a Libra you are a social sign, you realize the value of peace and tranquillity. Being alone provides the chance to contemplate life in your own good time, without distractions and interruptions. Although your intentions may be exemplary, expectations of what you and others are capable of achieving may be too high right now. A moderate approach needs to be taken. The inclination to eat and drink to excess must be curtailed or it could result in health problems now or in the future. Care with credit is advised. Be sure to include a few early relaxing evenings in your busy schedule over the ensuing weeks.

11. WEDNESDAY. Bumpy. This could be a trying, tiring, but exciting day as Mercury makes a positive connection with erratic Uranus and debates dreamy Neptune. Although major decision making isn't recommended, procrastination by other people could lead to frustration and annoyance. Concentration is limited as restlessness takes hold. The tendency to daydream instead of mentally focusing could cause problems. Spend some time composing a love song or painting an original masterpiece rather than trying to make sense of facts, figures, and an overload of demands and requests. Plan to do something totally different from your usual Wednesday night routine.

12. THURSDAY. Calm. With the Moon still gliding through your Virgo house of solitude, you will still prefer peace and serenity at least until lunchtime. Until then watch and wait rather than beginning any new project or moving into action. Emotions might be close to the surface and could spill over at any time. Virgo is the sign of service par excellence. However, with the Moon here a fussy or pedantic attitude is often seen, which could get people's backs up and create upsets or tension. Later in the day good humor and the urge to socialize return with a vengeance. Take time to pamper yourself without feeling guilty, especially if this is not your normal habit.

13. FRIDAY. Promising. There isn't any need to worry about today's date. Apart from a few minor obstacles, the day should hum along nicely. If you enter a competition, purchase a raffle ticket, or play the lottery you could be surprised by luck turning in your favor. A unique and challenging personal undertaking might be just what you need to display your capabilities to one or more important people. A sudden rise in responsibilities could mean you have to make some minor adjustments. Reschedule where you can to reduce the possibility of stress due to work overload. Social plans this evening should be memorable.

14. SATURDAY. Adaptable. A flexible approach can assist your efforts to overcome hurdles and stay on your chosen path. Before making any financial decisions, consider all of your options and think them through thoroughly. This is an excellent period to research methods of increasing income and reducing expenditure. Your positive spirit and determined effort will be rewarded. Extra exertion to promote your skills and expertise can produce financial advantages. If attempting to demonstrate your talent to the public at large, consider hiring an agent or management team to publicize your work or products.

15. SUNDAY. Exacting. A major planetary pattern has formed in the cosmic sky. Libra folks could be experiencing limitations and transformation of personal desires and ambitions. In addition, unsettling situations are apt to be occurring around home base. To cope with current influences, altering your outlook and perspective is required. Although this is a time of change, don't be persuaded by other people to follow their wishes if this is contrary to your desires. Money that comes in quickly is likely to go out in the same manner unless you can stem the flow and tighten the money drain. Check out the credentials of those with whom you conduct business; taking people at face value is not advisable right now.

16. MONDAY. Renewing. Enjoy today's more optimistic atmosphere. Mercury, planet of information, is now residing in Sagittarius, highlighting your solar sector of short travel and all forms of communication. A business trip to add contacts and customers should lead to desired results, with an increase in sales and goodwill. Be careful of a get-rich proposal around midday. Forget about gambling or playing any games of chance, or prepare to be parted from your hard-earned cash. A New Moon in Scorpio, your personal financial house, increases your focus on monetary matters. Over the next two weeks take the opportunity to implement new financial ventures and projects.

17. TUESDAY. Disciplined. Ambition and self-control are gifts now promised. Dreams and desires currently being sought could be found where never expected. This is a great day to practice your listening skills. If you are ready to engage in serious discussion with a relative, the stars are supporting your endeavor. Praise for your efforts could come from those higher up the ladder than you, which can be a wonderful boost to your self-confidence. Choose companions who are likely to talk about serious, deep topics rather than merely gossip. You will consider petty issues not worthy of your attention.

18. WEDNESDAY. Active. The atmosphere should be more easygoing today, with Scales optimistic and energetic. A brisk stroll around the neighborhood could get your heart pumping and provide an opportunity to increase your fitness level. If you are not on the job, a gossip session with friends or neighbors could put you in a good frame of mind. Running errands and performing personal tasks might have you on the go. The organized Libra could begin sourcing gifts, cards, and decorations to get ready for the upcoming festive season. A romantic interlude this evening can round off the day nicely, or you might prefer to curl up on the couch with a new novel or DVD.

19. THURSDAY. Passionate. Unless activity involves romance, you probably won't be in the mood for anything too strenuous or demanding. Affectionate Venus is in conflict with assertive Mars, creating tension in your love life. A committed relationship could be tested, challenging the depth of your union. With passion more likely to be on display than affection, couples shouldn't have any trouble adding extra zest in the bedroom. Libras who are in a blossoming new love affair should guard against comparing an old flame with a new one, which will only create tension and dissatisfaction. Being surrounded by those you love most will appeal this evening.

20. FRIDAY. Fair. A number of obstacles are slowing progress, but these are only minor and can be quickly and easily overcome. You may find it difficult to please yourself, let alone others, unless you are in familiar surroundings performing routine tasks. Puttering around at home, cleaning, making minor repairs, and focusing on household chores can be a positive way to utilize current cosmic forces. It might be time to begin cooking and baking and planning for the festive season. Emotional happiness and contentment come from being with family members, so opt for a night at home if possible instead of hectic socializing on the town.

21. SATURDAY. Happy. If your relationship with a family member has been a bit difficult, finding a way to overcome grievances and feel more comfortable should be easier now. A child could be anxious for your attention, which may add extra pressure to your already overloaded schedule. Giving your undivided attention at least for a short period can be helpful. By midnight tonight the Sun will enter the sign of Sagittarius, joining Mercury there until December 21. This provides you with the opportunity to meet and mingle with friends you haven't seen for some time. Socializing moves into top gear as you head into the holiday period.

22. SUNDAY. Enjoyable. A mini sabbatical could appeal this morning. Catching up on your beauty sleep or cuddling in bed can be the perfect beginning to the day. With socializing playing a major role in your life over the next few weeks, this is the time to make plans and become well organized. Bright ideas should be flowing freely, which will help with the many upcoming tasks that need a unique, creative touch. Purchasing gifts, arranging an end-of-year party, or planning a gathering of family members and friends will benefit from your original thoughts. The mood to party carries into activities planned for today, and whatever event you attend should bring pleasure.

23. MONDAY. Cautious. Remain clam and handle one task at a time. There is a lot to fit into your schedule, but rushing around in an uproar will just make matters worse rather than easier. When your ruler Venus is in dispute with excessive Jupiter, the word moderation needs to be clearly etched into your memory. Otherwise you could spend a small fortune without realizing it on food, alcohol, and entertainment. Postpone shopping for gifts; an overly generous attitude could increase the temptation to buy more than you intend. Delays or disappointment regarding a friend could overshadow a planned social event.

24. TUESDAY. Opportune. Life has a lot to offer to those born under the sign of Libra. Patience and self-discipline are abundant. Past efforts and accomplishments may be recognized, raising both your confidence and profile. Methodical planning can be the best way to obtain what is required. Progress comes through practical endeavors. The motivation to set goals and act on tasks that you would normally ignore moves to another level. Take the opportunity to go on a road trip with friends; you never know where this could lead, either now or sometime in the future. Social connections could be particularly useful, and mixing business with pleasure should add more dollars to your bank balance.

25. WEDNESDAY. Pleasant. A sociable, fun-loving frame of mind arrives with the advent of saucy Venus happily linked to excitable Uranus. Expect to receive a pleasant surprise some time within the next few days. For some Libras a marriage proposal could bring a thrill of anticipation. An intimate meeting this evening could excite the currently unattached. However, this is a time to enjoy the moment without holding out hopes of a long-lasting relationship. There is a possibility that a friendship could begin to have romantic overtones. If this is what you desire, it is time to make the first move. Good luck abounds, and finances should be looking up.

26. THURSDAY. Volatile. Conditions do an abrupt turn when it comes to love and money. In romance it is now time to proceed slowly and remove those rose-colored glasses. With a difficult contact between seductive Venus and foggy Neptune, senses and sensibility can be clouded. If in doubt, do nothing at all. Deceitful maneuvers by other people need to be guarded against. Your judgment may not be very sound. Avoid the temptation of shopping in stores that are open. An impractical mood makes you an obvious target. Creative activities will be fueled by the combination of raw talent, inspiration, and enthusiasm, leading to greater output and productivity. Enjoy a get-together, but don't promise anything to anyone.

27. FRIDAY. Tense. Libra folk need all the patience that you can muster now. Other people are unlikely to be cooperative, and a team effort that appeared to be moving along smoothly could come to a grinding halt. Mediation or compromise may be required before relationships can be put back on track. Be firm and sure about what you are seeking in a relationship. Avoid conveying mixed messages to your significant other. If you are not seeing eye-to-eye with a personal or business partner, it might be because one of you wants to handle things differently from the way they were done in the past. Initiate a discussion so you can talk about the best direction to take.

28. SATURDAY. Smooth. If you stay calm and centered, positive results can be achieved. With the lunar goddess sending mainly positive vibes, life should become easier as confusion and uncertainty regarding home and love life begin to disappear. With a sense of direction regained, and confidence in your own ability returning, this is the time to sort out money issues, research investment opportunities, and prepare to move into a better personal space. A shopping trip with your significant other or a friend can be fun, and you should do well when it comes to picking up quality items at bargain prices. A social occasion certainly shouldn't be dull or boring.

29. SUNDAY. Interesting. This is another day when there should be plenty of reasons to smile. An easygoing mood increases your charm and personality. Spending time with favorite people will enhance your enjoyment of the day. With abundant luck shining your way, you are likely to be in the right place at the right time. Any involvement with communication, from public speaking to writing out greeting cards, should proceed well. If you should need to talk your way out of a tight situation, you shouldn't experience any problems. It will be essential to keep all dealings aboveboard and avoid any dangerous areas.

30. MONDAY. Erratic. As the month winds down, you may feel you have been on a roller-coaster ride, with as many ups as downs. This trend continues today as talkative Mercury disputes with erratic Uranus. This is exactly how you may feel toward those who never stop talking or don't know when enough is more than enough. Restlessness and indecision peak, and negative or insensitive comments could test your patience. Don't take matters personally and, if possible, look on the funny side. Tomorrow a more peaceful atmosphere should prevail. Avoid haste, drive slowly, and walk instead of running.

December 2009

1. TUESDAY. Restless. Although the beginning of this month should flow quite smoothly, this is one of those days when you may feel unsettled and restless without knowing why. Dissatisfaction with the way your life is heading might be the cause. Adding variety to your daily routine can break the tedium and increase your enjoyment of looking forward to each day. If your love life has been a little up and down recently, it should now begin to settle down. With the transit of Venus in Sagittarius, your third house, from now until December 25, communication and interaction with friends and children should be more joyous than usual.

2. WEDNESDAY. Sensitive. Scales are likely to be in a hurry today, with one eye on the clock and the other on the overflowing in-basket. If you are trying to meet a deadline, take into account that the Full Moon is culminating in Gemini, increasing not only your sensitive feelings but those of everyone else in close proximity to you. This is an excellent period to complete a special project, sales report, or book manuscript. Keep an open mind and be receptive to other people's points of view. Uranus, the planet of originality, has now moved forward in the Pisces house of work, service, and health, so changes can be expected in some of these areas. Unsettling rumors that have been circulating on the job could be officially refuted, giving you an increased sense of security.

3. THURSDAY. Opportune. A much more relaxing day is likely, although you will be inclined to put extra effort in the career and professional arena. A business meeting can be informative and productive, with a number of nagging issues discussed and resolved. Valuable data could be received from a mentor, which may be the encouragement you need to look for a better paying position that also increases job satisfaction. Singles should not object if a friend wants to play matchmaker; a romantic opportunity could develop through such an introduction. Lucky Libras will be given lots of love and warmth and encouragement at home.

4. FRIDAY. Positive. Your ruler Venus happily connects with serious Saturn, bringing a practical, structured, realistic tone to romance and to fiscal management. During the next few days Libra shoppers will be determined to get value for money and will be more discerning with all purchases. In a discussion with an older relative, listen carefully. You could hear information that is transforming, setting you on a more positive path. The ties of love are strong. Libras who are in a new relationship should not be surprised if it takes on a more serious tone. This is a good time to consider beginning a family or adding a pet to your household.

5. SATURDAY. Buoyant. Love and blessings continue to surround you. Enrolling in a short course can increase your knowledge and expertise. In addition, it might be the meeting place for the unattached to find a romantic potential. Formulating plans for a child's education could keep Libra parents positively occupied. A major purchase can bring loads of enjoyment for the whole family. Mercury, planet of information, slips into Capricorn, your zone of home and family, which will focus attention on the domestic quarters. If you have plans to redecorate, look for inspirational ideas in magazines or on Internet sites catering in particular to homeowners.

6. SUNDAY. Enjoyable. You will enjoy a change of scenery. If you have been rushing around, socializing, shopping, and trying to keep on top of a heavy schedule, this is the time to do something that pleases you. Get out and about and you may even find a new haunt or store that you haven't noticed before. A friendship might be a little rocky, no longer delivering the companionship and comfort that it once did; don't feel guilty. People come in and out of your life for a reason, so just move on, cultivating new friends who fit into your current lifestyle. If you haven't brought out festive decorations for your home, now would be a good time to start. Take advantage of the party season and have fun.

7. MONDAY. Revealing. Your deep, penetrating mind combined with enhanced verbal skills will be of great assistance if you are giving a speech, delivering a lecture, or presenting a special honor. If you have a complaint that needs to be addressed, go right to the top person. Compassion could be hard to muster for someone you feel is not making the most of opportunities offered. However, you might need to put these thoughts aside and provide guidance and wisdom. Tact and diplomacy are in ample supply, helping to phrase your thoughts in the best way. This is a great time to visit a holistic healer or alternative therapist to obtain help with an ongoing ailment or to keep your body in top shape.

8. TUESDAY. Manageable. If a cloud descends on you today, rest and relaxation may be something you aim for but are unlikely to achieve. Although your Libra mental alertness remains accentuated, you might be inclined to ask awkward questions or suffer from foot-in-mouth disease. This could easily occur if anger or frustration overcomes you, so do your best to remain cool and detached. This should reduce the possibility of embarrassing yourself or someone else. Working on a project in secret can provide a great deal of satisfaction. A long soak in a warm bath before going to bed could be the perfect end to this tricky day.

9. WEDNESDAY. Vexing. Unhelpful cosmic influences prevail. The sensitive mood makes this a difficult day, at least until late in the afternoon. Escape from pent-up stress by going for a walk around the block, meditating, or finding a place where you can chill out for a little while. For most of the working day you will want to shun social activities and mixing with other people because the preference to work alone is strong. A change of plans could find you committed to finalizing a project that has been on the back burner for some time. An ongoing health condition could reappear, signaling that it is time to do something constructive about the problem now, not later.

10. THURSDAY. Vital. Although you could wake up feeling a little weary, a burst of vitality will fuel your motivation and drive. You could even help someone in bad humor become happy. Put this influx of energy into the right medium, which could include pursuing a personal ambition, achieving a cherished goal, or playing a competitive sport. Status improves as other people notice your achievements. Praise for your efforts from a superior could also include an incentive to keep up the good work or a bonus recognizing current accomplishments. Make evening plans that include getting together with friends.

11. FRIDAY. Bumpy. Imagination combined with insecurity could get the better of you. With tricky Mercury rubbing Neptune the wrong way, concentration and confidence are apt to take a plunge. The tendency to daydream rises. Instead of focusing on tasks at hand, your head may be in the clouds, which could bring the wrath of a superior. Be on guard for cheats, scammers, and double-dealers. If something looks too good to be true, it probably is. Whatever way a situation develops right now, someone is going to wind up disgruntled or disappointed. Although Libra intuition is enhanced, acting on a hunch would not be a bright move now.

12. SATURDAY. Fulfilling. The focus turns to ways to improve your financial situation and increase security. The urge to spend on loved ones could be the signal to begin or finish festive shopping. You have the intuitive ability to know what each of your nearest and dearest desires. An unusual purchase could turn out to be a collector's item, worth every cent you pay. There may be a chance to reignite a relationship with someone who has drifted away. Or ongoing difficulties with a friend could be resolved to everyone's satisfaction, with no more hard feelings standing in the way of an enduring friendship. Love and friendship are the perfect mix.

13. SUNDAY. Surprising. Breakfast in bed courtesy of your significant other would be a terrific beginning to this busy day. Tricky trends prevail, suggesting it would be wise to keep a low profile if possible. Decorating the house, writing out greeting cards, or preparing festive food may be the most productive way to keep busy and away from the firing line. A dispute about money could erupt when someone objects to what they consider an unfair distribution of household funds. Although this might not be a pleasant discussion, it would be better to bring the matter out into the open to reduce the chance of escalating resentment. Someone could give you a special treat or surprise gift.

14. MONDAY. Mixed. Ambiguous trends are in play as the Sun challenges erratic Uranus and smiles at abundant Jupiter. As a Libra you should thrive on the ensuing activity and disruptions that are likely throughout the day. However, there should be an equal amount of good luck, raising your spirits and adding pleasure to whatever you undertake. It could be all too easy to jump to conclusions based on biased or inaccurate information, so don't accept what you hear without first checking the facts. Remain optimistic, but beware becoming overly confident. A big ego will not serve you well.

15. TUESDAY. Creative. Take full advantage of current celestial trends which heighten insight, sensitivity, and understanding. Awareness of your own special talents can help you shine through in a magical way. With strong imagination and the ability to mentally visualize, any work that needs a special touch should progress well. Events should move in your favor. Success can come from converting people to your way of thinking. Your focus might not be strong, so minimize the possibility of errors by delaying filling out an application, sending important e-mails, or writing business letters. If you are considering resigning from your current position, postpone this action unless the decision was made some time ago.

16. WEDNESDAY. Exciting. You may receive good news, or someone may sing your praises. A long-awaited invitation can add excitement. You could finally acquire something desired for a long time. The New Moon in the sign of freedom-loving Sagittarius puts an extra spring in your step and a song in your heart. The way you communicate is in the spotlight. This is a time that messages can be conveyed in a powerful and positive way. Contact neighbors and relatives if you haven't been in a touch for a while. Finish writing cards, letters, and e-mails to the special people in your life.

17. THURSDAY. Fervent. Sexual energy is strong and focused as a romantic haze drifts pleasingly across the Libra landscape. Amorous Venus smiles at passionate Mars, signaling that this is the time to experience fun and enjoyment. It's the season to be merry, and although you may be in a frenzy with domestic chores and family demands, make time to strengthen loving bonds with your significant other. Roll up your sleeves and prepare for guests, finish small decorating chores, and discard clutter in your living quarters. If a new car is on your wish list, this is a good day to search for the perfect new set of wheels.

18. FRIDAY. Active. High spirits continue, although if you have thoughts of taking it easy these may be dashed. Even if a mountain of work is awaiting your attention, the industrious Capricorn Moon provides the energy to handle numerous tasks before festive celebrating gets under way. Listen to what a friend has to say; their words could have a very positive impact on your future plans. A sensitive family issue could be resolved during dinner, clearing the way for a happier remainder of the month. Home should be a haven. Don't feel guilty if you prefer family company instead of performing household chores.

19. SATURDAY. Intriguing. The sky is awash with planetary action. The indomitable duo of lover Venus and erotic Uranus is likely to wreak havoc on the love scene. This could further shake up an already rocky relationship. Beware thinking that the grass is greener, behavior that can lead to problems you would be better off without. Guard against impulsive action, and don't get carried away and spend more than you intended. A strange experience is possible, so be prepared for the unexpected. Singles should investigate a new venue or meet-and-greet method in an attempt to get to know interesting new romantic possibilities.

20. SUNDAY. Restrained. Look forward to an extremely pleasant day. Make time to socialize. Your outgoing personality will make you a star among family members and friends. People are counting on you, and it is unlikely that you will let anyone down. Beware overly benevolent gestures, however. Your generosity may know no bounds, which will not be good news for your budget if you need to finish holiday shopping. It will be easy to go overboard; the temptation to splurge on luxury items could be hard to resist. With your ruler Venus happily entwined with Jupiter, the planet of excess, luck is on your side. However, moderation is still essential. Buy a lottery ticket, enter a raffle, or take some other small risk; you may be very glad you did.

21. MONDAY. Dreamy. A wistful atmosphere prevails, making this the sort of day that romantic Libras love. It is an especially good time to be with your nearest and dearest, so you might prefer to remain at home rather than venturing outside. With your creative imagination extremely high, you can complete tasks that need an artistic touch. You may tend to take on too many responsibilities which could cause stress, so remember to pace yourself. The Sun now visits the sign of Capricorn, shining the spotlight on your home and family sector. You will probably prefer to entertain in the comfort of your own home rather than socializing in a public place.

22. TUESDAY. Hectic. Duty calls. If you will be hosting a holiday meal, make final preparations, stock up the fridge and pantry, and be sure you have enough chairs for your guests. There is a danger of going overboard with lavish catering and expensive gifts, so ask yourself if you can really afford to be so generous and whether it is necessary to do so. A pet could be the perfect present for someone who is alone, lonely, or has hinted about getting one. Even a goldfish in a bowl will give pleasure and comfort to a special person. Allowing youngsters to have some say in planning the holiday period will increase their sense of responsibility and participation.

23. WEDNESDAY. Productive. Family members are probably relying on you, but try not to get too stressed. If are a large amount of tasks remain to be done, make a list of priorities and methodically work from the most important down. In that way essential chores will be completed. As a Libra you tend to prefer quality to quantity, and things should be looking up in that area. If you are in the mood to shop, unexpected bargains can be found, assisting the household budget and helping you to make the upcoming holidays a little bit more special. With the excitement of Christmas, baking traditional treats and wrapping presents can include the whole family. Be sure to include both young and old in your plans.

24. THURSDAY. Festive. A strong competitive nature is evident, so take action and seize opportunities that come your way. Libras who are on the job can make good headway. Your natural leadership qualities and assertiveness can assist your climb up the career ladder. Although this is a busy festive time, don't allow yourself to become a doormat to the demands and needs of other people. A frenetic atmosphere may prevail at home, and it might be difficult to avoid getting enmeshed in the power plays of others. Family traditions will come to the fore, adding a special touch to celebrations. Spiritual activities could appeal, and attending a candlelight service should delight family members of all ages.

25. FRIDAY. Happy Holiday! As with most planned events, not everything will flow exactly as you envisioned. There may be a few obstacles to overcome, but these can add to the collection of family memories and recollections. Don't attempt to do everything yourself if hosting guests. Your vim and vitality could be lower than usual, making everything seem just a little bit harder and more stressful. Pay special attention to elderly relatives to ensure they are included in all that's going on; otherwise complaints could be upsetting. Your ruler Venus spreads blessings over the day with her entrance into Capricorn, your family sector. So Libras should find that a mostly calm and peaceful atmosphere will prevail on this holiday.

26. SATURDAY. Useful. This day will be very much influenced by mischievous Mercury. From now until January 15 the messenger planet will be moving in retrograde motion through Capricorn, your sector of real estate and family activities. It would be wise to limit purchases to essential items only and nothing major. Signing property leases and legal documents can be risky unless you double-check them for errors and hidden clauses. The post-Christmas sales are likely to excite you, and there should be plenty of quality bargains to tempt the savvy Libra shopper. Consider your goals for 2010 and begin making a list.

27. SUNDAY. Chancy. Life can be a balancing act, and there is no one that understands that more than a Libra. Today you can begin to unwind after the recent hectic round of socializing. Tiredness and lack of energy could be the encouragement you need to take it easy and rest. Playing computer games, enjoying the last of the leftover festive fare, and relaxing with a good book may be preferred amusement for those without social plans. If tempers become frayed from being cooped up, take a walk to burn off stress. Someone may be in a hurry to receive a promised payment, so if you owe money either pay in full or set a definite time when you can do so.

28. MONDAY. Intense. Your ruler sets the tone of the day, merging with intense Pluto and glaring at warrior Mars. Passion and emotional intensity are in force, and it is essential to keep alert for the green eye of jealousy. It definitely is the day to make love, not war. Personal attachments are more meaningful now. Your significant other could feel threatened or might be uncharacteristically possessive and controlling. A public display of emotions could be embarrassing and awkward if the situation is allowed to get out of hand. Good news can bring happiness to the family. Libras who are trying to conceive or adopt may experience luck now.

29. TUESDAY. Subdued. A serious atmosphere pervades the air. Focus on necessary tasks. Be careful when dealing with women who are older than you. Love takes a backseat, which you will probably be unhappy about. The romantic energy in your current relationship could be blocked, or your mate or partner might not be as responsive as usual, but don't react negatively. These influences will pass in a few days, so be proactive and show by your actions how much you care. Studying in order to constructively use your spare time or to further career advancement can be productive, particularly if you are hoping to increase your income in the new year.

30. WEDNESDAY. Uncertain. Emotions could still be unclear now for Scales who are in a committed relationship. However, absence can make the heart grow fonder for those living apart from a significant other, and you could be intently experiencing these feelings now. If possible, get in touch via e-mail or phone so you can renew loving bonds. Making a decision as to how and where to celebrate New Year's Eve could be difficult for Libras, known as the procrastinators of the zodiac. It might be wiser to make up your mind tomorrow, when you have a clearer idea of what entertainment will offer the most fun.

31. THURSDAY. Disconcerting. The cosmic dance of the planets sends an interesting mix of influences to end the year, but most of these are unsupportive. If a work bonus is not as high as you expected, or a promised pay raise or promotion hasn't come through, don't approach the boss today because you'll only get the runaround. Libras on the job may be very pleased at the end of the day, after encountering more than a fair share of upsets. With an eclipsed Full Moon in Cancer, you can expect cranky, emotional people to be out in force. A get-together of family members and friends may be the best choice if you would prefer a sedate gathering this evening rather than a wild night on the town.

WHAT DOES YOUR FUTURE HOLD?

DISCOVER IT IN *ASTROANALYSIS*—

COMPLETELY REVISED THROUGH THE YEAR 2015, THESE GUIDES INCLUDE COLOR-CODED CHARTS FOR TOTAL ASTROLOGICAL EVALUATION, PLANET TABLES AND CUSP CHARTS, AND STREAMLINED INFORMATION.

ARIES	0-425-17558-8
TAURUS	0-425-17559-6
GEMINI	0-425-17560-X
CANCER	0-425-17561-8
LEO	0-425-17562-6
VIRGO	0-425-17563-4
LIBRA	0-425-17564-2
SCORPIO	0-425-17565-0
SAGITTARIUS	0-425-17566-9
CAPRICORN	0-425-17567-7
AQUARIUS	0-425-17568-5
PISCES	0-425-17569-3

Available wherever books are sold or at penguin.com

Maria Duval, the famous clairvoyant, is making you this unusual offer:

Choose from the 33 wishes below those you'd most like to see come true in your life NOW!

Maria Duval

Maria Duval, the famous clairvoyant and medium, is making you this strange and truly amazing offer. She is ready to help you to realize your Secret Wishes, the wishes you cherish most, FREE OF CHARGE. All you have to do is choose from the list of 33 Secret Wishes below those you'd most like to see come true in your life, and then leave the amazing "powers" of Maria Duval to do their work...

Please note: offer limited to only 7 Secret Wishes per person.

Then what is going to happen?

As soon as Maria Duval is in possession of your "Special Form for Fulfilling Your Wishes", she is going to perform, on your behalf, a ritual known only to her which should allow your Secret Wishes to come true. You will have absolutely nothing special to do, other than to follow the very simple instructions that she is going to send you in a large, discreet envelope.

Only a few days after receiving your big white envelope, you should see the first beneficial effects of this special help. Then your life will take a new and quite astonishing turn!

You can expect some real "MIRACLES!"

That's right, "miracles" are going to occur in your life once Maria Duval has performed (free of charge) this very special ritual that should allow your Secret Wishes – whichever they may be – to become a reality in your life. You probably won't be able to believe your eyes, but each of the wishes you have asked for should come true.

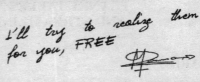

I'll try to realize them for you, FREE

Choose your 7 wishes NOW!

❏ 1. Win a lottery jackpot within a few weeks
❏ 2. Win a big prize ($10,000.00 minimum) on an instant-win scratch card
❏ 3. Win at the horse races
❏ 4. Immediately win a sum of money (indicate the amount you'd like to win on your special Form)
❏ 5. Have a monthly income of $10,000.00
❏ 6. Win everytime I go to the casino
❏ 7. Have enough money to buy a house
❏ 8. Sell or set up my own business
❏ 9. Get enough money to never have to work again
❏ 10. See my kids do really well in their studies
❏ 11. Get a new car
❏ 12. Travel around the world
❏ 13. Have enough money to help out my family
❏ 14. Make sure that my children and/or grandchildren have a happy life
❏ 15. Become the owner of properties that I could rent out
❏ 16. Succeed in an important exam or competition
❏ 17. Be the friend of wealthy people
❏ 18. Never have any more money problems
❏ 19. Buy a boat
❏ 20. Go on a cruise
❏ 21. Be and stay healthy

- ☐ 22. Have a country house
- ☐ 23. Get promoted at work
- ☐ 24. Find a job which is enjoyable and pays well
- ☐ 25. Find true love at last
- ☐ 26. Be madly loved by someone
- ☐ 27. Marry the person I love
- ☐ 28. Attract men
- ☐ 29. Attract women
- ☐ 30. Be on TV
- ☐ 31. Make new friends
- ☐ 32. Have more time to do things that I like
- ☐ 33. That my children have a substantial monthly income

So that's it! Have you chosen your 7 wishes? Then quickly complete the original of the Form below and return it without delay to Maria Duval.

Nothing to pay, everything is FREE!

Yes, Maria Duval wants to help you free of charge, and that's why she doesn't want any money in return for the help she's going to give you. All you need to do to benefit from Maria Duval's free help and to see your Secret Wishes coming true in your life is to simply indicate on your "Special Wish Fulfillment Form" the 7 Secret Wishes that you'd like Maria Duval to realize for you, and then return it as soon as possible to the following address:

Maria Duval c/o Destiny Research Center, 1285 Baring Blvd. #409, Sparks, NV 89434-8673.

Please, don't hesitate. Remember, you have nothing to lose, and EVERYTHING TO GAIN!

SPECIAL FORM FOR FULFILLING YOUR WISHES

Complete and return as soon as possible (by this evening, if possible) to:
Maria Duval c/o Destiny Research Center
1285 Baring Blvd. #409, Sparks, NV 89434-8673

YES, my dear Maria Duval, I accept your offer with pleasure. I would like you to try and realize the 7 Secret Wishes which I have indicated below FOR ME, FREE OF CHARGE.

I understand that I'll never be asked for any money in return for the realization of my 7 Secret Wishes, neither now nor later.

Subject to this condition, please see below the 7 Wishes I'd most like to see coming true in my life:

Indicate here the number corresponding to the 7 Wishes you'd most like to see coming true in your life (no more than 7):

I have chosen wish No. 4, so the amount I'd like to win is: $_____

In a few days' time, you are going to receive a large white envelope containing your secret instructions. Read them carefully, and I expect to see some big changes taking place in my life after a few days.

IMPORTANT NOTICE – Answer the following *confidential* questionnaire:

1. Do you have any financial problems?   ☐ yes ☐ no
   How much money do you urgently need?
   $_____
2. Are you unlucky (do you feel like you're born under a bad star)? ☐ yes ☐ no
3. Are you working?   ☐ yes ☐ no
   Are you retired?   ☐ yes ☐ no
4. Are you married or do you have a spouse?   ☐ yes ☐ no
5. Are there major problems in your love or family life?   ☐ yes ☐ no
6. Do you feel lonely or misunderstood?   ☐ yes ☐ no
7. Do you feel as if a spell has been cast on you, like someone has sent bad luck your way?   ☐ yes ☐ no

IMPORTANT – Please write below, in a few words, the question that disturbs you the most (IN CAPITALS):
_____
_____
_____

Age: I am ___ years old   Date of birth: _____
Hour of birth: _____ / _____   ☐ AM
(if you know it): Hour Minute   ☐ PM
Place of Birth: City/ Town: _____
State/Province: _____ Country: _____
I confirm my astrological sign is: _____

(IN CAPITALS) ☐ Ms. ☐ Miss ☐ Mrs. ☐ Mr.
FIRST NAME _____
LAST NAME _____
ADDRESS _____
_____
TOWN/CITY _____ STATE _____
ZIP _____   3D003
Email address: _____

American Federation of Astrologers SuperStar Course in Astrology

Want to study Astrology?
It's now easier and less expensive than you ever imagined Learn astrology at home, at your own pace, with the guidance of an experienced astrologer. Easy to follow lessons guide you from the basics of astrology all the way through chart interpretation and predictions. Then you'll be equipped to take the AFA certification exam.

The cost in only $415.00 including shipping; or, $165.00 including shipping, for each of the 3 sections, purchased individually.

AFA INC.
6535 S Rural Rd. Tempe, AZ 85283
480-838-1751 Fax 480-838-8293 Toll Free 1-888-301-7630
Email info@astrologers.com
Visit our website www.astrologers.com
Your ultimate source for astrology books & software!

FREE PARTY LINE

Make new friends, have fun, share idea's never be bored this party never stops! And best of all it's FREE!

Never Any Charges! Call Now!

712-338-7722

Only Regular Low Long Distance rates apply where applicable

Penguin Group (USA) Online

What will you be reading tomorrow?

Tom Clancy, Patricia Cornwell, W.E.B. Griffin,
Nora Roberts, William Gibson, Robin Cook,
Brian Jacques, Catherine Coulter, Stephen King,
Dean Koontz, Ken Follett, Clive Cussler,
Eric Jerome Dickey, John Sandford,
Terry McMillan, Sue Monk Kidd, Amy Tan,
John Berendt…

You'll find them all at
penguin.com

*Read excerpts and newsletters,
find tour schedules and reading group guides,
and enter contests.*

Subscribe to Penguin Group (USA) newsletters
and get an exclusive inside look
at exciting new titles and the authors you love
long before everyone else does.

PENGUIN GROUP (USA)
us.penguingroup.com

CelebrityPsychic.com

IRENE HUGHES
America's Most Accurate Psychic
AS SEEN ON TV

1-800-279-2775

as low as $2.79/min

---

psychic power
Empower Yourself Today

CALL NOW!
1st Time Callers Receive up to a **$50 SIGNUP BONUS**

1-800-243-4113

psychic**power**.com

Witches of Salem Network®
Our Witches Will AMAZE you!

First 2 Minutes FREE!

1-800-314-9168

as low as $2.79/min

US PAT. 5,802,156 • THE ZODIAC GROUP, INC. • MUST BE 18 YEARS + • FOR ENTERTAINMENT ONLY